THE ***Cruise*** *SHIPS*

Keeping fit on the aft decks of the *Nordic Prince*.

Resting at her New York berth between Atlantic crossings, the 963-foot *Queen Elizabeth 2* dominates this aerial view taken during the summer of 1985. The stern section of the *Bermuda Star*, the Chandris liner *Britanis* and Royal Caribbean's *Nordic Prince* can be seen to the left; the Home Lines' *Atlantic* is just visible to the right.

T H E

Cruise

S H I P S

William H. Miller

CONWAY
MARITIME PRESS

This book is dedicated to Peter Ising
for his friendship, his talent, and especially for his
creative genius

First published in Great Britain in 1988 by Conway Maritime Press
Ltd, 24 Bride Lane, Fleet Street, London EC4Y 8DR

ISBN 0 85177 429 6

Designed by Tony Garrett

Typesetting and page make-up by Inforum Ltd, Portsmouth

Printed and bound in Great Britain by
Butler & Tanner Ltd., Frome

Contents

AUTHOR'S NOTE

Over sixty passenger ship firms are included in this book. Had it not been for the obvious limitations imposed by its size, there might have been an even greater number. Certainly, firms such as Canadian National, Canadian Pacific (for their Alaska cruises), Naviera Aznar and relative newcomers such as Ocean Cruise Lines, Premier Cruise Lines and Western Cruise Lines had a perfect right to be included as well. I have covered in this book, however, what might be considered some of the more important and more interesting cruise ships.

The tonnage figures given are those most commonly quoted during the passenger ships' final years. All tonnages listed are for gross tonnage. The accommodation figures are the most accepted configurations.

ACKNOWLEDGEMENTS

In creating and organizing this book, special thanks are due to many people. My very special gratitude goes to Frank O Braynard, George Devol at the World Ocean & Cruise Society, Frank Duffy at Moran Towing Company, Vincent Messina, and to James Sullivan at Cunard. Deep appreciation goes also to several fine maritime photographers: Michael Cassar, Luis Miguel Correia, Alex Duncan, Antonio Scrimali and Roger Sherlock.

Important and enlightening anecdotes, conversations, shared memories and specially requested materials were provided by Barry Anderson, Cecil Spanton Ashdown, Captain Eric Ashton-Irvine, Captain Rolf Bassenberg, Captain Harry Biehl, Jeff Blinn, Philippe Brebant, the British Transport Docks Board, Blue Funnel Cruises, John Malcolm Brinnin, Carnival Cruise Lines, Bob Cummins, the Cunard Line, Gordon Dalzell, Goran Damstrom at Wartsila Shipyards, Philip Dawson, David de Havilland, Antoinette DeLand, John Draffin, Tom Dyer, Fekko Ebbens, Howard Franklin, Peter Fraser at Holland-America Line, Erik Frostenius, Y Fukawa, the Furness Withy Group, Tim Gallagher, Alvin E Grant, Johann Groothuizen, Lennart Hakanson at Cunard-Norwegian America, Peter Hagmann, Hapag-Lloyd, Hapag-Lloyd Shipyards, John Havers, R Izawa, F Leonard Jackson, Brenton Jenkins, Christian Kloster, Arnold Kludas, William Kooiman, Michael D J Lennon, Y Minami, Chris Montegriffo, Hisashi Noma, Stephen Parker, the Port Authority of New York & New Jersey, the Port of Le Harve Authority, David L Powers, Brian Price, Stephen Rabson at the P&O Group, Donald Reardon at American President Lines, H J Reinecke, Fred Rodriguez, Royal Caribbean Cruise Lines, Royal Viking Line, Captain Terry Russell, Richard Sandstrom, Schiffsfotos Jansen, Captain Heinz-Dieter Schmidt, Victor Scrivens, James Sesta, James L Shaw, Leslie Shaw, Sitmar Cruises, Captain Harry Smith, C M Squarey, Southern Newspapers Ltd, Fred Stindt at Matson Lines, Cees Tensen, Jacob van den Berg, Nico van der Vorm, Captain Frederik van Driel, Captain Cornelius van Herk, Dr Wolfgang Vieweg, Everett Viez, Steffan Weirauch, Alan Wells, Howard Whitford, Wilton-Fijenoord Shipyards, Len Wilton at Astor Cruises, Barry Winiker and the World Ship Society Photo Library. Special thanks also to Conway Maritime Press for accepting this project.

In December 1985, I had the very good fortune to sail aboard the *Rotterdam*'s annual Christmas cruise. We departed from a wintery New York, bound for the warmth and sunshine of nine tropical ports in the Caribbean. Although she was a majestic, still stunning liner, often called 'the grande dame of the North American cruise fleet', there was also an historic, rather sad note to the journey. After twenty-five consecutive Christmas holiday sailings from New York, this would be her last. Hereafter, like so many cruise ships before her, she would sail from Florida, geographically closer to warm-weather destinations and supposedly even more convenient and practical for the legions of air-sea travellers from Middle America. In fact, the *Rotterdam* would rarely visit New York again. The cruise industry, which had become an international force by the sixties after the jets had taken over almost all of the traditional ocean liner routes, had prompted many changes. Among these, the once busy liner-filled docks of New York, Southampton, Rotterdam, San Francisco and Melbourne were replaced by the likes of Miami and Port Everglades, San Juan, Piraeus and Vancouver.

Still perfectly maintained, the *Rotterdam* made, I am quite sure, a most beautiful sight as she made her way along the Hudson River, then out into the Lower Bay, passing the Narrows and under the Verazzano Bridge and finally into the open Atlantic. Built in 1959, as the flagship of the entire Dutch Merchant Marine and noteworthy as the first Atlantic liner to do away with the conventional funnel, she was designed as a 'convertible' vessel. With a few doors opened here and there, she could be changed, with considerable ease, from a two-class transatlantic liner to an all-first class cruise ship. The *Rotterdam* alternated these roles for about a decade. In 1969, her transocean passenger trade had almost completely disappeared and she was refitted as a full-time cruise ship.

There are many loyalists to cruising and to particular cruise ships. There was certainly a good number among the *Rotterdam*'s 1089 passengers in December 1985. Many had travelled in the ship before, including some passengers from her prestigious around-the-world cruises. Others included a family of twelve who were on their nineteenth consecutive *Rotterdam* Christmas cruise, two elderly sisters who had made every one of the ship's holiday cruises (beginning in December 1959) and several who had been on her maiden crossing from Rotterdam to New York (in September 1959).

As the *Rotterdam* steamed south, making an average of 18 knots (there is no pressing need for great speed on cruise voyages), we had the increasingly rare opportunity to experience the climatic transition from cold weather to warm. On deck, coats and jackets soon gave way to sweaters and then to swimming and sunning attire. Large numbers began to gather on the open decks and the pool became a very popular amenity.

The *Rotterdam* visited a large selection of whitewashed and palm-fringed ports: Nassau, San Juan, Tortola, Martinique, Grenada, La Guaira, Curacao, Antigua and St Thomas. Mostly, these were all-day stop-overs that afforded passengers those cherished bonuses of cruising: shopping, sightseeing and shoreside swimming. Temporarily, the ship became almost deserted – silent lounges, rows of empty deck-chairs and a definable silence that was only broken by the working staff. Shortly before departure, the last of the passengers returned to the ship, 'their home away from home', often laden with tropical purchases: wooden sculptures, straw hats and those perennial favourites – duty-free alcohol and perfume.

At Nassau, the *Rotterdam* was berthed in company with four other liners: the *Royale*, *Mardi Gras*, *Carnivale* and *Emerald Seas*. Each of these had been adapted for cruising as well. The *Royale* had been Costa's *Federico C.*, built for three-class service to Latin America. The *Mardi Gras* and *Carnivale* had been transatlantic ships, the *Empress of Canada* and *Empress of Britain* respectively, sailing for Canadian Pacific (the latter ship had also sailed for the Greeks as *Queen Anna Maria*). The *Emerald Seas* had the most diverse background, however. Built towards the end of the Second World War, she had five earlier names for an equal number of shipowners.

As we approached the Puerto Rican coast, on a flawless afternoon, the *Queen Elizabeth 2* swept past us on the port side at an impressive 28 knots. Almost at the same moment, the blue-hulled *Norway*, the largest cruise ship of all, was steaming in the opposite direction, on the starboard side. From some distant aerial vantage point, one might have seen the overall group: the last transatlantic liner, the Dutch flagship and the former *France*.

At Tortola, the hundred-passenger *Newport*

Clipper arrived at midday. She represents a new and increasingly popular generation of yacht-like cruisers that call at more remote ports along more exotic routes. At La Guaira, the port for Caracas, we were berthed in company with two Cunarders: the aforementioned *QE2*, possibly the most fabled and surely the most publicized liner afloat, and the exquisite *Sagafjord*, bought from the Norwegians and regarded in some circles as the finest cruise ship afloat. The *QE2* is perhaps best known for her diversity of travel offerings, ranging from overnight sailings 'to nowhere', to transatlantic crossings, to an annual three-month circumnavigation, while in contrast the *Sagafjord* has a reputation for longer, more expensive cruises.

The world-wide cruise industry is a multi-billion dollar industry and one with a very promising future. The offerings remain varied, ranging from overnight visits to the Bahamas, the Mexican Riviera and the Greek isles, to fortnights in the Norwegian fjords, the Black Sea and the Far East, and voyages to more exotic destinations such as the Amazon, the Galapagos and even the 'lost islands' of the South Seas.

This book has been created as a sequel to *The Last Atlantic Liners* and *The Last Blue Water Liners*. It deals with most of the passenger ships of the past quarter century, the majority of which were not covered in either of those earlier books. Some are sleek, very contemporary types with raked bows, vast lido decks and even cocktail lounges attached to their funnels, while others are aged, often well-worn veterans that had extensive earlier careers before being pressed into cruise service. Some ships offered nothing but deluxe, all-first class cruise service – pure cruising, if you like – such as the club-like *Caronia* and *Andes* while others, such as the combination ships of the Orient Overseas Line, offered cruise-like sailings as part of their round-trip passenger-freight sailings.

All of these ships are, however, part of maritime history, members of 'the great parade of ocean liners'.

William H. Miller,
Jersey City, New Jersey,
Summer 1986

P&O's 41,923-ton *Oriana* was commissioned in late 1960 for the two-class passenger run between England and Australia via the Suez. By 1973, hard-hit by aircraft competition and the loss of most of her traditional passengers, she, like so many other liners included in this book, was refitted as a one-class vessel and used for cruising.

P&O Group

one

BRITISH
CRUISE
SHIPS

CUNARD LINE

CARONIA

It is most fitting that this book begins with the *Caronia* because she was the first large ocean liner designed specifically for leisure cruising. Cunard had created the illustrious *Queens*, the *Mary* of 1936 and then the *Elizabeth* of 1940, especially for a luxurious transatlantic express run, between New York, Cherbourg and Southampton. A smaller and somewhat slower liner, the *Mauretania* of 1939, was built as a 'relief ship', to sail on a slightly more extended service between New York, Cobh, Le Havre and Southampton. She too was to have a running-mate, a ship of comparable size and speed (about 35,000 gross tons and 23 knots), but these plans were disrupted by the Second World War. Soon after the hostilities ended, the Cunard directors at Liverpool did some serious rethinking about this new ship, in fact they cast a serious eye towards the future of ocean liner trading. In view of the great success of the prewar sisters *Carinthia* and *Franconia*, a pair of 20,000 tonners

When commissioned at the end of 1948, the 34,172-ton *Caronia* was the largest single-stack liner afloat. Even her tripod mast then rated as the tallest of its kind at sea. Affectionately known as the 'Green Goddess', she is shown departing from Hamburg during one of her summer-time North Cape cruises.

Schiffsfotos Jansen

Eric Ashton-Irvine Collection

The *Caronia* was quite similar in decoration and style to the giant *Queen Elizabeth*. This, her Observation Cocktail Bar, was decorated in late art deco style.

from the mid-twenties that spent considerable time on long, luxurious cruises, a new luxury ship particularly for all-first class cruising seemed appropriate.

Some plans and sketches were brought out soon after the war had ended, but then were reviewed modified and improved somewhat so that, in early 1946, an order was placed with an old friend to Cunard, John Brown & Company at Clydebank in Scotland, for a 34,000 tonner, which was to be Britain's biggest postwar liner. She would not be out-sized for some years, until the summer of 1960, when the 37,600-ton *Windsor Castle* was commissioned. The new Cunard ship, *Caronia*, was to be fitted with traditional steam turbines that would provide a service speed of 22 knots, and to have a maximum capacity of 932 passengers, which as required could be divided in transatlantic fashion between 581 in first class and 351 cabin class. Adding to the ship's all-luxury image would be the absence of tourist-class quarters. The décor was to be typical of Cunard for the period, much of it reflecting the style of the late thirties. There would be glossy veneers and chromium lamps, oversized club chairs and swirl carpets. In later years, it would be often said that this liner was, in fact, a miniature *Queen Elizabeth* within. There was a great similarity in the décor and decoration of the Cunarders in those years, the only difference being in the dimensions of the actual passenger spaces. The style of Main Lounge on the combination liner *Media*, finished in 1947, could clearly be traced to the earlier *Mauretania* and even the giant *Queen Elizabeth*. The distinctive and ever-popular last three-stacker, the *Queen Mary*, was said to be the grandest of all. Perhaps this new cruising liner would be the cosiest of all as she had a club-like quality about her. Amidst the traditional, however, there would also be some novelties: the first permanent outdoor pool on a Cunarder and every stateroom, down to the least expensive, with private bathroom facilities.

Launched on 30 October 1947, HRH Princess Elizabeth did the honours. A royal baptism was indeed appropriate for Britain's biggest postwar passenger ship and also as a mark of respect to Cunard's distinguished and heroic war record. Sent down the ways and into the Clyde to roaring cheers that briefly brightened the end-of-war austerity and gloom, she was named *Caronia*, after an earlier Cunarder, a two-stacker which plied the North Atlantic from 1905 until 1932.

Once moved to John Brown's fitting-out dock, several more novel features became apparent. She was painted overall in four shades of distinctive green. Publicity material suggested that this was to enhance heat resistance in tropical waters (she was as much as 10 degrees cooler on board than the more traditional black-hulled *Queen*s and other Cunard liners), but the choice was also a strong bid to give the new ship a distinctive identity and distinguishing feature. It was a success, as soon after she was commissioned, she was affectionately dubbed the 'Green Goddess', a nickname she carried through to the very end of her Cunard days. Her general design was also quite different, particularly from the more conservative earlier Cunarders. The *Queen Mary* was a successor to the design of the old *Aquitania* of 1914, and the second *Mauretania* clearly a first cousin of the larger *Queen Elizabeth*, with twin funnels balanced between twin masts, but the *Caronia* was given one large stack. In fact, this stack ranked as the largest funnel afloat for some years thereafter. A very tall tripod mast was placed over the wheel-house section. This new *Caronia* was in yet another way quite unlike most other liners of her time. When the all-green, single-stack *Caronia* finally entered service at the very end of 1948, she attracted considerable attention.

Cunard had at first suggested that the *Caronia*

With glossy veneers, oversized chairs and large windows overlooking the sea, the Main Lounge aboard the *Caronia* had a club-like atmosphere. The room rose two decks in height and had a portrait of Princess Elizabeth (now Her Majesty the Queen) and the Duke of Edinburgh at the far end.

A corner of the *Caronia*'s writing room.

would spend considerable time on the North Atlantic, sailing in tandem with the *Mauretania*, and then cruise only periodically. In fact, she would rarely cross that northern route. Her mainstay would be cruising, mostly on very long and very expensive trips. Her pattern of service remained the same for most of her Cunard days: a three-month trip each January, either around the world, throughout the Pacific or to South America and Africa, would be followed, in May, by a six- or eight-week Mediterranean trip, which terminated at Southampton (the fares of which included first-class return in any other Cunarder within a year's time). She would then recross to New York in late June, in preparation for a six-week summer cruise to Scandinavia and the fjordlands; this too would terminate at Southampton. Following another west-bound crossing, she would set off on a two-month Mediterranean-Black Sea cruise. She then returned to Southampton once again; her annual overhaul was traditionally scheduled for December, with special Christmas leave for her hand-picked staff. In January, in preparation for the annual pattern to repeat itself, she again crossed westbound to New York, but usually on an extended routing that might include stopovers at Trinidad, Barbados, Kingston, Nassau and/or Bermuda.

The *Caronia*'s schedule for 1961 read:

World cruise, January 28th from New York to Las Palmas, Madeira, Tangier, Malaga, Palma de Majorca, Barcelona, Villefranche, Naples, Messina, Catania, Malta, Piraeus, Rhodes, Alexandria, Port Said, Port Suez, Port Sudan, Aden, Bombay, Colombo, Singapore, Bangkok, Hong Kong, Kobe, Yokohama, Honolulu, Long Beach, Acapulco, Balboa and Cristobal. Fares from $2875 for 95 days.

Spring Mediterranean cruise, May 8th from New York to Madeira, Tangier, Palma de Majorca, Malta, Piraeus, Dubrovnik, Venice, Catania, Messina, Naples, Villefranche, Barcelona, Malaga, Gibraltar, Lisbon Cherbourg and Southampton. Fares from $975 for 39 days.

Scandinavian cruise, July 1st from New York to Reykjavik, Hammerfest, North Cape, Lyngseidet, Trondheim, Aandalsnes, Merok, Bergen, Stavanger, Oslo, Stockholm, Helsinki, Visby, Sopot, Copenhagen, Hamburg, Queensferry, Oban, Dun Laoghaire, Glengarriff, Le Havre and Southampton. Fares from $1175 for 45 days.

Mediterranean cruise, August 29th from New York to Las Palmas, Tangier, Malta, Catania, Messina, Naples, Villefranche, Barcelona, Palma de Majorca, Malaga, Gibraltar, Lisbon and Ponta Delgada. Fares from $600 for 21 days.

Mediterranean-Black Sea cruise, September 24th from New York to Madeira, Casablanca, Tangier, Malta, Yalta, Odessa, Constantza, Istanbul, Alexandria, Haifa, Piraeus, Dubrovnik, Venice, Catania, Messina, Naples, Villefranche, Barcelona, Palma, Malaga, Gibraltar, Lisbon, Cherbourg and Southampton. Fares from $1110 for 52 days.

'The *Caronia* was a grand and luxurious floating clubhouse', according to Captain Eric Ashton-Irvine, a former master of the ship.

We carried many passengers year after year, many of them living on board for months at a time, and who were given precision, manor-house service. Cunard's best and most senior staff members were selected to serve aboard the *Caronia*. They rarely said 'no' to passenger requests. Most of the guests travelled for travel's sake, in fact there were very few places that they had not already been. The *Caronia* was a safe and familiar refuge where they could rest, be pampered and be entertained. These passengers, often of the millionaire class, often gave large and lavish parties on board, frequently for as many as 300 of their fellow voyagers. Of great note were the elaborate theme parties that required costumes or special attire. The *Caronia*'s style, reputation and unique status in the world's passenger fleet was and remains unique.

In the early sixties, as the transatlantic trade began its deep and steady decline, Cunard attempted to increase its cruise offerings, trying to find alternatives for a fleet of ageing, money-losing 'indoor' ships. Even the mammoth *Queen*s were sent to the tropics, mostly on short trips such as New York to Nassau, and Southampton to Las Palmas in the Canaries. But with limited amenities for warm weather voyaging, such as vast lido decks and open-air pools, and dark, almost sombre, non-air conditioned interiors, their potential for success, especially financial success, was quite limited at best. Cruising in the *Queen*s seemed to have far more nostalgic, sentimental overtones. For example, for $125 for a five-day round-trip to Nassau, Americans flocked aboard the venerable *Mary* for what they suspected to be the twilight years of one of the world's greatest ocean liners. By 1966, Cunard was losing as much as £15 million a year on its passenger operations. Company managers were faced with the inevitable: an aged fleet that had lost its competitive edge to the likes of a new generation of far more contemporary cruise ships such as the *Oceanic*, *Sagafjord* and *Kungsholm*. Even the mighty *Queen Elizabeth*, which at a cost of £1.5 million had just been modernized and upgraded for extended use until as late as 1975 in the cruise trades, failed to escape the axe. In the thirteen months between September 1967 and October 1968, Cunard retired five liners: the two *Queen*s, the sisters *Carinthia* and *Sylvania*, and the *Caronia*. While the first four ships were primarily victims of a vanishing transatlantic trade, the 'Green Goddess' – the former doyenne of the long-distance cruise business – had been suffering from slightly different infirmities: escalating operational costs (she consumed the most fuel, for example, of all big Cunarders), dwindling passenger loads (especially the die-hard, loyalist passengers), and long-cruise competition from the likes of the Swedish American, Norwegian America and Holland-

America lines.

After a half-filled Mediterranean cruise in the late summer of 1967, the *Caronia* sailed empty from New York to Southampton. Like so many of her British-flag contemporaries, she was then offered for sale and sat along the Southampton Docks for weeks, then months, looked after by small maintenance crews as prospective buyers made their curious inspections. Among these groups were the voracious scrap merchants of the Far East. As the *Caronia*'s green colouring steadily began to fade and as great streaks of rust lined her once immaculate hull, rumour was that a Yugoslav firm, Dumas Turist, wanted her for use as a floating hotel to be permanently moored along the Dalmatian coast. The plans never materialized. Instead, in the summer of 1968, just months before the last of the *Queen*s, the twenty-eight-year-old *Elizabeth*, was to be retired, the *Caronia* was sold to Greek-financed, Panama-flag owners known as the Universal Line. At New York, the same buyers were listed as the Star Line. This was only the beginning of the mysteries and uncertainty that would cloud the future of the former Cunarder. Taken to the Mediterranean and renamed *Columbia* and then *Caribia*, she was given a less-than-satisfactory refit, first at Piraeus and then at Naples. In her final Cunard years, as the Company lost millions, much maintenance had been deferred. This, combined with the effects of her advancing years, meant she was almost desperately in need of some extensive repairs and refitting.

The *Cariba* returned to New York in early 1969, and in direct competition with Cunard's smaller *Franconia*, then used on the weekly New York–Bermuda run. She was scheduled for two-week Caribbean sailings in winter, and weekly seven-day runs to Bermuda and Nassau at other times during the year. Large advertisements appeared in newspapers and magazines, with particular emphasis on the ship's glamorous heritage and well-known former name. Most unfortunately, all of this came to a thundering halt during the ship's second sailing. She would never carry fare-paying passengers again. On 5 March, while sailing off Martinique, the *Caribia* suffered a serious engine room explosion. Her passengers had to be sent ashore and later flown home and the disabled, powerless ship given an expensive and embarassing tow back to New York. This heralded the beginning of a five-year saga of debt and law suits, trouble with local authorities and unpaid crew mem-

Eric Ashton-Irvine Collection

Each November, interrupting her traditional cruise programme, the *Caronia* had her annual overhaul. In this view, she is at Harland & Wolff's graving dock at Southampton.

bers, frequent rumours of reactivation and the visible decay of a once great and grand liner. After being briefly examined at the Todd's Eire Basin Shipyards in Brooklyn, the *Caribia* sat at anchor for a time in the outer harbour, off Gowanus Flats, and then was sent to lay-up berths, first in Brooklyn, then between Piers 84 and 86 along Manhattan's fading 'Luxury Liner Row' and finally to Pier 54, another city dock located at the foot of West 14th Street, which ironically was a terminal used by Cunard until the early 1950s. Various reports hinted that the ship's financial woes were at last settled and that she would resume cruising, from Miami and then from San Juan to the Caribbean, and from Port Everglades on three- and four-day runs to the Bahamas. Other stories suggested that the Chandris Lines wanted her for the Australian migrant trade, the Lauro Lines for Mediterranean cruising, C Y Tung for a combination floating university-cruise ship and, possibly the least accurate, that Cunard wanted to repurchase their former ship for conversion to a Caribbean cruise ship.

In February 1974, with little hope in sight other than a final voyage to the ever-hungry Taiwanese shipbreakers, the owners of the *Caribia* announced an auction. Nostalgic fans, steamer buffs and the curious stepped aboard the cold, musty, badly weathered and ill-kept liner. Anything and everything even remotely removable, from wood panels in the former Smoking Room to dressing tables in the suites, to cooking utensils in the galleys, were price-tagged. The ship was just about stripped bare; anything that was not sold went to the shed on Pier 56. Two months later, on 27 April, under the care of a large ocean-going tug, the *Caribia* set off for Kaohsiung, Taiwan via the Panama Canal. Like almost all voyages to the scrapyard, it was a long and tedious affair. On 11 July, she finally reached Honolulu. Reports of flooding and leaks went largely unnoticed. A month later, on 12 August, she put into Guam during very heavy weather – this was to be her end. Lashed by ferocious winds and violent seas, the empty hulk was thrown on a local breakwater and broke into three pieces. She posed a hazard to navigation so the US Coast Guard quickly intervened, took charge and then promptly dismantled the wreckage. The story of the first large cruise ship had ended.

CARMANIA AND FRANCONIA

In the early 1950s, the Cunard Company ordered what were to be their last traditionally styled transatlantic passenger ships, a quartet of sisters especially for the St Lawrence trade to Quebec City and Montreal (and to Halifax and often New York in deepest winter). Named *Saxonia*, *Ivernia*, *Carinthia* and *Sylvania*, they were commissioned at yearly intervals beginning in the summer of 1954. They were designed for year-round North Atlantic service but rather soon fell out of step as off-season, winter-time cruising became more and more of a profitable alternataive to the ailing transocean runs. In hindsight, Cunard should have been more forward-thinking. There were no open-air pools, no air conditioning and far too few cabins with private bathrooms, all amenities essential to the demanding American cruise market. Consequently, these ships were forced to remain on the freezing winter Atlantic, often sailing with only a quarter of their 900 or so berths filled.

As this foursome steadily made less and less profit, Cunard selected two of them, the *Saxonia* and *Ivernia*, for major transformations. They would even receive new names, *Carmania* and *Franconia* respectively, and would become dual-purpose liners, working as Atlantic ships in peak summers and tropical cruisers for the remainder. In extensive conversions at their builder's yard, the John Brown plant at Clydebank, they were repainted overall in Cunard's 'cruising green' (in imitation of the fabled *Caronia*), given large lido decks with kidney-shaped pools and all of their staterooms were fitted with at least private toilets and showers. Air conditioning was extended throughout the ships and most of the public rooms were redecorated and improved (and even included some experimentation, particularly with their double-deck Main Lounge, a design later adopted on the *Queen Elizabeth 2*). The refitted *Carmania* resumed Cunard service in April 1963, the *Franconia* in July. At first, both ships spent their winters in the Caribbean, the *Carmania* sailing from Port Everglades and the *Franconia* from New York.

At about the same time, Cunard was offering cruises in almost all of their other passenger liners as well. In December 1963, the legendary *Queen Mary* made two six-day trips between Southampton and Las Palmas with fares beginning at £59. A month later, the *Mauretania* set off from Southampton on a thirty-six-day Caribbean cruise, with fares starting at £160, to Las Palmas, Trinidad, La Guaira, Cristobal, Port au Prince, Kingston, Vera Cruz, Port Everglades, Nassau and Ponta Delgada. In February 1966, the *Sylvania* went to the Mediterranean from Southampton for twenty-eight days, calling at Le Havre, Gibraltar, Naples, Piraeus, Alexandria, Beirut, Haifa, Messina, Tangiers and Lisbon, with fares from £210. The *Carinthia* offered a thirteen-day sailing from Liverpool to Madeira, Tenerife, Las Palmas and Gibraltar for £89.

By spring 1967, with transatlantic services curtailed even further and with the Furness-Bermuda Line's contract in hand, the *Franconia* was assigned to weekly service between New York and Hamilton, Bermuda. Her season generally extended from March to November. This operation lasted until 1971. Meanwhile, the *Carmania* spent her winters in

An atmospheric, late afternoon photo of Cunard's *Carinthia* at Liverpool. She was the third of the four Canadian-class liners built by the Company between 1954 and 1957. In addition to passengers, she had six cargo holds, three forward and three aft.

the Caribbean (and was joined by the *Franconia*) and the remainder of the year, from May through to September, cruising from Southampton. A sample listing from 1971 included:

May 21	Atlantic Isles, 13 days, from £125
June 4	West Africa, 14 days, from £140
June 18	Mediterranean, 13 days, from £125
July 2	Mediterranean, 13 days, from £125
July 15	Northern Cities, 16 days, from £170
August 1	Mediterranean, 13 days, from £140
August 14	Mediterranean, 14 days, from £155
August 28	Mediterranean, 14 days, from £155
September 11	Mediterranean, 13 days, £125
September 25	Mediterranean, 14 days, from £140

That autumn she was based in the Mediterranean, sailing on five consecutive fly-sail voyages from Naples or Palma de Majorca.

However, by the early 1970s Cunard was once again faced with an increasingly competitive industry. The *Carmania* and *Franconia* were ageing and becoming less and less profitable so were scheduled for withdrawal by the end of 1971. They were to be replaced by two smaller, supposedly more efficient ships, the sisters *Cunard Adventurer* and *Cunard Ambassador*. These two elderly Cunarders were laid-up at

Southampton and later rested together in Cornwall's River Fal. They were to have been sold to the Greek flag Chandris Group of Companies, for Australian migrant service as well as cruising, then to Japan's Toyo Yusen K.K. for Pacific cruises but neither sale materialized. In August 1973, both were sold to the Nikreis Maritime Corporation, a Liberian intermediary, which was acting as agent for the Soviet Union's Black Sea Steamship Company of Odessa. They were given refits and then renamed the *Leonid Sobinov* and *Feodor Shalyapin* respectively. More information on their subsequent careers is given in Chapter 8.

QUEEN ELIZABETH 2

The *Queen Elizabeth 2*, best known as the *QE2*, is perhaps the most publicized and possibly the most prestigious cruise liner of modern times. She has been in more newspaper headlines, television news broadcasts and documentaries, and featured in more glossy magazines than any other contemporary passenger ship, superliner class or otherwise. Even the *Norway*, the radically renovated former *France*, which is some

The last of the great Atlantic superliners, Cunard's *Queen Elizabeth 2* received enormous publicity and attention in her inaugural year, 1969. Here, during one of her transatlantic crossings in her first months, she is berthed at Le Havre. Shortly afterwards the French stopover was changed to Cherbourg.

3000 tons larger and therefore the world's largest liner (in 1986), has not quite captured the public's or the media's attention to the same degree.

Soon after her launching at the John Brown yards at Clydebank, on 20 September 1967, noted author John Malcolm Brinnin wrote an extended piece in *Holiday* magazine entitled 'The New *Elizabeth*'. He described the launching scene.

It is the day of the royal visit that will launch the 736th oceangoing vessel to be built downriver from Glasgow at the famous old shipyard of John Brown Ltd. The Queen is on the viewing stand. With the pressing of a button, she releases a bottle of champagne on a ribbon that swings on target, into the bow. After a long pause, the ship slides down the ways with a prolonged whoosh, hits the water in a haze of metallic dust from the drag chains, and bobs in the Clyde like an apple in a tub. 'May God bless her,' says Her Majesty, 'and all who sail in her.' The *Queen Elizabeth 2* is at last in her element.

Having been plagued by some early mechanical problems and resulting delays that cost an additional £3 million, the $80 million *QE2* finally crossed the North Atlantic for the first time in May 1969. Cunard had earlier designed a far more traditional three-class liner dubbed the *Q3*, which would replace only the *Queen Mary* but the *QE2* design was the result of far more thought, research, experimentation and foresight, and replaced both of the older *Queens*. In view of future demands, particularly in the 'cruising seventies', the *QE2* – intended to be the last of the supposed Atlantic superliners – was designed and created as a

contemporary cruise ship that would spend only about half her time on the customary Atlantic route, on five-day crossings between New York, Cherbourg and Southampton. For the remaining months, she would cruise, sometimes for as little as two nights, or on longer trips to Bermuda, the Caribbean, the Canaries, the Mediterranean and Scandinavia, and in later years (from 1975) on one long, luxury wintertime run, usually around the world, for about ninety-five days. Her cruises departed not only from New York and Southampton, but from ports such as Bremerhaven, Rotterdam, Boston, Baltimore, Philadelphia, Norfolk, Port Everglades, San Francisco and Los Angeles.

John Brinnin described the concept of the new and presumably last Cunard *Queen*.

For the better part of each year, the *Queen Elizabeth 2* will cruise. In this service, she will operate on a classless basis, the only discrimination among the passengers being the prices they pay for their staterooms. But on the Atlantic run in high summer season, she will try to mitigate the rigidity of the old sea-going class system. While designations of first class [with 564 berths] and tourist class [with 1441 spaces] will be kept, she will attempt to maintain the sense of a largely 'open ship', with 'premium' accommodation for the well-heeled and no hint of austerity in accommodation for anyone else. Like the old *Queens*, however, she will hold to

Port Authority of Le Havre

banded funnels and a wall of lighted portholes sliding through the transatlantic night. It's a way of life that somehow belongs to other people, in a setting borrowed equally from La Scala and Radio City Music Hall. It's a chokered dowager, immensely alone amongst the pillars of the Main Lounge, being served tea by twelve white-jacketed stewards. It's the picture-palace baroque of foyers and staircases with murals of fawns and Dianas, and the rest of the personnae of mythological kitsch. It's Crêpes Suzette flaming out like brush fires all around the dining room; jowly tycoons in jockey caps and muffin-shaped ladies in cardboard tiaras. It's *The Times*, 'top people and First Class Passengers Only'.

When Cunard recently moved its headquarters from a grandiose Victorian landmark on the Liverpool waterfront to a remodelled railway hotel in Southampton, the old image was abandoned along with the marble fireplaces and Adam ceilings of stately boardrooms in which it was nurtured. The Company's newly appointed executives are young and, as one of them put it, 'not too Cunardy'.

the Establishment tradition of catering to an elite, an elite whose badge is the money to pay for a Main Deck Suite Deluxe and meals in the Verandah Grill and perhaps to those of sounder credentials listed in *Who's Who* and *Debretts*, who may still be invited to dine with the captain.

The 963-foot *QE2*, slightly smaller than the two earlier *Queen*s, was a radical departure from all previous Cunard liners. The new flagship, with her unconventional single funnel device, did not even wear the Company's familiar colours of black and orange-red. The name Cunard was painted in red letters along her forward superstructure just below the bridge section. Within, the veneers, oversized leatherettes and English chintzes were replaced by sleek creations of chrome and aluminium, vinyl, formica and even plastic. There were two pools on deck, a disco, a casino for gaming, at least three different restaurants and a coffee shop, an arcade of shops and a sheltered courtyard on the uppermost deck. The *QE2* was said to be a major turning point in ocean liner design and decoration, a theme enhanced by Cunard's advertising slogan at the time, 'Ships have been boring long enough.'

John Brinnin added,

Not the least of Cunard's problems is how to break an image without endangering a reputation. To hundreds of thousands of passengers who sailed on the *Queen*s, and to millions of other people who have been led to believe that 'Getting there' in the company of diplomats and debutantes 'is half the fun', the Cunard image [by the late sixties] stays in mind like a beloved antique. It's not only huge black-

Cunard Line

With just inches on each side, the *QE2* passes through the Panama Canal during her first cruise around the world, in the winter of 1975.

Now, well past her fifteenth year and supposedly half way through her expected lifespan, the *Queen* has settled into an established route pattern. She is still legendary and alluring, sometimes profitable and – despite her frequent woes with problem boilers and electrical systems, breakdowns and disruptions in her hard-placed schedules, and mixed reviews of her onboard services – is still the best-known liner afloat. She is the last super-ship still plying the Atlantic route out of New York, a service in which she is said to earn her best profits. According to James Sullivan, one of Cunard's senior vice presidents at New York:

The success of the *Queen* in Atlantic service is not just with nostalgic voyagers yearning for the good old days, but with a new generation of travellers, people who want to experience the ultimate travel experience. In 1986, our transatlantic bookings were up 35 per cent over 1985. The *QE2* is a glorious combination: we can offer the vestiges of the Old World, the grand heritage of Cunard, as well as the latest trends in ocean travel – from health spas to special dining to an elaborate guest lecture programme.

The *Queen* is much more than just a cruise ship in the Caribbean. She's in a class by herself, still the last of the great Atlantic superliners. She is an extraordinary large luxury ship, carrying 1800 or so passengers and as many as 60 or 80 cars, at speeds as high as 28½ knots, with onboard facilities such as kennels for pampered pets, a large array of shops, the Golden Door Spa and a computer learning centre. We must cater to all kinds of passengers, particularly passengers looking for new travel experiences. The transatlantic crossings, in particular, offer an experience of a lifetime. We've even made them more attractive, such as the combination of one-way by the *QE2* and one-way by the Concorde. Added onto the ship's fare, the cost of the Concorde is only $699 [1986]. Other offerings include deluxe tours of Europe, an Orient Express programme and even the opportunity of buying a car in Europe and bringing it home on the *Queen*.

Surely the most glamorous of the *QE2*'s cruise voyages is her annual three-month trip around the world. On 15 January 1986, for example, she set off from New York on a three-month circumnavigation, which called at Port Everglades, Playa del Carmen, Puerto Limon, Balboa, the Panama Canal, Callao (for Lima), Valparaiso, Puerto Montt, Strait of Magellan, Montevideo, Sao Paulo, Rio de Janeiro, Capetown, Durban, Mombasa, the Seychelles, Karachi, Bombay, Colombo, Penang, Singapore, Bangkok, Hong Kong, Taipei, Pusan, Kagoshima, Yokohama, Honolulu, Lahaina, San Francisco, Los Angeles, Acapulco, the Panama Canal, Cristobal,

Cartagena, Port-au-Prince, Kingston, Port Everglades and return to New York. Fares ranged from $17,000 to $325,000 for one of the top-deck duplex suites. Brian Price, a former cruise director on the *Queen*, remembered some of the earlier world voyages.

The long winter-time trips around the world catered to an exceptional group of passengers – the King of Malaysia comes to mind – who could afford the very best. Every aspect of the voyage, from the food to the shore excursions to the onboard entertainment, required months of advance planning. The three-month voyage might call on as many as thirty ports in twenty-five different countries and cover over 30,000 miles.

James Sullivan added,

Similar to our transatlantic programme, the world cruise is a very unique experience. It must not only be an exceptional voyage, but it must be upbeat and vibrant. We must look after the passengers' mental, physical and even financial well-being. Consequently, we offer an extensive lecture programme as well as sports and dietary programmes. There are even sessions in investing and estate planning. It is not just where we go, the ports of call, but what we do onboard that is very important. World cruising is, of course, far different from the days of the *Caronia*. Today, there are fewer passengers who make the full voyage. More and more, we have 'segment passengers', who come aboard for two, three, possibly five weeks. Segment travel is the future of world cruising.

From October 1986 until well into the following spring, the *QE2* underwent her most extensive refit, called her 'transplant-facelift' by one writer. It took place at the Lloyd Werft Shipyards at Bremerhaven at a cost of $162 million. The original steam turbines have been replaced by brand-new diesel electric engines and there were structural changes and alterations, redecorating and considerable improvements. According to Eric Parker, the chairman of Cunard in Britain, 'At completion, this work will ensure that the *QE2* will be able to operate competitively for at least another twenty years or well into next century.'

CUNARD ADVENTURER AND CUNARD AMBASSADOR

These 14,100-ton cruise ships, ordered from the now defunct Rotterdam Drydock Company, the builders of such liners as the *Nieuw Amsterdam* of 1938 and the *Rotterdam* of 1959, were quite small by Cunard standards. They were, however, considered practical investments for the early seventies, when smaller, higher-capacity cruise ships were considered the promise of the future. The pair were initially ordered by the Overseas National Airways, an American charter airline, who wanted to diversify into world-wide cruising, Cunard later bought a 50 per cent share in them. However, when Overseas National faced some financial woes, Cunard bought the sisters outright. The Southampton management felt that they would be ideal replacements for the ageing, less profit-making sisters *Carmania* and *Franconia*.

Similar to the *QE2*, the traditional Cunard image and style was shunted aside. The ships would never visit Britain. Their tall funnel devices were painted all white and their interiors were a combination of flashy chromiums and zebra stripes, multi-coloured umbrellas and rubberized deckchairs. Even their names would be different, abandoning the old 'ia' nomenclature. The *Cunard Adventurer* was delivered in December 1971, and the *Ambassador* in the following October. They each had a maximum capacity of 806 passengers and were employed mostly in Caribbean waters. The *Ambassador* also ran a series of summer season sailings between New York and Bermuda, and made two special trips out of New York City, sailing along the upper Hudson River to a point just off Kingston Flats (in June and October 1973). The author was aboard the autumn sailing, which was enhanced by the rich colours of the river-side foliage. It was a three-day sailing in all, the final time was spent idling about in the open Atlantic off the New Jersey coast.

Both ships were less than successful in Cunard hands. Brian Price, who served in the *Cunard Adventurer*, recalled, 'Unfortunately, this little liner was plagued with lots of engine trouble, but was held together by the high and noble spirits of her crew.' There seemed to be no end to her mechanical maladies, which were compounded by a fire in the Caribbean, in July 1973, and then a collision with Costa's *Carla C.* at San Juan in February 1976. The *Cunard Ambassador* fared even less well. On 15 September 1974, while sailing on a 'positioning voyage' without passengers, off the Florida coast, she was badly damaged by fire. Beyond economic repair, she sat idle for a time, first at Key West and then at Bermuda, before being sold to C Clausen A/S, a Danish shipper well known for its interest in the sheep-carrying trades. With her former passenger quarters gutted and then restyled, the former cruise ship's new capacity was for 30,000 sheep. Renamed *Linda Clausen*, she plied a very different run, between Australia and the Middle East. In 1980, she changed hands and was sold to Middle Eastern interests and placed under the Qatar flag, first as the *Procyon* and then as *Rascan*. On 3 July 1984,

Quite different from the earlier Cunarders that once plied the North Atlantic, the *Cunard Countess* (shown here) and her sister ship, the *Cunard Princess*, are smaller cruise ships designed especially for warm-weather voyaging.

The *Cunard Countess* at San Juan, Puerto Rico.

Cunard Line

exactly ten years to the day that her former sister suffered a fire in the Caribbean, the former *Ambassador* burned as well, while sailing in the Indian Ocean on a voyage between Jeddah and Singapore. Once at Singapore she underwent an inspection, was judged to be beyond economic repair and was subsequently sent off to Taiwan that autumn for scrapping.

The *Cunard Adventurer* ended her Cunard service in the autumn of 1976, just as the newer and slightly larger *Cunard Countess* and *Cunard Princess* were entering service. The older ship was sold to the Norwegian Caribbean Lines, given a major refit (which included the creation of a new twin-funnel exhaust device) and then re-entered service, in May 1977, as the *Sunward II* on three- and four-day cruises to the Bahamas from Miami.

CUNARD COUNTESS AND CUNARD PRINCESS

According to Captain Harvey Smith, operations superintendent in the Caribbean for Cunard,

The *Cunard Countess* and *Cunard Princess* were to have been two of eight identical sister ships. MGM, the well known film company, were to own the other six. The ships were to have been positioned throughout the world – the Caribbean, the Mediterranean, even the Indian Ocean and the South Pacific – for what was to be a boom in long-distance air-sea cruising. The plan was to build the ships in Denmark in eighty days and then outfit and complete them in another eighty days in an Italian yard. This was, of course, quite impossible. In fact, the other six ships never left the drawing boards.

These newest Cunarders, improved versions of the *Cunard Adventurer* and *Cunard Ambassador* and over 3000 tons larger, were constructed at the Burmeister & Wain shipyards at Copenhagen and then towed to La Spezia in Italy, to the Industrie Navali Merchaniche Affine shipyards. The *Cunard Countess* was delivered in the summer of 1976 but the *Princess*, originally to have been named *Cunard Conquest*, was delayed by a shipyard fire in April 1976, and was not introduced until March 1977.

Her Serene Highness Princess Grace of Monaco named the *Cunard Princess* at New York's newly renovated Passenger Ship Terminal, the three finger piers that had been part of 'Luxury Liner Row' during the busy transatlantic era. As the former Grace Kelly released the customary bottle of christening wine, the American cruise industry fell into a temporary slump, caused by increasing fuel costs and the consequence of escalating passenger fares, which prompted Cunard to call their new vessel 'the last cruise ship'. Within two years the building of new ships as large as 40,000 tons had begun.

The *Countess* has served almost without interruption in the Caribbean, sailing on weekly cruise trips out of San Juan (except for a special charter to the British Government, in the spring of 1983, to the Falklands). Afterwards, she underwent an extended refit at Malta. The *Princess* has since served in the Caribbean, along the Mexican Riviera and to Alaska during the summer. Between June and November 1979, she was chartered to Italy's Lauro Lines, repainted in their colours and sent on two-week Mediterranean cruises out of Genoa. A year later, in October, despite loud protests from the struggling British maritime unions, she was transferred to the Bahamian flag and began carrying a multinational staff. She was extensively refitted, also on Malta, at the end of 1985.

The Cunard passenger fleet, which had as many as twelve liners in transatlantic service in the 1950s, is now an international cruise firm with five passenger ships. The *QE2* remains the flagship and plies a diverse pattern of trade, ranging from weekend 'party cruises to nowhere', to five-day Atlantic crossings, to

her ninety-five-day annual circumnavigation. The much smaller *Cunard Countess* and *Cunard Princess* remain solely in North American service, sailing on one- and two-week voyages. Two further liners, the ultra-luxurious *Sagafjord* and *Vistafjord*, which were acquired with the purchase of Norwegian America Cruises in 1983, work international schedules. They are discussed in Chapter 3 on pages 75–77.

ROYAL MAIL LINES

ANDES

The original South American passenger trades were usually divided between a deluxe first-class market, who wanted nothing but the best in accommodation and standards, if not for one-way travel then for round-trip cruise-like voyages, and a vast, very lucrative, but far less demanding trade in tourist or third class. Mostly, these passengers travelled southbound, to new lives on the South American continent. The greatest number of these third-class passengers from Northern waters would board at specially arranged calls in both Spain and Portugal, at ports such as Vigo and Lisbon. Homebound, these lower deck quarters were often quite empty, filled possibly with students or budget tourists.

One of Britain's finest cruise ships of all time, a ship that followed the deluxe standards of Cunard's fabled Caronia, *the Royal Mail Lines'* Andes *had a devoted, loyal following of passengers that travelled in her year after year. All-white and capped by a large yellow funnel, she was also among the finest looking of ocean liners.*

Britain's Royal Mail Lines was one of the most prominent firms in the Latin American passenger trade. In the prewar years, they were known especially for the twin motor-liners *Asturias* and *Alcantara*, built in the mid-twenties and acclaimed for their superb accommodation. They were highly successful ships and they had three classes on board, first, second and third.

Although Royal Mail's competitors already included not only other British shipping lines, but French, Dutch, German, Spanish and Italian companies as well, they were most concerned by the news, in the mid-thirties, that the Compagnie Sud-Atlantique was planning a fast, new liner. This was the 30,500-ton *Pasteur* of 1939. Royal Mail had to keep pace and so went to Harland & Wolff at Belfast for their largest, grandest liner yet. Designs were created for the 25,600-ton *Andes*, smaller than the new French ship, but a vessel that was intended from the start to be the finest British-flag liner on the Latin American trade.

Despite elaborate publicity efforts, extensive planning, accelerated work schedules and capacity lists of maiden voyage passengers, neither the *Pasteur* nor the *Andes* undertook their inaugural runs, both of which were scheduled for September 1939. Weeks before their intended departure dates, Germany invaded Poland and thrust almost all of Europe into the Second World War. The *Pasteur* was sent to Brest and laid-up for safety while the *Andes* was still at her fitting-out berth at Belfast, so she was consequently hurriedly refitted in war-time greys for use as a troop transport. Her new passenger fittings remained mostly in warehouses. Her commercial maiden sailing was not until January 1948, nearly nine years off schedule.

The *Andes* performed heroically throughout the war years, travelling out to the Pacific, the Far East and to South Africa. Released and then returned to Royal Mail during 1947, she was handed over to her Belfast builders and then, with only slight modifications, restored to her intended prewar standard. Unlike the earlier Royal Mail liners, however, she would not carry third class passengers, but 324 in rather exceptional first class accommodation and 204 in slightly less sumptuous second class. She was intended and always used for the 'up market' trade.

Paired with the older *Alcantara*, which survived until 1958, the *Andes* used her 21-knot service speed to maintain a sixteen-day schedule between Southampton and Buenos Aires with calls en route at Cherbourg, Lisbon, Las Palmas, Rio de Janeiro, Santos and Montevideo. She developed instant popularity and a very devoted and loyal following. Periodically, she was sent off on all-first class cruises, to the Mediterranean, West Africa, Scandinavia and even on a special mini-cruise, in June 1953, to participate in Her Majesty the Queen's Coronation Review off Spithead. She was one of 160 ships present for that glorious occasion, one that will never be repeated on such a scale again.

When Royal Mail directors reviewed the future of the South American passenger run, in the mid-fifties, it was decided to build three new combination liners – the sisters *Amazon*, *Aragon* and *Arlanza* – with three-class accommodation as well as substantial space for freight, particularly for carrying beef northward from the Argentine. The very popular *Andes* would be converted to a full-time cruise ship. Following her final Royal Mail South American sailing, in November 1959, she was sent to the De Schelde shipyards at Flushing in the Netherlands for a two-stage transformation that was carried out after a forty-six-day winter cruise to the Caribbean and Florida. When this work was completed the *Andes* set

off on her first official cruise, on 10 June 1960, and she was immediately equated with Cunard's legendary *Caronia*, the 34,000-tonner that was internationally known for her impeccable cruising standards. With only 480 berths in a 25,000-ton hull, the *Andes* now seemed even more spacious, in fact very like a large, white yacht. This new career, which would last for over a decade, would bring the ship even greater acclaim. Her style was that of an almost bygone era of sea travel.

John Draffin who served in the purser's department aboard the *Andes* in the second half of the sixties recalled her high standard and popularity.

She was an exceptionally elegant ship, much like a floating clubhouse. Sailing day from Southampton was like the first day back at school. Almost all the passengers were 'regulars' and therefore knew one another. The *Who's Who* of Britain would be aboard. Passengers in the best suites brought along their own servants. There were, of course, more crew members than needed, but then that was the standard that Royal Mail preferred. There were special facilities and considerations for older passengers. On some voyages, we had more wheelchairs aboard than many hospitals. While we always carried a full dance band, the demand was, in fact, for very limited entertainment. Ironically, in her latter years, in the second half of the sixties, our biggest competitor was the *Reina del Mar*, which was basically a tourist class-style cruise ship that sailed for Union-Castle, but which was owned by Pacific Steam Navigation, a division of the Furness Withy Group, which also owned Royal Mail. However, while the *Reina del Mar* catered to corporate Britain, the *Andes* carried aristocratic Britain.

Bob Cummins served in the stewards' department on the *Andes*, also in the second half of the sixties.

This exceptionally beautiful liner was in the highest class, possibly even more so than some of the famed Cunarders, with the rather obvious exception of their world cruise ship *Caronia*. The *Andes* was a floating clubhouse, filled with gentry and millionaires, who met two or three times a year on board. With about 500 passengers served by an equal number of staff, we had a one-to-one service ratio. It was all very English: mid-morning bouillon, ritual afternoon tea, formal dinners at one sitting. As stewards, even we had to don formal dinner suits and the response to almost any request was either 'Yes, Madam' or 'Yes, Sir'. We cruised on long, luxurious trips – from Southampton to the Mediterranean, Scandinavia, West Africa and even farther afield such as around continental Africa, to South

America and the West Indes, North America and even out to the Pacific.

In 1967, the *Andes* was reconditioned and modernized in two stages, in May to June and in December. Her boilers were retubed, which supposedly guaranteed she would last through the early 1970s. However, she was facing a dilemma becoming more and more common for British-flag ship operators, caused by escalating operational costs in the face of declining passenger loads. John Draffin remembered these rather bitter years.

The *Andes* was becomingly increasingly more expensive, especially after that devastating British Seamen's Strike in the spring of 1966, which lasted six weeks and cost some £4 million. Unfortunately, her problems were doubled as she began sailing with fewer and fewer passengers. Royal Mail brought in some rather brash, flashy entertainment in an effort to recruit new passengers, but which instead managed to alienate members of the older set. The Furness Withy Group, having just closed out its Furness-Bermuda Line operations at New York, thought of building two new 20,000-ton cruise ships, one of which would replace the *Andes*. Having all the contemporary amenities and intended to be based in the Caribbean mostly, they were to be quite innovative as 'bed and breakfast' ships. The cabin accommodation would be included in the fares, but there would be additional, quite separate charges for the onboard restaurants. Alternatively, passengers had the option of dining ashore. Also, there were ideas of converting one of the *Amazon* sisters into a cruise ship as well as rebuilding a large freighter with passenger cabins. However, the final decision was that Furness and Royal Mail saw container ships and bulk carriers as far better investments. The days of passenger shipping were clearly numbered as far as they were concerned.

Gordon Dalzell, an ardent cruise enthusiast from Appleby-in-Westmorland in Cumbria, also recalled the final years of the *Andes*.

She was immaculate, had old-world atmosphere and a very definite club-like atmosphere. There were two large launches especially for port calls, one of which was used often by a very rich passenger and therefore known as his 'private chariot'. In the last seasons, she had passed her best: the pipes were bursting, the air conditioning would break down and there would be plumbing problems. But most of the passengers were deep loyalists and accepted these problems and discomforts. I don't think that the *Andes* was a spectacular vessel, just a good, old-fashioned solid ship.

Furness Withy Group

The *Andes* had a palatial, prewar luxury about her – apparent in these photos of the Warwick Room (above) and the bedroom of a luxury suite (below).

The winter schedule of 1971 was to be the last for the venerable *Andes*. Two of her final cruise voyages were among her most diverse: a forty-day sailing that departed from Southampton on 10 January and called at Las Palmas, Luanda, Durban, Capetown, Dakar and Lisbon, and then, on 20 February, a nostalgic thirty-nine day run to Lisbon, Tenerife, Rio de Janeiro, Recife, Trinidad, Curacao and Madeira. As a member of the diminishing group of prewar luxury liners, she was given a tearful send-off from Southampton that May. With her masts partially stumped for bridge clearance and in the hands of a small delivery crew, she merely had to cross the

F Leonard Jackson

Channel for delivery at Ghent in Belgium. She was handed over to the local shipbreaking firm of Van Heyghen Freres and subsequently broken-up.

A rare occasion at Liverpool's Gladstone Dock: Canadian Pacific's twin sister ships *Empress of Britain* (left) and *Empress of England* (right) are berthed together.

CANADIAN PACIFIC LINE

EMPRESS OF BRITAIN, EMPRESS OF ENGLAND AND EMPRESS OF CANADA

The enormous Canadian Pacific Company was well known for its transatlantic *Empress* liners, ships that sailed the St Lawrence route between Montreal, Quebec City and then across to Greenock and Liverpool. In the ice-clogged winter months, these ships sailed to Saint John, New Brunswick. However, by the late fifties, as the Atlantic trade began its losing battle with jet aircraft, the winter-time Atlantic crossings were curtailed more and more in favour of more lucrative cruising, mostly from New York to the Caribbean.

The twin sisters *Empress of Britain* and *Empress of England* were the Company's largest postwar liners, both registered at some 25,000 tons and with space for about 1050 passengers (or 650 on cruises). The *Empress of Britain*, built by Fairfields of Glasgow, was delivered in April 1956; the *Empress of England*, having come from Vickers-Armstrongs at Newcastle, appeared exactly a year later. The *Empress of Britain* had one further distinction: she was Britain's first fully air-conditioned liner. Though they were only fitted with portable deckside swimming pools and few

of their cabins had private facilities, it seemed to matter very little in those early years. Both ships spent their winters at New York, sailing on ten- to twenty-one-day Caribbean trips.

The success of this pair, both on the summer season Atlantic trade and in winter cruising, led to a third liner, an improved and larger ship, that was geared more towards cruising. Named *Empress of Canada*, she came from the Vickers-Armstrongs yards at Newcastle and was introduced in spring 1961. Considered the most luxurious *Empress* and flagship of the Canadian Pacific fleet (many incorrectly thought of her as the flagship of the Canadian Merchant Marine as well), she made several Caribbean trips each winter, but in the earlier seasons was also sent on a long, luxurious trip through the Mediterranean. On her first such sailing, which departed from New York on 9 February 1962, she set off for sixty-one days to Tenerife, Madeira, Casablanca, Gibraltar, Tunis, Malta, Alexandria, Beirut, Haifa, Cyprus, Rhodes, Samos, the Dardanelles, Istanbul, Limnos, Piraeus, Milos, Iraklion, Kotor Bay, Dubrovnik, Venice, Catania, Messina, Naples, Villefranche, Barcelona, Palma, Oran, Malaga, Tangier and Lisbon. Minimum fares began at $1675.

By the early sixties, however, as the North Atlantic trade slumped further still, all three *Empress* liners were rescheduled for further cruising. The *Empress of Britain* was chartered to the Travel Savings Association (the TSA as it was more commonly known), a creation of entrepreneur Max Wilson by which travellers invested their money in a savings plan and inexpensive cruises were forms of interest. The ship sailed not only from Liverpool and Southampton to the Atlantic Isles, West Africa, the Mediterranean and Caribbean, but from Capetown to the Indian Ocean and South America. A two-week cruise from Britain to Tangier, Monte Carlo, Valencia and Corunna was priced at £110 in first class and £35 in tourist class. Thirty-one days to Las Palmas, Trinidad, Curacao, Kingston, Barbados and Madeira cost £242 in first class and £76 in tourist class.

Unfortunately, Mr Wilson's travel scheme fell on hard times and was eventually dismantled. In February 1964 with her charter gone and little prospect of further service on the Atlantic, the *Empress of Britain* was sold off, to the Greek-owned Goulandris Group for the Greek Line services between the Mediterranean and New York (and for winter cruising as well). Delivered a year later and then refitted, she resumed sailing as the *Queen Anna Maria* in the spring of 1965. Ten years later, with the Greek Line in financial collapse, she changed hands once again, this time going to the Carnival Cruise Lines of Miami for whom she still sails as the *Carnivale*.

The *Empress of England* remained with Canadian Pacific until spring 1970, when she too was sold off. Passing to the Shaw Savill Line, who had very ambitious plans to expand their British and Australian cruise services, her new life as the renovated *Ocean Monarch* was little more than a complete financial and operational disaster. She was broken-up on Taiwan in 1976. The *Empress of Canada*, suffering from increased British-flag operating costs and more competitive US cruise industry, was to have followed her former running-mate under the Shaw Savill house-flag, supposedly as the *Dominion Monarch*. The transfer never took place and, after a brief lay-up along the Tilbury Docks, in the winter of 1971–72, she was sold to a newly created firm, Carnival Cruise Lines of Miami. She was renamed *Mardi Gras* and then refitted and upgraded during her earliest Caribbean cruises out of Miami. Her success led to the prompt

The last of Canadian Pacific's transatlantic liners, the *Empress of Canada* of 1961 was also designed for winter cruising from New York to the Caribbean and to the Mediterranean. She terminated the St Lawrence service in November 1971. She is shown above, in one of F Leonard Jackson's superb photos, approaching the Princess Landing Stage at Liverpool.

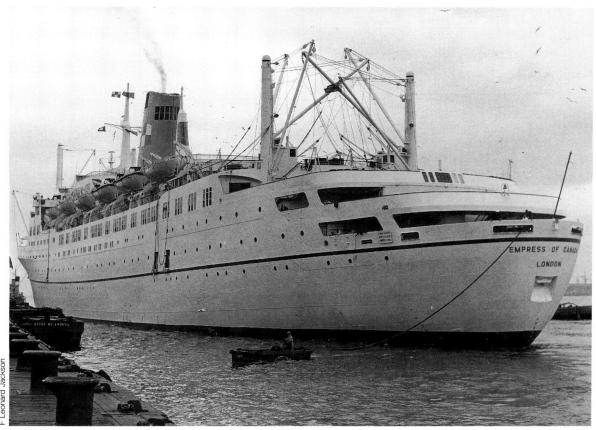

acquisition of two other second-hand liners, her one-time fleet mate, the *Empress of Britain*, and Union-Castle-Safmarine's *S. A. Vaal*, renamed *Carnivale* and *Festivale* respectively. Carnival added a succession of four brand-new liners, the *Tropicale*, *Holiday*, *Jubilee* and *Celebration*, and by the mid 1980s is considered the busiest cruise firm in the world. They are discussed in more detail in Chapter 9.

UNION-CASTLE LINE

REINA DEL MAR

When the Pacific Steam Navigation Company of Liverpool decided to replace their aged, but very popular *Reina del Pacifico* (built 1931 and 17,800 tons) in the mid-fifties, they returned to the same shipbuilders, the noted Harland & Wolff company at Belfast. While this replacement would be a modern vessel, including amenities such as full air-conditioning and far more passenger cabins with private facilities, she would still have a substantial cargo capacity (five holds in all) and the traditional three classes (207 berths in first class, 216 in cabin class and 343 in tourist) similar to her predecessor. Launched on 7 June 1955, as the *Reina del Mar*, the 'Queen of the Sea', she was Pacific Steam's new flagship and their final liner.

The routing to the west coast of South America via the Panama Canal was one of the most extensive for any major passenger ship. It was a trade then, in the fifties, still supported by large numbers of port-to-port and interport passengers, sea travellers who might remain aboard the ship for weeks or for as little as one or two nights. After departing from the Liverpool Docks, she would call briefly at La Rochelle in France and then Santander and Corunna in Spain before crossing the mid-Atlantic to Bermuda, Nassau, Havana, Kingston, La Guaira, Curacao, Cartagena, Cristobal and the Panama Canal, La Libertad, Callao, Arica, Antofagasta and finally a turnaround at Valparaiso in Chile. There would be well-to-do South Americans and diplomats in first class, businessmen and merchants in cabin class (equivalent to today's airline club classes) and then budget tourists, students and migrants in tourist class.

She was a strikingly handsome ship, painted overall in white, offset by a single, tapered yellow funnel. She had a forward mast only, and all rigging was attached to the funnel. There were three cargo holds forward, worked by six booms, and two aft,

which were handled by four booms. The first-class quarters were exceptionally comfortable and luxurious, and included two deluxe suites; all the other staterooms had private bathrooms. Cabin class, slightly smaller and less ornate, included one- to four-berth cabins. The rooms in tourist class had one- to six-berth cabins. Unfortunately, the *Reina del Mar* had only about five years of profitable service. Like so many other passenger firms, her owners could not have fully envisioned the swift, merciless invasion of jet aircraft. In a very short time, months in fact, almost all of the *Reina del Mar*'s South American passengers had deserted her in favour of airline travel.

Though reports circulated that the liner would be retired from British-flag service or sold off to the ever-growing Chandris Lines, she was in fact quite fortunate in securing an extensive charter that began in 1963. Mr Max Wilson's Travel Savings Association was then well into its rapid expansion. Supported by the likes of Canadian Pacific and Union-Castle, Mr Wilson's concept was to offer inexpensive 'fun in the sun' cruise voyages. He had already chartered such ships as P&O's *Strathmore* and *Stratheden*, and Canadian Pacific's *Empress of Britain* and *Empress of England*. The *Reina del Mar* was the ideal all-year-round cruise ship.

Once retired from three-class South American service, she was sent to Belfast and structurally rebuilt for full-time cruising. A new, highly successful and extremely popular life began for the *Reina del Mar*. John Havers, an ardent historian of ocean liners from Southampton and former member of staff with Union-Castle, recalled the rather elaborate transformation.

Here was a three-class liner successfully converted for one-class cruising. Her capacity increased from 766 berths to 1047 by extending the number of berths in some original cabins and then adding 135 new staterooms, which were built in the former cargo spaces. The restaurant was enlarged, and the deck space and superstructure extended forward of the bridge, making a large, new Coral Lounge with 650 seats and the longest bar afloat. Above the bridge, just forward of the funnel was the new cinema, on top of which was a viewing area of open deck, which surprisingly brought passengers very close to the radar scanner, but which they were warned to keep well clear of. All of the passengers had to pass through the original first class corridors, which were very narrow and on one visit which I found to be very congested.

F Leonard Jackson

The *Reina del Mar* made some sailings for Mr Wilson, including a maiden crossing to New York for the 1964 World's Fair, but his TSA operations soon fell on hard times. Among other problems, companies like Union-Castle resented his success with low-fare cruising. The British & Commonwealth Shipping Company, the owners of Union-Castle, were, in fact, the managers of the *Reina del Mar*. As Mr Wilson's

In the colours of her first owners, the Pacific Steam Navigation Company, the *Reina del Mar* is being manoeuvred by tugs at Liverpool in preparation for an outward sailing to the Caribbean and west coast of South America.

Restyled as a one-class cruise ship and painted in Union-Castle colours, the *Reina del Mar* became exceptionally popular, sailing not only from Southampton but from Capetown.

Michael D J Lennon

Everett Viez Collection

In her original guise, with three funnels, the *Queen of Bermuda* sailed regularly on six-day cruises between New York and Bermuda. However, in the view above, she was on an extended eight-day cruise that included a call at Nassau. She is anchored off Paradise Island.

The *Queen of Bermuda* returning to New York in April 1962 following a major refit in which she was modernized and given a new single, tapered funnel. Her bow had also been reshaped and extended, and full air-conditionung installed throughout her passenger accommodation.

Vincent Messina Collection

TSA fell into deeper financial trouble, British & Commonwealth gradually became the sole stockholder. Eventually, TSA was dissolved and the ship's operations transferred to Union-Castle's passenger department. The standards on board, if not quite as crisp and as luxurious as first class in the big Mail ships on the Cape run, were improved and brought into conformity with Union-Castle's overall image. By November 1964, the *Reina del Mar* – while still owned by Pacific Steam Navigation, a part of the large Furness Withy Group which also included the rival Royal Mail Lines – was repainted in Union-Castle colours. It was not until as late as September 1973, not long before the ship's retirement, that she was sold outright to Union-Castle. This sale reflected Furness Withy's decision in the early seventies to phase-out its remaining passenger interests, which included Royal Mail's cruising programme with the *Andes* and no less than six liners sailing for another sister company, the Shaw Savill Line.

Thousands cruised with the *Reina del Mar* each year. From April to October, she sailed from Southampton to the Canaries, West Africa, the Mediterranean and Scandinavia. For the remaining months, following low-fare, all one-class 'positioning trips' between Southampton and the South African Cape, she cruised from South Africa's largest port on voyages to the Indian Ocean and even across to South America.

Although laid-up at Southampton for six weeks in spring 1966, during a major British Seamen's strike, she was perhaps hardest hit in 1973 when the cost of fuel oil dramatically jumped from $35 to $95 a ton. Though still often filled to the very last berth and highly regarded by the British travelling public, she was suddenly, like so many other older liners, unable to earn her keep. Just as Union-Castle had decided to phase-out its last remaining mail ships to South Africa (which was to be finalized by the end of 1977), the management reluctantly had to include the *Reina del Mar* as well. In fact, the Company decided to end passenger trading altogether.

The 1974 season was the *Reina del Mar*'s last. Decommissioned in April the following year, she was briefly laid-up in Cornwall's River Fal to await her fate. There were rumours that she would be converted to a permanently moored youth hostel at the Royal Albert Dock in London. The Greeks, Italians and even the Soviets had a look over her, but it was a tense time for ageing, fuel-hungry passenger ships and she was thus sold, along with five other British liners, to Taiwanese breakers. She reached Kaohsiung on 30 July 1975, and then sat untouched for several months before being broken-up in the winter of 1975–76.

FURNESS-BERMUDA LINE

QUEEN OF BERMUDA

One of the Port of New York's best known and most beloved ships was the *Queen of Bermuda*. For most of each year, at precisely three o'clock on Saturday afternoons, she departed on her regular run: six-day cruises to Hamilton, Bermuda. She would reappear at her usual berth, at Pier 95, at the foot of West 55th Street, by 8.30 the following Friday morning.

Built by Vickers-Armstrongs at Barrow-in-Furness, the *Queen*, as she was most affectionately called, was delivered in the spring of 1933 as a three-funnelled near-sister to the *Monarch of Bermuda*, which was completed two years earlier. They shared the Bermuda trade until the outbreak of the Second World War, in the late summer of 1939, when both returned to Britain for use in military service. Used as

an armed merchant cruiser and then as a troop transport (with a capacity enlarged from 733 peacetime berths to over 4000 for war-time), she sailed for a while with her third 'dummy' funnel removed.

She was restored and returned to commercial service in the winter of 1949 and two years later was joined by the smaller, more yacht-like *Ocean Monarch*. In the early sixties the latter vessel was frequently detoured to two-week cruises, both to the St Lawrence and to the Caribbean, while the *Queen* was sent to Port Everglades, Florida for winter-time trips to the Caribbean. She underwent a major refit between October 1961 and March 1962, at the Harland & Wolff yards at Belfast, and re-emerged with improved passenger amenities, a new raked bow (increasing her length by some 20 feet, to 590 feet overall) and a new, single, tapered funnel replacing the original three stacks.

The 1960s saw something of a revolution in American cruising in particular. A new generation of specially built or redesigned cruise ships, with vast lido decks and large pools, saunas and discotheques, began to appear, especially on one-week sailings to ports such as Bermuda and Nassau. The beloved *Queen of Bermuda*, then past thirty, appeared more and more dated. This competition intensified at the same time as operational and staffing costs increased and the US Coast Guard introduced new, very stringent safety regulations. Without another costly refit, the *Queen of Bermuda* would be unable to meet those standards. In view of these conditions, the Furness management in London reluctantly decided to terminate the Furness-Bermuda cruise service (only cargo operations would remain and then these too would be ended).

The *Queen of Bermuda* terminated her owner's service in November 1966, and then, having been sold to Faslane shipbreakers in Scotland, she crossed the North Atlantic under the care of a greatly reduced maintenance staff.

OCEAN MONARCH

When the prewar *Monarch of Bermuda* burned out while undergoing her postwar refit in 1947 and was sold off, Furness Withy were forced to contemplate a replacement. Rather than build a larger ship comparable to the 22,500-ton *Queen of Bermuda*, Company directors selected a smaller, more intimate design that could easily alternate between weekly New

Furness Withy Group

Furness-Bermuda's *Ocean Monarch* looked much like a small cruising yacht. She was designed for weekly service between New York and Bermuda and extended cruises.

James L. Shaw

Reina del Mar, the former *Ocean Monarch*, on fire in Perama Bay, in May 1981. This photograph was taken several days after the destructive blaze began; her upper decks and single funnel have collapsed within the superstructure.

York–Bermuda sailings and longer two-week cruises. Similar to the style of Cunard's big *Caronia*, which was finished in 1948, this new liner, named *Ocean Monarch*, was an all-first class liner with amenities such as a permanent outdoor pool, a full range of handsome public rooms and private bathroom facilities in every passenger stateroom. Her design even resembled that of the Cunarder, with a single mast mounted above the bridge section and a single raked funnel. Only very limited cargo space was provided in the overall design.

Built by Vickers-Armstrongs at Newcastle, the 516-foot *Ocean Monarch* was delivered in spring 1951. She had space for 440 passengers (later reduced to 414) and she sailed in company with the *Queen of Bermuda* on Saturday afternoons towards Bermuda, but steamed to St George's rather than Hamilton.

She returned to New York on Friday mornings and remained in port overnight.

Furness decided to end its American cruise operations, thus the *Ocean Monarch* was retired, in the late summer of 1966, just months before the retirement of the older *Queen*. Laid-up for a time in the River Fal, she went to rather unusual buyers in the following summer, the Balkanturist Company under the Bulgarian flag. Renamed *Varna*, she continued cruising, but in the Mediterranean and Black Seas, and later also sailed on charter voyages. In the early seventies, she returned to North America for a series of summertime trips out of Montreal along the St Lawrence and to the Canadian Maritime provinces. She also made several longer voyages that called at Bermuda.

During 1973, the *Varna* was used mostly by British tourists, cruising from Nice within the western Mediterranean on fly-sail packages. Shortly thereafter, she was adversely affected by the sudden increases in fuel costs and spent the following years in lay-up. In February 1979, after having been sold to Greek buyers, I recall seeing her at Perama Bay, near Piraeus, painted overall in anti-corrosive orange-red and undergoing a structural refit. She was lying amidst a large assortment of both passenger and cargo ships, a group that also included such liners as the *Australis*, *Ellinis*, *Olympia*, and *Bergensfjord*. There were various reports regarding her future. One speculated that she was to be renamed *Riviera*, with the intention of running Mediterranean cruises from

Suva on Fiji was among the most popular calls for P&O liners, including those on cruises from both the American West Coast and from Sydney. In this view, the *Arcadia* has just arrived and disembarked her passengers and the *Oronsay* is approaching the wharf and is about to offload another 1200 passengers.

Venice, but this never materialized, another, that she was to have been chartered to a newly formed firm known as the World Cruise Lines for summer season New York–Bermuda cruises. Yet another report suggested that she was to become the *Venus* for both New York and Florida cruising. In fact, in 1981 whilst still at her lay-up moorings at Perama, she was rechristened *Reina del Mar* and it was intended that she should sail to Scandinavia and the North Cape in summer and the Mediterranean for the remainder of the year. On 28 May 1981 whilst undergoing repairs and a refit she was swept by fire. Burning from end to end and badly damaged, she later capsized and became a total loss. Her remains poked above the local waters, not far from the sunken remains of the *Rasa Sayang* which burned out just months previously, when she too was in Greek hands. The *Varna*'s wreck has been removed.

P&O-ORIENT LINES

ORCADES, HIMALAYA, CHUSAN, ORONSAY, ARCADIA, IBERIA AND ORSOVA

In 1960, the merger of the P&O Steamship Company and its long-time rival on the UK–Australian trade, the Orient Line, created the largest deep-sea passenger ship fleet on earth. In all there were sixteen passenger ships: the *Arcadia, Iberia, Himalaya, Chusan, Canton, Stratheden, Strathmore, Strathnaver, Strathaird, Carthage* and *Corfu* from P&O, and the *Orsova, Oronsay, Orcades, Orion* and *Orontes* from the Orient Line. The elder, prewar ships were gradually phased out and sold off, namely the four *Strath*s, the *Orion* and *Orontes*, and P&O-Orient Lines (as they were called until 1966, when they reverted to the P&O name only) added their largest, fastest and most luxurious liners yet, the 41,900-ton *Oriana* and the 45,700-ton *Canberra*. It was intended that these ships, with their extensive facilities, large capacities and vastly improved tourist-class amenities, would 'revolutionize' the Company's most important service, from Southampton via the Suez Canal to Fremantle, Melbourne and Sydney. Additionally, it was hoped they would enhance the firm's expansion into world-wide passenger shipping, particularly into the upper Pacific and to the North American west coast, which was becoming increasingly more important and profitable. P&O-Orient liners began to appear in major ports throughout the world and were scheduled for longer round-trip voyages, that might last up to four and five months.

At the same time as P&O-Orient began the expansion of its port-to-port services it intensified its cruise programmes. These were well-known before the war and had been resumed to some extent in the early fifties. All of the major liners were rescheduled to cruise sailings, which were usually made between their long-distance voyages rather than on a regular pattern. The only possible exception during the late sixties was probably the 24,200-ton *Chusan*, which was used increasingly for cruise sailings from Britain. By the very end of the decade, cruise sailings began to increase in the P&O schedules, especially as the Australian trade began its gentle and then swift, almost abrupt decline in 1972–73. Two-class cruising,

with separate accommodation and different fares for first- and tourist-class passengers, as on ordinary line voyages, began to give way to all one-class operations, with full run-of-the-ship privileges. Onboard activities and entertainments changed as well. Howard Franklin, the noted lecturer on horticulture, served with P&O for over a decade and has done seven world cruises and over a hundred voyages, mostly of the two- and three-week type. He recalled,

My sea-going career began with a phone call, out of the blue, in 1970, from P&O in London. They had just decided to put a cultural lecture programme on some of their liners. I was to offer one of three topics, the others being bridge and art. Prior to that time, P&O had only port lectures and ballroom dancing instruction. My first cruise was a three-week trip in the *Oriana*, from Southampton to the Caribbean. There was lots of sea time and therefore lots of lecturing. Subsequent trips followed on board the *Arcadia*, *Orsova*, *Canberra* and later, the *Sea Princess*, added to the fleet in 1979. My favourite of all was the *Arcadia*, which had a very cosy, club-like atmosphere. She was a real ship in the older tradition, on board which you always felt welcome.

The Company had other cruise operations as well, such as sailings to the South Pacific islands and northward to the Orient from Sydney, and from San Francisco and Los Angeles to Alaska (in the summers and begun by the *Arcadia* in the late sixties), and also

A sample P&O cruising schedule for the summer months of 1971 included:

June 11th	*Canberra*	Palma, Piraeus, Naples, Barcelona – 14 days
June 13th	*Orcades*	Lisbon & Ceuta – 6 days
June 13th	*Chusan*	Amsterdam, Alesund, Narvik, North Cape, Copenhagen, Amsterdam – 14 days
June 20th	*Orcades*	Lisbon, Gibraltar, Palamos, Palma, Madeira – 13 days
June 26th	*Canberra*	Lisbon, Madeira & Vigo – 8 days
June 27th	*Chusan*	Casablanca, Tenerife, Madeira, Lisbon, Vigo, Amsterdam – 14 days
July 4th	*Oriana*	Naples, Piraeus, Lisbon – 12 days
July 4th	*Orcades*	Lisbon, Malaga, Villefranche, Malta, Palma – 14 days
July 16th	*Chusan*	Amsterdam, Bergen, Narvik, North Cape, Trondheim, Copenhagen, Amsterdam – 14 days
July 17th	*Oriana*	Gibraltar, Elba, Piraeus, Palma – 13 days
July 17th	*Canberra*	Tenerife, Madeira, Barcelona, Naples, Vigo – 14 days
July 23rd	*Orcades*	Messina, Kotor, Corfu, Gibraltar, Lisbon – 15 days
July 30th	*Oronsay*	Gibraltar, Ajaccio, Cannes, Palma, Vigo – 13 days
July 31st	*Oriana*	Palma, Istanbul, Naples, Lisbon – 14 days
July 31st	*Chusan*	Lisbon, Casablanca, Lanzarote, Madeira, Amsterdam – 13 days
August 1st	*Canberra*	Izmir, Piraeus, Naples, Alicante, Vigo – 14 days
August 8th	*Orcades*	Lisbon, Ibiza, Naples, Cannes, Gibraltar – 13 days
August 13th	*Oronsay*	Tenerife, Salvador, Santos, Rio de Janeiro, Dakar, Madeira, – 29 days
August 14th	*Chusan*	Malta, Venice, Kotor, Piraeus, Barcelona, Tangier, Vigo – 20 days
August 15th	*Oriana*	Palma, Lisbon – 7 days
August 20th	*Iberia*	Naples, Kotor, Corfu, Ceuta – 14 days

Y Minami

A night-time view of the Yokohama Ocean Terminal in 1966, with P&O's *Iberia* in the foreground and the *Oriana* just behind her. The former was on a cruise from the United States, the latter from Australia. Just to the left of the *Iberia*'s funnel is Sitmar's *Fairsky*, another cruise ship which had sailed from Australia.

to the Mexican Riviera. There were several unsuccessful ventures, however. Between April and October 1970, the 240-passenger combination liner *Chitral*, last used on the dwindling London-Far East service, was sent to Genoa, Italy for a series of air-sea Mediterranean tours. Three years later, the giant *Canberra* was moved to New York for a ten-month 'experimental' schedule on one- and two-week Caribbean trips. In direct competition with the likes of Cunard and others, and in an area where the P&O name was barely known, these *Canberra* cruises were so poorly booked that the ship was laid-up for several weeks at Wilmington, North Carolina.

Beginning in 1972, the older, immediate postwar generation of liners began to lose both their profits

James L Shaw

A sad photograph taken at Kaohsiung on Taiwan of P&O's *Orsova*, which had arrived on 14 February 1974, moored alongside Home Lines' *Homeric*, which had arrived on 29 January. Both had been handed over to the shipbreakers and were awaiting their turns to be dismantled.

and usefulness. The Australian line voyages had all but disappeared completely, oil prices were just about to increase at a startling pace, the wages for all-British staff ships were causing havoc with the Home Office accountants and all of these factors were compounded by new, far stricter safety and operational codes being enacted by the Board of Trade. The extensive refits and upgrading which would be necessary to bring these vessels up to Board of Trade standards would be quite uneconomic. Therefore, almost all of these older ships became weakening investments. The *Iberia* led the 'parade to the block', to Kaohsiung on Taiwan, in September 1972, the *Orcades* went in February 1973 and the *Chusan* followed that June. The *Orsova* reached the East on her final trip in February 1974 and nine months later, the *Himalaya* arrived as well. The *Oronsay* was retired in October 1975 and the *Arcadia*, after being reprieved for Australian cruising from Sydney, finally ended this generation of ships in February 1979.

ORIANA AND CANBERRA

When commissioned in December 1960 and June 1961 respectively, this team of superliners (the *Oriana* having been ordered by the original Orient Line and the *Canberra* by P&O) were the most outstanding and newsworthy passenger ships in the British fleet since the *Queen Elizabeth* of 1940. To emphasize their size, speed and capacity, it was often reported that these new liners could easily be equated with the transatlantic *Queens*. The *Oriana* was not only the largest liner yet built in England, at Vickers-Armstrongs at Barrow-in-Furness, but the fastest ever to sail the Australian route. Her maximum speed was slightly higher than that of the *Canberra*. The latter, which was built by Harland & Wolff at Belfast, had the proud distinction of being the largest liner yet built for a service other than the North Atlantic. Although both ships primarily sailed on what was really a three-week 'express run' out to Australia, they were often sent into the Pacific and travelled via Panama and South Africa as well as the Suez route.

In 1973 the passenger division of the P&O Lines became P&O Cruises. The older ships were being retired and the last of the once frequent line voyages had just about drawn to a close. The *Oriana*, with 638 first class and 1496 tourist class berths, was converted to a 1700 berth one-class vessel; the *Canberra* was modified from having 596 first class and 1616 tourist class berths to 1737 one-class berths. Soon after, as fuel oil prices, in particular, began their dramatic escalation, there were frequent reports that the thirteen-year-old *Canberra* might go to the scrapheap. Rumours were that the twenty-year-old *Orsova* would be converted for full-time cruising as a replacement. This idea never materialized. Both the *Canberra* and *Oriana* survived, cruising on two- and three-week sailings from Southampton and then spending their winters, from December until April, sailing from Sydney on an annual three-month world cruise. However, although large, well-known and mostly profitable, such ships were not to the liking of every P&O loyalist. Leslie Shaw of Rainham in Kent began sailing with P&O in 1935 and forty years later travelled in the *Oriana* on a three-week Caribbean cruise. 'With 1700 passengers aboard, she was far too big for our liking. Actually, we saw passengers on the return boat train from the Southampton Docks to London that we hadn't even seen aboard the ship.'

The histories of both big ships have been marked by a string of mishaps and misadventures. The *Canberra* suffered serious engine problems off Malta in January 1963 and the *Oriana* had two fires, in June and August of 1970. Gordon Dalzell was aboard Shaw Savill's *Northern Star* when the *Oriana* caught fire in Southampton Water on her August outward sailing.

I remember seeing the pall of smoke on the horizon caused by the nasty blaze in the *Oriana*'s engine room just after she left the Southampton Docks. Suddenly, all of these little tugs sped out to the crippled ship and, as the fire was extinguished, she was towed to the King George V Graving Dock. The passengers were kept aboard and most of them remained as food was sent over from the other liners in port. Finally repaired, she sailed about a week later, missing a few ports on her itinerary to catch up on her schedule.

In the summer of 1973 the *Canberra* went aground twice in the Caribbean. Mr Dalzell was aboard the *Oriana* a year earlier on another unusual arrival.

It was 1972, the *Oriana*'s last full year as a two-class liner, which many passengers actually preferred. We were on a Mediterranean cruise, to Naples, Piraeus, Beirut and Gibraltar. On her previous cruise, she had had some berthing problems at Piraeus and so there was some apprehension for this return call. As an alternative, we anchored in one of the smaller local bays. For one of the first shore visits, we left the ship in lifeboats rather than tenders. Unfortunately, we went to the completely wrong landing basin, in the completely opposite direction. As passengers,

P&O Group

A rare occasion at Sydney when P&O's largest liners were in port together. The *Oriana* is outbound having left her berth at Pyrmont. The *Canberra* remains at dock, being replenished, at the Overseas Passenger Terminal.

we just assumed that the young mate in charge knew what he was doing. We were lost in some obscure yacht basin in the pitch dark – completely stuck! Finally, the boat was freed at midnight. When we returned to the *Oriana*, the officer in charge greeted us with 'You're the boat that's been missing. We didn't know where you were, but we knew you would turn-up eventually!'

The *Oriana* left Southampton for the last time in November 1981 and cruised from Sydney in Pacific waters. She remained in this service until March 1986, when she was retired from nearly twenty-six years of P&O service. She has since been converted to a convention and reception centre at Beppu in Japan.

The *Canberra*, following heroic duties in the South Atlantic during the Falklands crisis and then a festive return to Southampton in July 1982, took on renewed popularity – despite her twenty years of age and continual service. Presently, she cruises from Southampton from April to December and then makes an annual 90-day world cruise each January.

SEA PRINCESS

Because the twenty-five-year-old *Arcadia* was earmarked for withdrawal from her cruising base at Sydney, in early 1979, P&O sought a replacement, a ship of more 'up market' style. Just coming on the sales lists was the 27,600-ton *Kungsholm*, the celebrated Swedish American Line flagship, well known for her long, expensive cruises. She had latterly been in Norwegian hands and had also been under the Liberian flag for a short time. She was bought in September 1978, by a P&O holding firm, the Sea Leasing Corporation of London and renamed *Sea Princess*. Sent to Bremen, West Germany, she was given a thorough overhaul and alterations that resulted in the elimination of her forward dummy stack and then the heightening and alteration in shape of her second funnel, causing considerable unhappiness amongst steamer buffs everywhere. One long-time P&O officer later reported, 'I hated to go ashore from the *Sea Princess* for I knew that I would have to return and face her profile'. Her earlier, serenely beautiful good looks had been destroyed.

Michael D J Lennon

Just having been refitted at Bremen, P&O's *Sea Princess* made a short call at Southampton, in January 1979, while outbound for Sydney where she was assigned for two- and three-week Pacific cruises. In spring 1982, she was reassigned to Southampton-based cruising.

Used for over three years exclusively in Australian cruising from Sydney, she proved to be better suited to the UK market and replaced the *Oriana* at Southampton in the spring of 1982. She began seasonal winter cruising from Port Everglades to the Caribbean in December 1985 and full-time North American operations a year later.

Shaw Savill's *Southern Cross* of 1955 was the first major liner to have her engines and therefore her funnel mounted aft. This created considerable midships deck space. She was revolutionary for her time, and carried 1100 passengers, all tourist class quarters.

SHAW SAVILL LINE

SOUTHERN CROSS AND NORTHERN STAR

When the Shaw Savill Line, a part of the large Furness Withy Group, decided to expand its Australia-New Zealand passenger operations in the early fifties, they ordered a most novel liner. Built by Harland & Wolff at Belfast and named by Her Majesty the Queen in August 1954 as the *Southern Cross*, she was the first major liner, at over 20,200 tons, to have her engines and therefore her funnel mounted aft. She

Alex Duncan

was fitted with space for tourist class passengers only, with a total of 1100 berths, and would carry no commercial cargo whatsoever. She plied a most unusual route: continuous seventy-six-day voyages, travelling from Southampton to Trinidad, Curacao, the Panama Canal, Tahiti, Fiji, Wellington, Auckland, Sydney, Melbourne, Fremantle, Durban, Capetown, Las Palmas and then return to Southampton. Frequently, in her earlier years, she reversed this pattern and sailed in the opposite direction.

So successful was the *Southern Cross*, not only with one-way passengers and around-the-world cruise passengers, that Shaw Savill designers created a larger, improved version, a ship of 24,700 tons that was delivered by Vickers-Armstrongs at Newcastle in the summer of 1962. A year previously, in June 1961, this vessel had been named *Northern Star* by the Queen Mother. With a higher capacity than the *Southern Cross*, of 1437 total berths, again all in tourist class, she served on a similar seventy-six-day itinerary. From 1968, cruises, from Southampton as well as from Sydney, were interspaced in these ships' extensive schedules. Gordon Dalzell recalled this pair.

The *Southern Cross* was, in fact, the better of the two – cosier and supposedly offered better times. Aside from her Southampton sailings, she also offered cruises from Liverpool. The *Northern Star* had a very good reputation at first, but poor health reports eventually gave her a poor name. I especially recall the newspaper headlines of the weekend before we were to sail in the *Northern Star* [1972]. She was condemned as unhygenic, in fact unfit to sail. The kitchens were said to be filthy. This bad publicity was to scar her for the rest of her days.

Hindered by rapidly escalating operational costs and increasing competition, the *Southern Cross* was withdrawn in March 1971 and laid-up, first at Southampton and then in the River Fal. Amongst other rumours was one that she would become a floating leisure centre off the Cornish coast. She was sold subsequently, in March 1973, to the Greek-flag Ulysses Line and then underwent a long, frequently deferred, two-year refit at Piraeus. She resumed sailing in June 1975 as the *Calypso*. Sold again in September 1980, she now sails as the *Azure Seas* for the Panamanian-flag Western Cruise Lines on the Los Angeles–Mexico route.

The *Northern Star*, troubled by mechanical and engine problems during 1974, which included an engine room explosion off Venice on 12 June, was finally withdrawn in October 1975. Although only thirteen years old, she could find no buyers on the sales lists and went to Kaohsiung breakers. She was broken-up in the spring of 1976, after a comparatively brief career.

OCEAN MONARCH

In the late sixties, Shaw Savill, in a flush of enthusiasm and excitement, decided to expand its passenger operations, particularly with a view to one-class cruising. Canadian Pacific's *Empress of England* was bought in February 1970, and was sent on some initial line voyages to Australia prior to being scheduled for an extensive refit and modernization at the Cammell Laird yards at Birkenhead. She was renamed *Ocean Monarch* and her berthing scheme was increased from 1058 berths in two classes to 1372 in one class. The refit, which proved to be one of the longest and consequently costliest in British ocean liner history, stretched from September 1970 until October 1971. Gordon Dalzell recalled seeing her, at

A busy day at Gibraltar as three liners arrive with British tourists from Southampton. Shaw Savill's *Ocean Monarch* is in the centre, Union-Castle's *Reina del Mar* to the left, and Chandris Lines' *Ellinis* is at the outer end of the dock.

Chris Montegriffo

H J Reinecke

Converted from a prewar peace-time trooper, the *Dunera* resumed British India's educational cruises in 1961. Here she is moored at the Overseas Landing Stage at Hamburg during a summer-time Northern Cities cruise.

Easter 1971, at Cammell Laird's. 'She was caught in continuous strikes and delays at the shipyard. Only partially rebuilt when we saw her, she was a grey, rusting hulk that sat untouched.'

Her first cruise was from Southampton in October 1971. Gordon Dalzell was aboard her in the following season.

She was booked solid for a Southampton–Mediterranean cruise, but there was a delay in sailing because the health inspectors were being exceptionally thorough following earlier problems with the *Northern Star*. I recall that there were no or very few deck-chairs and instead we sat on life-rafts. The promenade windows would not open and the emergency doors had to be opened and ropes stretched across them for safety. As the air conditioning was less than effective, the passengers were gasping. Finally, the Company bought some deck-chairs, but these were very inexpensive, light-weight aluminium types. In quick time, they were collapsing due to salt air decay. Shaw Savill had to buy still more chairs.

Overall, the ship was tatty-looking, indeed past her best. She was a ship spoiled. Extra cabins had been built in the former cargo hatches and were the smallest ever, with two berths each. She listed all the way to and from the Mediterranean and I recall an engineer who said that she actually sailed better that way and that she had actually been balanced to sail at a list. It was also the first time that stewardesses and waitresses in the restaurant were being used by Shaw Savill. As the air conditioning remained faulty, it seemed impossible to get cool and I recall sitting quite wet in the cinema. Docking at Izmir, we didn't bother stopping at the end of the quay and went straight into the wall with an almighty thud. We knocked a chunk of concrete out of the dock wall and lost some paint on her stem.

The *Ocean Monarch* sailed for Shaw Savill for just five years. She was retired in June 1975, and then sold to Taiwanese breakers. Her remains were scrapped in the following winter at Kaohsiung, quite close to her former running-mate, the *Northern Star*. It was the end of the Shaw Savill liner fleet.

BRITISH INDIA LINE

DEVONIA AND DUNERA

Although the British India Steam Navigation Company was registered at London, it was perhaps best known for its second home-port services in India, which ran from Bombay and Calcutta, to the Persian Gulf, East Africa and the Far East. It also ran a fleet of peace-time troop ships that were chartered to the British Government. In the thirties, when the trooping seasons slumped, several of these ships were used for a novel and notable concept in ocean travel: educational cruising. A comparatively small number of adults were carried, usually in the upper deck, first-class quarters; the remainder of the ship, mostly the lower deck dormitories, was given over to students, who travelled at specially reduced fares. Lecture programmes were geared to the ports of call and appropriate themes and topics. The first educational cruise was on board the 9200-ton *Neuralia*, and set off in July 1932. Such sailings were suspended during the Second World War, and were not resumed until 1961, with the *Dunera*.

The *Dunera*, completed in 1937, by Barclay Curle at Glasgow, was created as a peace-time trooper for British India. Her sister, the *Dilwara*, had been delivered two years earlier (and decades later, in 1960, was sold off to the China Navigation Company and became their *Kuala Lumpur*). Two other near-sisters were P&O's *Ettrick* (later sunk during war service in 1942) and Bibby Line's *Devonshire* (which was sold to British India in 1962 and became the *Devonia*).

The 12,600-ton *Dunera* had a peace-time trooping capacity of 123 in first class, 95 in second class, 100 in third class and 831 in troop quarters. After war service, she sailed out to the Mediterranean, the Middle East, and colonial outposts such as Hong Kong and Singapore. However, once the British Government decided to airlift more and more of her overseas troops, the need for ships such as the *Dunera* and the *Devonshire* declined. The former was taken in hand and converted for educational cruising. In 1961,

P&O Group

the first year British India resumed such cruise sailings, *Dunera* made fifteen cruises and carried an impressive total of some 9700 passengers. The *Devonshire*, having been bought outright by British India and then refitted at Glasgow as the *Devonia*, was introduced in the following year. The *Dunera* had a capacity for 188 adult passengers and 834 students; the *Devonia* for 194 adults and 834 students. Each ship was fitted with six lecture halls and had student dormitories of from twenty to forty berths each. Captain Terry Russell, now with the P&O-Princess cruise fleet, served in both of these veteran liners in the mid-sixties.

On these ships, our entertainment equipment consisted of one record player per ship. We created all other events and, of course, all of them blended with the exceptional lecture programmes. At best, I recall these ships managed a sluggish 12 knots. In fact, the *Dunera* was fitted with Sulzer diesels that had been exhibited at the Geneva Industrial Fair of 1931. The ships were cooled by the old Punkah forced air system. The adult passengers had the services of a wonderful Indian bath steward. My own cabin, as a junior officer, opened onto the deck and I had to go along the outside just to get a bath.

Cruises, often of two week's duration, sailed from various UK ports including Southampton, Tilbury, Liverpool, Greenock, Invergordon, Grangemouth, Avonmouth, Swansea, Sunderland, Dundee, Immingham, Portland and Plymouth as well as from several overseas air-sea terminals such as Genoa, Venice, Malta, Tripoli and Gibraltar. So successful and instantly popular were these sailings that the *Dunera* and *Devonia* ran a combined total of forty-one

Another converted peace-time trooper, the *Nevasa*, was among the most popular of all British cruise ships of the 1960s and early 1970s. She is seen here in the Mediterranean; the Royal Navy's HMS *Bulwark* can be seen to port.

cruises during 1964, carrying 27,535 students and 6655 adults, which represented a four-year total of 94,246 passengers. In 1965, forty cruises were scheduled and forty-eight a year later.

Both of these older ships had reached retirement by 1967 and were replaced by the specially converted *Uganda*, added to educational cruising in February 1968. The *Dunera* went to Spanish breakers at Bilbao; the *Devonia* to Italians at La Spezia.

NEVASA

Completed in July 1956, by Barclay Curle at Glasgow, the 20,500-ton *Nevasa* (named after a small Indian village some hundred miles east of Bombay) was British India's largest passenger ship of all. She was intended from the start to be a peace-time trooper and was built for a special fifteen-year government charter (which would later be considerably shortened). Her accommodation was arranged for 220 in first class, 100 in second class, 180 in third class and for 1000 troops who would be berthed in eight large dormitories.

She sailed mostly out to the Mediterranean and the Far East until 1962 when her government services were abruptly terminated and her trooping duties ended. Shortly thereafter, another British trooper, Bibby Line's *Oxfordshire*, ended British trooping by sea altogether. The *Nevasa*'s fate was unclear and, for over two years, she was moored in the River Fal. It was not decided until November 1964 that she

Roger Sherlock

The *Uganda* preparing for her maiden voyage in August 1952. Her black hull was later painted white. She was among the last British passenger ships to be used on the colonial East African run. She was withdrawn in 1966, and then converted for educational cruising. Her sister ship, the *Kenya*, terminated British India's African liner trade three years later.

would be converted for educational cruises and would be sent to Falmouth to undergo a £500,000 refit. The accommodation was reorganized for approximately 300 first class and 1100 student passengers.

The *Nevasa* resumed sailing in October 1965, mostly on two-week cruises. She soon established herself as a popular ship. Leslie Shaw has fond recollections of her.

We had our first school-ship cruise in 1972, aboard the *Nevasa* on which there were some 300 adults separately divided from 900 or so youngsters. Our first trip was a seven-day run to La Pallice [in France], Vigo and Oporto. We liked this rather unique concept in ocean cruising. There were excellent lectures on board and you could always ask questions afterward. There were no professional performers, but instead the officers entertained. There were also lots of quizzes. Most of the adult passengers tended to be getting-on a bit, but were great fun and very interested in travel for travel's sake. One hundred out of the 300 adults would be teachers and another fifty would be connected to schools. When we were booked once again on the *Nevasa* in 1975, the voyage was suddenly cancelled. Due to the abrupt increases in fuel oil costs, the *Nevasa* could no longer earn her keep.

The *Nevasa* was delivered by a greatly reduced crew to Kaohsiung, on 30 March 1975, and was later broken-up for scrap.

UGANDA

The *Uganda* and her sister ship, the *Kenya*, were built in the early fifties for one of Britain's strongest colonial routes, to the East African coast via the Suez Canal. They were the largest British India passenger ships of their time and, until decolonization, which began in the early sixties, were highly profitable investments. As the trade finally declined, the *Uganda* was withdrawn, in December 1966; the *Kenya* terminated the service entirely in June 1969.

After being extensively rebuilt at Hamburg, during 1967–68, the *Uganda* took up a new career as an educational cruise ship. Like her predecessors, she sailed from various British ports including London, Southampton, Liverpool, Edinburgh, Falmouth and even northerly Aberdeen. Her voyages, mostly of a fortnight's duration, went to the Mediterranean, West Africa, the Baltic, the Norwegian fjords and even the Scottish isles. Her accommodation had been enlarged, with her original 300 berths (167 in first class and 133 in tourist class) increased to berths for 306 adults and 920 students. The adults used the old first class quarters; the students had specially built dormitories.

Alan Wells was cruise director aboard the *Uganda* and has some fond, sometimes mournful memories of this last British India liner and her distinctive 'lost era' cruising.

Following extensive duty in the South Atlantic as a hospital ship during the Falklands campaign, the restored *Uganda* prepares to sail on her first educational cruise, on 28 September 1982. Here, also berthed along the Southampton Docks is the P&O flagship *Canberra*.

P&O Group

There was total segregation between the adults and the children. The only time the children appeared in the adult section was during the children's fancy dress. They passed through the Music Room, itself much like a Victorian drawing room. The kids also ran a fun fair in their quarters, having darts, cards and raffles, and to which the adults were invited.

To many who remember her, *Uganda*'s cruises were reminiscent of grander ship-board days like the evocative 1930s. Alan Wells certainly agreed.

The elevator operator, for example, was a bearded Indian, straight out of the Imperial Raj, who wore white gloves. On Ladies' Night, all the women were given a list of all dances and then proceeded to have it filled-in.

There was an entertainments' officer [the cruise director] and a hostess, but that was it. You did everything. At other times, the gaps were filled by officers and staff. For example, the Casino Night was worked by the officers. Social life on board often included private cocktail parties, especially since many of the *Uganda*'s passengers were regulars and were therefore previously acquainted. The Captain also hosted several parties of his own, using his dayroom which connected onto a canvas-covered verandah. We also ran a daily tote-, hat- and flower-making sessions, bingo, classical concerts, deck sports and tournaments. Evenings included frog racing and a ship's concert, which was done entirely by the officers. I recall our

singing surgeon, the plumber-magician, the chief engineer who did a monologue, the engineers who staged a corps d'ballet and all of this emceéd by the deputy captain. There was also an Indian band, always a quartet, that played before lunch just like in some grand seaside hotel.

Alan Wells was also fascinated by the décor of this 'period' ship.

The public rooms included a rather splendid ballroom with a Victorian flavour and with windows along each side looking out onto the sea and aft onto the pool. The other public room was the Smoking Room, complete with leather chairs and mounted elephant tusks. Indeed, it was like a gentlemen's club from last century. Nothing ever happened here – just chats and drinks. It was a quiet space.

The theatre was one area where the adults and children merged for the superb specialty port lectures. The back rows of seats were reserved for the adults. Of course, on the *Uganda*, all of the shore excursions were included in the passage fares [a fifteen-day cruise with excursions had fares beginning at £80 in 1969].

The service aboard the *Uganda* became very well known and was one of her best features.

The *Uganda* was staffed in the hotel areas by Indians, which was customary for British India ships. It was service of a lost age. It was all ultra-efficient and cheerful. Chairs were always lifted and pushed, and waiters seemed to catch knives before they fell. Most of the tables in the restaurant were round and the officers appeared far more often for dinner. The food was, of course, quite magnificent and also included a deserts trolley. Every night without fail, the headwaiter would inquire about the quality of the meal. Of course, there were lots of curries. There was also more dressing for dinner, far more black tie and long gown.

The passengers that travelled in the *Uganda* were often a special type.

They were mostly retired professionals and consequently the age range was rather high. There were virtually never any children travelling in the adult quarters. The passengers tended to be regulars, who came year after year after year. We also had lots of retired military. Many of the passengers knew one another from prior sailings. They were always a great audience and wonderfully good-hearted. They always helped to decorate the lounge before a party or special occasion. They were a well-travelled group, the type of passengers who liked lots of non-fiction in the library.

Leslie Shaw has called the *Uganda* his favourite passenger ship.

She was the most friendly ship we ever travelled in.

P&O Group

P&O Cruises' *Spirit of London*, later the *Sun Princess* for Princess Cruises (a P&O subsidiary), is shown in the dramatic setting of Alaska's Glacier Bay. These northern sailings from Vancouver are among the most popular of all summer voyages.

While there was no professional entertainment, the officers gave superb presentations, which often included hilarious slapstick. The quizzes were often a real battle as we would frequently have many teachers aboard. While most of the passengers tended to be getting-on in age, they were always great fun. I have a special memory of my wife's birthday aboard the *Uganda*. Not only was a cake presented, but there was a gala birthday parade into the restaurant in her honour. The band played especially for the occasion.

Unfortunately, just prior to *Uganda*'s Falklands service as a hospital ship, during the spring and summer of 1982, the number of school-ship bookings had slumped. Inflation had put them out of reach of many young people and their families. In autumn 1982 she resumed cruise sailings for a brief time until she was chartered to the government and used as a transport between Ascension and the Falklands. She was decommissioned in April 1985, returned to home waters and was later moored in the River Fal to await disposal. A special committee was formed to save 'Britain's last colonial liner' but inevitably she was sold to Taiwanese breakers (in late spring 1986). She capsized in a typhoon at Kaohsiung and remains on her side at the time of writing (1987).

PRINCESS CRUISES

SPIRIT OF LONDON/SUN PRINCESS

Princess Cruises was an innovator in North American cruising. In the mid-sixties, Mr Stanley MacDonald, a Seattle based entrepreneur, saw a bright and very promising future in an as yet untapped cruise area, from Los Angeles to the so-called Mexican Riviera, to such ports as Acapulco, Mazatlan and Puerto Vallarta. He chartered Canadian Pacific's 6600-ton *Princess Patricia*, which normally sailed on the seasonal (April to October) Vancouver–Alaska run, for the first winter periods of these cruises. Although not an ideally suited ship (there were no outdoor pools, for example), she proved to be very popular as well as profitable. This led to two, far more important charters, of the Italian-flag liner *Italia* of 12,200 tons and then the *Carla C.* of 19,900 tons. Although they were advertised as the *Princess Italia* and the *Princess Carla*, they were not officially renamed. Operations soon expanded to year-round schedules and included summer-time sailings to Alaska and longer trips to the Caribbean and Florida via the Panama Canal.

Britain's P&O Lines began, by the early seventies, to re-examine its position in North American cruising. Their ships, such as the *Arcadia* of 1954, were not only ageing, but becoming less and less competitive when compared to some brand-new tonnage. The Norwegian Caribbean Lines of Miami, which was owned by Klosters Rederi of Oslo, had had enormous success in the Caribbean since their first voyages in 1966. By 1970, they had ordered yet two more passenger ships, a pair of sisters later named the *Southward* and *Seaward*, from Italy's Cantieri Riuniti del Tirreno e Riuniti SpA shipyard of Genoa. However, greatly increased construction costs for the second of these ships prompted her intended Norwegian owners to lose interest. She was placed, in her incomplete state (and therefore suitable for some modification), on the sales lists and was promptly bought by P&O specifically for American West Coast operations. She was completed in the autumn of 1972 and delivered to her London owners. Although P&O might have used one of their singular geographically-themed names, the management decided that a fresh image was required and one which American tourists could easily identify. She was named *Spirit of London*. Captain Bob Ellingham recalled this period in P&O passenger history.

At first, we worked as the P&O Lines, using the brand-new *Spirit of London*. We had developed a good following. Aptly, we intended to acquire two more cruise ships, the Norwegian *Island Venture* and *Sea Venture*, which were to become the *Spirit of Liverpool* and *Spirit of Southampton*. But, at the same time [1974] as we bought out Princess Cruises from Mr Stanley MacDonald, we realized that that Company had an even stronger following. Consequently, we took the Princess concept with the *Spirit of London* becoming the *Sun Princess*, the *Island Venture* the *Island Princess* and the *Sea Venture* the *Pacific Princess*.

The *Sun Princess*, the smallest member of the P&O-Princess fleet, currently divides her year between summers in Alaska and winters in the Caribbean.

PACIFIC PRINCESS AND ISLAND PRINCESS

In the late sixties, in the surge of interest in the expanding American cruise industry, particularly in the Caribbean area, Norwegian shippers Oivind Lorentzen and Fearnley & Eger, amongst others, created Norwegian Cruiseships A/S, which was better known as Flagship Cruises. Two 19,900-ton sister ships were ordered from the West Germans, from the Nordseewerke shipyards at Emden. Although this yard only had limited experience in cruise ship construction the results were most impressive.

Completed in May and December of 1971 as the *Sea Venture* and *Island Venture*, each had a high standard of accommodation for 646 all-first class passengers (750 was absolute maximum capacity). Their passenger facilities included two outdoor pools (one of which was covered by a retractable glass Solardome), a gymnasium, sauna, closed circuit television system and as many as fifteen deluxe suites and twenty-eight deluxe cabins. Their public rooms were appropriately named the Starlight Lounge, Carousel Lounge, International Lounge, Bridge Lounge and the Skaal Bar. There was also a casino, aft lounge-bar and a restaurant. Sailing mostly from New York, the *Sea Venture* was used primarily on the seven-day Bermuda run; the *Island Venture* was used on longer trips to the Caribbean.

In late 1974, however, an irresistable sum was offered for *Sea Venture* and *Island Venture* and despite having established strong reputations they were sold rather suddenly to the P&O Group for their Princess subsidiary on the American West Coast. Thereafter, Flagship Cruises expected to rely on chartered tonnage, namely Holland-America's *Veendam*, which was to become the *Sea Venture II*. However, this plan never

P&O Group

The *Island Princess* is shown undergoing her annual overhaul, between cruises, at Burrard Yarrow's shipyards at Victoria in British Columbia.

materialized and instead, at the end of 1975, they purchased Swedish American Line's famed *Kungsholm*, which retained her well-known name, but under Liberian colours. Flagship Cruises ended their passenger services less than three years later, in 1978, when the *Kungsholm* was sold to P&O as well, to become the *Sea Princess*. The earlier *Sea Venture* and *Island Venture* were placed under the British flag and staffed with British officers and personnel from international hotel departments and became the *Pacific Princess* and *Island Princess* respectively. They were assigned to cruise services from San Francisco, Los Angeles, Vancouver, San Juan and Port Everglades, sailing to Alaska, the Mexican Riviera, the Panama Canal and the Caribbean.

The *Pacific Princess* has since gained special recognition, being widely identified as the set for the television series 'The Love Boat'. Captain Ellingham, who in fact has a noticeable resemblance to actor Gavin MacLeod, who portrayed Captain Merrill Stubbing, the master of the fictional 'Love Boat', has been on board during several filming sessions. 'This very popular television series began on the *Sun Princess* and then moved to the *Pacific Princess*. It's been a stroke of genius, but we've also helped our competition as well.'

Princess Cruises has been a major part of the four billion dollar American cruise industry. They have become almost synonymous with 'The Love Boat' series, even though it was sometimes filmed aboard the Royal Viking and Sun Line cruise ships, and even the Far East-based *Pearl of Scandinavia*. In 1979, *Time* magazine reported that the continued growth and widespread popularity of cruise travel in the United States was due primarily to three factors: first, appealing air-sea package plans that deliver passengers with same-day-ease to such 'warm weather' embarkation ports as Miami, Port Everglades, San Juan and Los Angeles; second, the expansion of onboard activities and diversions; and third, the impact, particularly across Middle America, of 'The Love Boat'. The series, watched by as many as thirty million viewers, has inspired many people to take their first cruise. Widely considered the best travel value of all, travellers often become 'repeat passengers' or at least begin to sail on other cruise ships. A recent survey aboard the *Pacific Princess* indicated that 18 per cent of her passengers had booked the ship after seeing 'The Love Boat'. Each weekly episode is said to be worth over $8 million in advertising. Also, while the series is filmed mostly in a Hollywood studio, cast members and guest stars do appear on about six cruise sailings each year. Princess Cruises, which is based in Los Angeles, frequently notifies travel agents and former passengers of these special 'Love Boat filming' cruises often as much as six months in advance. Mostly, these cruises are prompt sell-outs and some passengers are asked to appear as 'extras' in the filming sequences.

Apart from running their high standard cruise ships, Princess has been particularly instrumental in developing entertainment. Traditional diversions such as bingo, skeet shooting and cha-cha classes have been added to, to include specialty lectures on such topics as wine-tasting, gourmet cooking, beauty and fitness, financial investing, classical music and even Hollywood nostalgia, murder mysteries, oceanography and astronomy. There have been special theme cruises that are marketed to special interest groups, such as Jazz Cruises, Golf & Tennis Cruises and even No-Smoking Cruises.

Although both the *Pacific Princess* and *Island Princess* have been based primarily at San Francisco and Los Angeles for Alaska (in summer-time only),

Mexican Riviera and trans Panama/Caribbean cruises, they have also been used for six- and eight-week Pacific/South Seas sailings and, during 1985, within the Mediterranean. Beginning in December 1986, the *Island Princess* was detoured to Australia for several months, on cruises from Sydney to the South Pacific islands, as a replacement for the retired *Oriana*.

ROYAL PRINCESS

Reminiscent of the royal christenings of earlier years, HRH the Princess of Wales travelled to the Southampton Docks on 15 November 1984 to name Britain's largest liner in well over a decade, the 44,348-ton *Royal Princess*. At first thought to be even larger than P&O's *Canberra* (44,807 tons), the new ship has been dubbed 'Britain's most expensive cruise liner' and, by the North American cruise industry, one of the most outstanding new vessels of the 1980s. She also ranks as the largest British liner to be built abroad, having come from the noted Wartsila shipyards of Helsinki in Finland.

Designed especially for the increasingly competitive and highly demanding American cruise trades, the *Royal Princess* is a radical departure from the earlier P&O liners such as the *Oriana* and *Canberra* and a well-planned improvement of ships like the more contemporary, but far smaller Princess cruise ships. At the time of her maiden voyage, a 'positioning trip' across the mid-Atlantic from Southampton to Florida (and then on a seventeen-day trans Panama Canal cruise to Los Angeles), P&O-Princess enthusiastically heralded her as 'unlike anything currently sailing'. Her most outstanding novelties were perhaps in her cabin accommodation: 1200 passengers were all berthed in outside staterooms.

She has twelve passenger decks and a unique feature of her overall design is that almost all of her 600 passenger cabins are positioned in the ship's upper decks while the main public deck and dining room are, in fact, located on two lower decks. This allowed nearly a third of her cabins to be fitted with private verandahs – a great asset on her scenic Alaskan and Panama Canal cruises. All the cabins contain two beds that can be readily converted to a queen size bed, and all have a bath and shower. Each cabin is also fitted with a colour television that offers a special onboard information system, teletext, four off-air channels, two video channels and one live onboard channel. Each stateroom has a mini-refrigerator.

P&O Group

A special occasion at Southampton, on an early November morning in 1984, as the *Canberra* arrives in her first meeting with the newest member of the P&O Group, the *Royal Princess*.

The public areas of the ship include a hotel-styled Purser's Lobby, with exceptional wood, brass and marble artefacts, the Horizon Lounge with top-deck panoramic views and the twin-level Princess Court. There are also two acres of open decks, including a promenade which encircles the entire ship. There are two large outdoor pools plus two additional splash pools. One of the pools includes a special waterfall and another, considered the largest swimming pool afloat, is especially designed for swimming laps. The health centre includes a fully equipped gymnasium as well as a sauna and two whirlpools.

George Devol, the president of the World Ocean & Cruise Society (which is based at Stamford, Connecticut), was most impressed with the new *Royal Princess*. In June 1985, he wrote, as part of his appraisal,

When planning this new ship, P&O-Princess not only wanted a new cruise vessel, but they also wanted one that would be clearly different from the other new ships that have been built recently. Actual construction of the *Royal Princess* began in April 1982. There are three specific design features that help make this ship different from others. Although she is not the first ship to feature all-outside staterooms, she is the first of a newer breed to have such a feature. She is, however, the first to have all outside staterooms with the large majority of them placed in the superstructure instead of the main hull configuration. The

Southern Newspapers

HRH the Princess of Wales inspecting the *Royal Princess*, the new liner that she had just christened along Southampton Docks on 15 November 1984.

Royal Princess also has the distinction of having the largest number of staterooms, 152 in all, with private verandahs. The second design feature is the vast amount of unobstructed open deck space. While a quick glance at a brochure or photos of the ship do not draw out this feature, it clearly becomes evident once you are aboard. Highlighting the large amount of open deck space is a wide, full walkaround promenade on the Dolphin Deck, and a series of terraced walkarounds located forward on the Observation, Sun, Aloha, Baja and Caribe decks. This forward area is so arranged that when passengers are viewing a transit of the Panama Canal (or sailing in Glacier Bay in Alaska), there is never a 'fight' to find a perfect viewing point. So well

The impressive modern décor in the Princess Court aboard the *Royal Princess* is a good example of the 'hotel at sea' concept; the obvious ship-board style is clearly missing.

Wartsila Shipyards

The Continental Restaurant aboard the *Royal Princess*.

Wartsila Shipyards

designed is the forward portion of the ship that we can't think of a single other ship that would even come close to offering the same viewing comfort to their passengers. The third significant design feature is the patterning of the interior décor along the lines of the newer style hotels. While you occasionally hear the comment that today's new ships 'look too much like floating hotels', the fact is that this is something that has been done in passenger ship design since the turn of the century! While other new ships have tended towards a more 'European' look in their décor, the *Royal Princess* follows more of a 'California' style, with soft colour schemes, atriums and plenty of 'real' plants.

Mr Devol continued,

While there are a number of technological features of the *Royal Princess* about which we might go into detail, there is one aspect that is of interest to all and that concerns the ride of the ship in choppy seas. Although the overall design of the hull is similar to many other new cruise ships, her Wartsila shipbuilders appear to have made a technological breakthrough in the way she handles in rough seas. This was best brought to light by what we experienced once during our cruise. In an area below Acapulco, called the Gulf of Theuantepec, which is known for its freakish weather (and similar in some ways to Cape Hatteras on the American East Coast), strong winds and high seas can build up in very short periods of time. We experienced the full force of such an occurence when, under bright blue skies, the winds picked up to over 70 miles per hour (Force 12) and the seas built up to 20 and 25 feet in height. Normally, under such conditions, a ship would not only be tossed about quite a bit, but would also have to substantially reduce speed. The *Royal Princess* did neither, keeping an even keel. There was very little motion for the size and ferocity of the seas and so little effect by this freakish weather that the ship's master, Captain John Young, maintained her scheduled $18\frac{1}{2}$ knot speed for the entire time we were in the Gulf.

The British cruising fleet has undergone enormous change and transition in the passage of the thirty-five or so years between the *Caronia* and the *Royal Princess*.

UNDER THE
STARS AND
STRIPES

AMERICAN PRESIDENT LINES

PRESIDENT MONROE AND PRESIDENT POLK

The American President Lines, based at San Francisco, were, for some years following the Second World War, the most important passenger line trading across the Pacific. American President provided the best links out to the Far East, for the Japanese had barely resumed their passenger services and Britain's P&O-Orient Lines did not appear in this area in full force until the late fifties.

In 1940, the Company ordered seven 9200-ton combination passenger-cargo ships, the sisters *President Jackson*, *President Monroe*, *President Hayes*, *President Garfield*, *President van Buren*, *President Polk* and *President Adams*, for their around-the-world service, which included a westbound transpacific sailing and a transatlantic sailing. It was planned that the ships would be commissioned by the end of 1941, but they were soon taken in government hands for military duties. By 1946, however, only two of this class, the *Monroe* and the *Polk*, had been returned to American Presi-

dent. They were restored for commercial service and teamed with a series of twelve-passenger freighters as their running-mates.

The *Monroe* and the *Polk* were high standard vessels with space for ninety-six first-class passengers only and made continuous a hundred-day or so circumnavigations. Although the ports of call sometimes varied, the usual routing was from New York to Cristobal, Balboa, Acapulco, San Francisco, Honolulu, Yokohama, Kobe, Hong Kong, Singapore, Penang, Colombo, Cochin, Bombay, Karachi, the Suez Canal, Port Said, Alexandria, Naples, Marseilles, Genoa, Leghorn and then across the mid-Atlantic to New York. While the ships had a berth at Jersey City, just across the Hudson River from the New York City steamship piers, they broke their schedules to make freight-determined 'coastal swings'. These were ten- to fourteen-day cargo voyages which, after off-loading the passengers and most of the important freight at New York, called at Boston, Philadelphia, Baltimore and Hampton Roads, and then returned for a final call at New York before the next outward world voyage. Though many passengers made the entire cruise around the world, interport sailings were also available, particularly across the Atlantic and the Pacific.

American President had planned to add three new 13,000-tonners in 1951 to this world service, which were to have been named *President Jackson*, *President Adams* and *President Hayes*. Each was to have accommodation for 204 first class passengers and to carry considerable freight. However, the sudden outbreak of war in Korea while they were still under construction prompted a drastic change in plan. The US Government recalled the three ships and had them completed as large troop transports. They were renamed the *Barrett* (later the training ship *Empire State*), the *Geiger* (later the *Bay State*) and the *Upshur* (which became yet another cadet training ship, the *State of Maine*).

The earlier *President Monroe* and *President Polk* remained in passenger service until the end of 1965. The *Polk* completed her final sailing that October; the *Monroe* in December. Thereafter, passenger demands were quite adequately handled by a new generation of fast, luxuriously appointed twelve-passenger freighters. The *Polk* was sold to Ganderos De Mar S/A, flying the Liberian colours and was refitted as the cattle carrier *Gaucho Martin Fierro*. She sailed mostly in the Argentine trade until scrapped on Taiwan in

The 9200-ton *President Monroe* is a fine example of the classic combination passenger-cargo design of the 1940s; she could carry cargo in five holds as well as 96 first-class passengers. She is shown arriving in New York Harbor, at the conclusion of one of her three-month voyages around the world.

The twin-funnelled *President Wilson* and her twin sister ship, the *President Cleveland*, were the most popular transpacific liners of the postwar years. They were also the best known American President liners. Apart from carrying port-to-port passengers, they also took travellers on round-trip sailings that were sold as full cruises.

1970. The *Monroe* went to Greek owners, the John S. Latsis Line, and became the *Marianna V*. She too was broken-up on Taiwan, but a year earlier, in the summer of 1969.

PRESIDENT CLEVELAND AND PRESIDENT WILSON

During the Second World War, the US Government built several series of specially designed military troop transports. The P2SE2R1 class, ordered from the Bethlehem Shipyards of Alameda, California, consisted of ten 17,000-ton ships. However, once the war was drawing to a close, the orders for the last pair, which had been laid down in 1944 and which were to have been named the *Admiral D.W. Taylor* and the *Admiral F.B. Upham*, were cancelled. The hull sections were finally launched two years later, in June and November 1946 respectively, then laid-up and eventually offered for sale to commercial buyers. The American President Lines, which had lost almost all its passenger tonnage, saw great potential in these hulls for completion as first-rate passenger ships on a revived California–Far East service. The *Admiral Taylor* was finished in November 1947 as the *President Cleveland* and the *Admiral Upham* as the *President Wilson* in the following April.

They were fitted out as the finest transpacific luxury liners of their time. Their facilities included two outdoor pools, air conditioning, a string of suites and deluxe staterooms, handsomely decorated public rooms and amenities such as a gift shop, barbers,

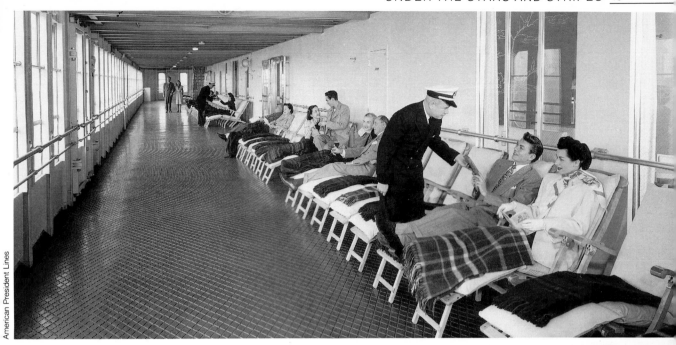

American President Lines

A typical scene along the enclosed promenade of the *President Wilson*.

beauty salon and dog kennels. In their earlier years, when they sailed primarily as port-to-port passenger ships, their accommodation was arranged in a three-class configuration, divided between cabin class, tourist class and third class, then between 324 in first class and 454 in tourist class, figures which were amended in their later years to 304 in first class and 380 in economy class and finally to 511 all-one class (and even as few as 300 one-class during some special cruises).

Donald Reardon served with the American President Lines as their senior naval architect and recalled these sister ships.

While they had been ordered as troop ships, the *Cleveland* and the *Wilson* were not conversions, but planned as passenger ships pretty much from the keel up. They simply used the same hulls and machinery as planned for the troopers. However, since their topside weight as passenger ships was greater than that of the troop ship design, it was necessary for stability purposes to build the superstructure above the Boat Deck, and including the twin funnels, of aluminium. The life-boat davits were also originally of aluminium. Nevertheless, both ships still had to carry considerable fixed and liquid ballast. The design of the *Cleveland* and *Wilson* was the result of close cooperation between the Maritime Commission, the George G. Sharp

American President Lines

The handsome Main Lounge aboard the *President Wilson* was decorated in a sleek, postwar American style that included mirrored walls and an ornamental fireplace. △

American President Lines

Located on the forward end of B Deck, the California Dining Room aboard the *President Wilson* had murals with Polynesian themes. ▷

The sitting room of a first class suite aboard the *President Cleveland*.

American President Lines

The American President Lines' terminal along the San Francisco waterfront during 1959. The passenger liner *President Hoover* (with her grey hull) is berthed in the centre of three Company freighters, the *President Garfield*, *President Jackson* and *President Taft*. The liner *Leilani*, laid-up on the lower right, was soon to be acquired by American President and refitted as their *President Roosevelt*.

Company [noted naval architects] and the American President Lines. They proved to be very dependable ships and were highly popular with the public.

The *Cleveland* made 199 voyages for American President, all in the Pacific and nearly all of them to the Far East, which usually meant a forty-three-day round-trip between San Francisco, Los Angeles, Honolulu, Yokohama, Manila, Hong Kong, Kobe, Yokohama, Honolulu, returning to San Francisco. Only a few short trips were made to Hawaiian islands. The *President Wilson* completed 200 voyages for American President Lines and which were nearly all transpacific. She did, however, make several cruises – to Alaska, Mexico and the Hawaiian islands and made several long cruises. In 1972, she made a sixty-five-day cruise from San Francisco to the Mediterranean and Black Seas. The ports of call included Acapulco, Cristobal, Port Everglades, Casablanca, Piraeus, Yalta, Odessa, Constantza, Istanbul, Rhodes, Barcelona and Lisbon. [Two years earlier, in the summer of 1970, she had cruised to Northern Europe and Scandinavia on a fifty-eight-day itinerary that read San Francisco, Los Angeles, Acapulco, Balboa, Cristobal, Kingston, Bermuda, Lisbon, London, Oslo, Copenhagen, Stockholm, Helsinki, the Kiel Canal, Amsterdam, Le Havre, Bermuda, Kingston, Cristobal, Balboa, Puerto Vallarta and then return to Los Angeles and San Francisco.] In 1973, her last voyage was a ninety-five-day cruise around the world.

Mr Reardon gave insight into the early day economics of both *President* liners.

Although primarily passenger ships, they did carry an average of some 1500 tons of general cargo, including a fair amount of refrigerated items. A large number of pineapples, for example, were picked-up in Hawaii for transport to Hong Kong and Japan, and then large amounts of ethnic Oriental foodstuffs were carried from Hong Kong and Japan to Hawaii for the large number of Orientals living in those islands. Mail, automobiles, Conex boxes [early small containers] and assorted other cargoes were also carried, but had to be limited and stowed so as not to interfere with the sailing schedule of a passenger liner.

Also, of interest I think is the fact the chief engineers on both vessels served on board for the full time American President operated the ships. Captain and later Commodore Hobart J Ehman served as master of the *Cleveland* for twenty-one years until he retired after having sailed with APL and its predecessor, the Dollar Steamship Company, for forty-six years. Captain and later Commodore Joseph D Cox served as master of the *President Wilson* for twenty-three years. Captain Ehman while skipper of the *Cleveland* received a citation from the US Navy for rescuing eleven crewmen whose P2 Neptune patrol bomber crashed at sea 400 miles from Guam. Captain Cox while on the *Wilson* received the Meritorious Service Award – and the *President Wilson* the Gallant Ship Award – for rescuing the crew of the Italian freighter *Agia* in rough Pacific seas in 1964.

In the early seventies, as operating costs continued to rise, especially for American-flag passenger ships, American President decided to end its liner services. The Company's Pacific crossings were the

Donald V Reardon Collection

last to be provided on a regular basis under any flag. The *President Cleveland* was withdrawn in January 1973 and, a month later, she hoisted the Panamanian colours as the *Oriental President* for Oceanic Cruises Development Corporation, a division of the ever-growing C Y Tung Group of Hong Kong. It was expected that she would sail for another Tung subsidiary, the Orient Overseas Lines, but soon after her arrival at Hong Kong, she was laid-up. Little more than a year later, in June, she was delivered to Kaohsiung breakers.

The *President Wilson* was decommissioned by American President, on 9 April 1973; she was their last passenger liner. Eight days later, she too was sold to the Tung Group, placed under the Panamanian flag and renamed the *Oriental Empress*. She was used briefly in an around-the-world cruise service, but was a struggling victim of the dramatic fuel price increases of the mid-seventies. Laid-up briefly in 1974 and then reactivated for some Far Eastern sailings, she was moored in a Hong Kong backwater beginning in September 1975. A decade later, in a greatly neglected state and with rather mysterious bow damage, the former *President Wilson* followed her sister to a Taiwanese scrapyard.

PRESIDENT HOOVER

When I travelled for fifty days aboard the twelve-passenger container ship *President Taft* to the Far East during the summer of 1978, several of the crew recalled the passenger ship *President Hoover*. She was warmly regarded, held in high affection and was noted for her good rapport both with passengers and staff alike. In many ways, she was the ideal vessel and, by almost everyone, she was fondly dubbed the 'Happy *Hoover*'.

Built in 1939, by the Bethlehem Steel Company of Quincy, Massachusetts, as the *Panama*, she was the flagship of a trio of identical sisters built for the Panama Line service between New York and the Canal Zone. Soon called to war duties, she did yeoman work as the transport USS *James L Parker*, sailing to ports around the world. Released in 1946 and then restored for commercial service, she resumed Caribbean sailings as the *Panama* and was joined by her sisters, the *Ancon* and *Cristobal*, all of which are discussed later in this chapter under the Panama Line.

By the mid-fifties the Panama Canal passenger and cargo trades had begun to wind down, so the *Panama* was withdrawn. She was handed over to the US Government, who, avoiding the possibility of having to place the eighteen-year-old ship in 'mothball' reserve, sold her to the American President

Lines. The passenger services to the Far East, then being maintained by the aforementioned *President Cleveland* and *President Wilson*, could do with assistance. This smaller ship was the ideal vessel, with five cargo holds and very comfortable quarters for 216 all-first class passengers. There was an open-air pool, a series of very fine public rooms (designed in the late thirties by Raymond Loewy, noted for his skill at streamlined design) and private bathrooms (and, in some cases, private verandahs) for all cabins. While not quite as large as the *Cleveland* and *Wilson* (10,000 gross tons compared to 19,900 tons) nor as fast (having a 17 knot service speed against the 20 knots of the two bigger ships), the *President Hoover*, as she was renamed in January 1957, was well suited for the six-week transpacific run between San Francisco, Honolulu, Yokohama, Kobe, Hong Kong and Manila.

In May 1962 the *President Hoover* was replaced by the larger, more luxuriously appointed *President Roosevelt*. She was laid-up for a time and was eventually cleared by US Government restrictions and sold, in December 1964, to International Cruises, a Greek-flag subsidiary of the fast-growing Chandris Group. In the previous two years, Chandris had also purchased two other prominent American liners, Matson's original *Lurline*, which became the *Ellinis*, and then United States Lines' *America*, which was rebuilt as the *Australis*. Both these larger ships were specially refitted (and given vastly increased all-tourist class capacities) for the booming Australian migrant trade; the former *President Hoover*, renamed the *Regina*, was altered for year-round cruising. Her capacity was tripled, to 650 berths, and it was intended she should open a new Chandris cruise service between Southampton, Spain, Portugal and the Canaries. Instead, however, she was sent to the Mediterranean (and occasionally into the Black Sea), sailing mostly from Venice and Piraeus on one- and two-week crusies and then later for winter Caribbean service out of Curacao. Highly successful and the acknowledged flagship of Chandris Cruises, the sister firm to the big liner services of the Chandris Lines (Australia, around-the-world, etc), she was transferred to the Panamanian flag in 1967. Her name was changed slightly, to *Regina Prima*, in early 1973, just as Chandris bought West Germany's *Bremen* and renamed her as the *Regina Magna*. The smaller ship was renamed in order to avoid confusion, especially as both ships were operating in European waters.

In 1979, at the age of forty, the ex-*President Hoover*

was laid-up permanently in Greece's Perama Bay, near Piraeus. Rusting and untouched, she was finally broken-up at Aliaga in Turkey in 1985.

PRESIDENT ROOSEVELT

Few liners have endured more ownership and name changes. Having been the *General W P Richardson*, the *Laguardia* and then the *Leilani*, the *President Roosevelt* later became the *Atlantis* and presently sails as the *Emerald Seas*. In all, she has served six different owners under three different flags: the United States, Greece and Panama. She sailed for American President, possibly as their best known roving cruise ship, from 1962 until 1970.

A rather unsuccessful ship during most of her early years, she was built as one of the last of eleven P2S2R2 troop ships (a slightly larger version of the class from which the *President Cleveland* and *President Wilson* emerged) at the Federal Shipyards at Kearny, New Jersey. With a capacity for 5200 troops, she saw some military and then postwar government service, but then was selected in a scheme to convert some of these purpose-built troopers to commercial passenger ships. She was rebuilt at the Ingalls Shipyard at Pascagoula, Mississippi, with 609 passenger berths and time chartered to the American Export Lines for whom she sailed as the *Laguardia* on their transatlantic service between New York and the Mediterranean. She was an expensive ship to operate as she had fuel-hungry engines and extra hull plating (from her troop ship design) that caused added drag and therefore further drain on her fuel consumption, so in 1951 she was returned to the US Government. After being briefly used again as a troop ship, she was laid-up for two years from November 1952. She was refitted in 1955–56 (this time with 650 all-tourist berths) and renamed *Leilani* by the Hawaiian Steamship Company who planned to operate her, as a rival to the long-established Matson Lines, between San Francisco and Honolulu. Again unsuccessful, she went to lay-up, along the San Francisco waterfront, in January 1959.

The *Leilani* was bought by American President in 1960 and then sent to Seattle for an $8 million conversion and modernization to a luxury cruise ship. Renamed *President Roosevelt* and intended to replace the smaller *President Hoover*, she reappeared in the spring of 1962, with 456 all-first class berths only, for both transpacific line voyages as well as cruises.

American President's descriptive literature read:

This ship is a multi-million dollar American resort hotel. It has spacious, air-conditioned rooms – all with a private bath. It has luxurious lounges and intimate bars. It features one of the world's finest restaurants, and a supper club for after-dinner dancing. It has a heated swimming pool, outdoor recreation areas, sun decks, game courts and card rooms. It has room service, a hospital, laundry service, barber shop and beauty salon. Each stateroom on the *President Roosevelt* cost as much to design, build, decorate and furnish as many entire homes would cost ashore. The reason is obvious in the splendid fabrics, carpets and custom-made furnishings. If you look closely, you'll see it in many other things as well. The air conditioning, for example, is of a new and completely silent type. It does not simply recirculate the air, but constantly adds fresh air at a controlled temperature which you can regulate yourself. The wardrobe closets are more than 'hanger deep'. Your clothing hangs straight and wrinkle free. In the tiled bathroom, you will find a regulator which blends hot and cold water to the temperature you desire. Connecting accommodations are available in every cabin grade on the *President Roosevelt*. In addition to suites and lanais [deluxe staterooms], there are thirty-two pairs of connecting rooms. Practically any room arrangement can be made available at your convenience. The ship offers country club relaxation. The casual atmosphere of the Pacific Lounge provides a favourite get-together spot aboard ship. Thick carpeting, comfortable chairs and picture windows create pleasantly informal surroundings, ideal for entertaining. Just aft is the Cocktail Lounge. On beyond is the Game Room, followed by the Roosevelt Room – the ship's library and reading room. Just forward of the Pacific Lounge is a special soundproof Club Lounge with record player and Coke machine for teenagers, or for private parties and meetings.

In just a few years, however, the demand for transpacific crossings began to decline. American President's response was to build two new container-passenger ships. The specifications released in spring 1968 revealed that these new ships would accommodate 225 first class passengers and have space for 678 containers. The passenger quarters would be placed aft, the freight area forward. The preliminary details showed ships 780 feet long and capable of 26 knot service speeds. Neither ever left the drawing boards. Some years earlier, in the mid-fifties, American President contemplated building the largest liner ever for transpacific service. They planned to name her *President Washington*. According to the excellent *Damned by Destiny*, written by maritime historians David L Williams and Richard P De Kerbrech,

This new ship was to be something of a duplicate of the *United States*. She would be, in fact, some 10,000 tons smaller with an estimated gross tonnage of 43,000, an overall length of 956 feet and a passenger complement of 1450 divided between three classes. The *President Washington* was also considered for the installation of nuclear instead of plant/ boilers for military reasons [for easy conversion to a wartime troop ship if needed] and, as a twin-screw ship, would have had the very credible speed of 29 knots. Unfortunately, she too never left the design tables.

American President began to schedule more and more cruises by 1968–69. The *President Roosevelt* was sent off on various luxury runs, from three-day weekends southward to Ensenada in Mexico, to two-weeks to Alaska, three weeks in the Caribbean and three-month around-the-world cruises. In March 1970, she set off on a sixty-five-day trip to the Mediterranean, which after departing from San Francisco and Los Angeles called at Acapulco, Balboa, Cristobal, Kingston, Piraeus, Rhodes, Haifa, Naples, Nice, Palma de Majorca, Madeira, St Thomas, Cristobal, Balboa and Mazatlan.

However, her soaring operational expenses, combined with a rapid increase in foreign-flag cruise ship competition prompted American President to sell the *President Roosevelt*. She was bought for $1.8 million, in 1970, by the Chandris Group for Greek-flag cruise service. Given yet another $8 million facelift, she appeared, in June 1971, as the *Atlantis* on the weekly New York–Bahamas cruise trade. However, once again less than financially successful, she was sold at the end of 1972 to the Eastern Steamship Lines of Miami, who still sail her as the *Emerald Seas* on overnight cruises to Nassau and Freeport. Apparently, in this, her sixth career, she has at last been a success.

ALCOA STEAMSHIP COMPANY

ALCOA CAVALIER, ALCOA CLIPPER AND ALCOA CORSAIR

On 13 November 1943, the keel was laid for the *United Victory*; she was the first of 500 'Victory' ships. A mere two months later, she was launched from the now long defunct Oregon Shipbuilding Yards at Portland and was commissioned on 28 February 1944 – in just over three months! It was an exceptional, highly demanding period for shipbuilding. The 'Victorys', at 7600 tons and 455 feet in length, were designed as substantial improvements on the earlier-built 'Liberty'

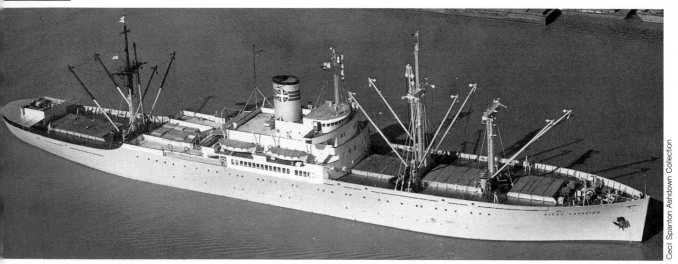

The *Alcoa Cavalier* and her two sister ships were combination passenger-cargo liners that were built on a 'Victory' ship hull. They each had very fine accommodation for ninety-five passengers. The ship is shown arriving at Mobile, following her round-trip voyage to the Caribbean.

ships. They had larger cargo capacities, greater speeds (15–16 knots as compared to 11 knots of the previous class) but more importantly, with the Allied victory finally in sight, they were intended for post-war commercial service as well. The 'Libertys' were first and foremost war-time emergency cargo vessels. It was intended that the 'Victorys' would play an important role in peace time. The *United Victory* and her sisters proved themselves admirably.

After the hostilities and when over a hundred of these ships had been cleared for foreign-flag service, a number were converted for passenger operations. America itself used three for passenger trading. This trio was actually too late for the war and their government building contracts were cancelled. Instead, they were sold on the ways to the Alcoa Steamship Company and finished to their specifications. Consequently, there was extensive use of aluminium, particularly in the superstructure and thus these ships served as something of a floating showcase for Alcoa's chief product. High standard passenger accommodation was also fitted, with space for ninety-five travellers aboard each ship. All staterooms had private facilities and, in addition to a fine group of very attractive public rooms, the passengers had use of an outdoor lido deck and swimming pool. The first of these, the *Alcoa Cavalier*, was delivered in March 1947 and was followed by the *Alcoa Clipper* and *Alcoa Corsair* in April. The *Alcoa Cavalier* actually spent her first year sailing from New York to the Caribbean while the other two were based at New Orleans. However, they were eventually all teamed together, offering sixteen-day cruises to Kingston, Santo Domingo, San Juan, Puerto Cabello, La Guaira, Guanta and Port of Spain on Trinidad. At the latter

port, each ship loaded their most important cargo: bauxite for the return voyage to Mobile (and then to New Orleans).

The Alcoa trio had over a decade of profitable and dependable service. However, by 1960 the passenger operations were becoming too expensive and they were in stiff competition with the more modern cruise ships then coming into service. On 22 October 1960, while on her last outbound sailing from New Orleans to the Caribbean, the *Alcoa Corsair* was severely damaged in a collision with the Italian freighter *Lorenzo Marcello*. The *Corsair* had a 150-foot gash in her side and twelve passenger cabins were ripped open. Five passengers and five crew were killed and over a dozen were injured. The *Corsair*, in danger of sinking, was beached along the banks of the Mississippi River, near Empire, Louisiana. Later refloated and then towed to a dry dock, she was, in the opinion of Alcoa engineers, beyond economic repair. In the following March, she was put up for public auction, still with the huge gash along her side, and sold to American Bulk Carriers Incorporated. Her new owners had her repaired and returned to freighter service in March 1962, although for some reason they retained her Alcoa name. A year later, she was renamed *Rye* and shortly thereafter developed serious mechanical problems while on a voyage from Houston to Bombay. In September 1963, she sailed to Kobe, Japan and was scrapped.

The *Alcoa Cavalier* and *Alcoa Clipper* were transferred, after also being withdrawn from passenger service in 1960, to the US Maritime Administration. In 1963, they were sent to the Federal Reserve Fleet and laid-up. The *Cavalier* was declared surplus in 1968, removed from the 'mothball fleet' and broken-up at New Orleans. A year later the *Clipper* shared the same fate and she was scrapped at Baltimore. For some years, the Alcoa Company carried only a dozen or less passengers aboard its cargo vessels and then finally discontinued passenger services entirely.

DELTA LINE

DEL MAR, DEL NORTE AND DEL SUD

The Delta Line which was based at New Orleans built three very well appointed passenger-cargo ships just after the Second World War. Named *Del Mar, Del Norte* and *Del Sid*, they were constructed by the Ingalls Shipyards as Pascagoula, Mississippi in 1946–47 and were specially noted at the time (as were the aforementioned Alcoa sister ships) for the advanced use of aluminium in their superstructures. Their overall designs and silhouettes reflected to a considerable extent 1930s streamlined style. They had light grey hulls, white upperworks and silver masts and booms, and were among the first vessels to have funnels which were actually large 'dummies', the exhaust being released through two short uptakes placed farther aft. Another novel feature was the circular shape of their forward superstructures, which created some unusually shaped forward staterooms. The accommodation for 120 first class passengers, which also had a rather glossy streamlined style, included the novelty of a circular stairwell. Along with such facilities as a permanent outdoor pool and a private bathroom in every cabin, were a gift shop, barbers, library, enclosed promenade and an open-air deck café.

The three ships were routed on a seven-week itinerary, departing from New Orleans for Barbados, Bahia, Rio de Janeiro, Santos, Montevideo and Buenos Aires. On the return sailings, they omitted Barbados and instead called at Curacao and then sailed onward to Houston before terminating their voyages at New Orleans. Minimum round-trip fares were priced at $900 in 1959. They were popular ships for some years, but were finally affected, after two decades of service, by less costly foreign-flag competitors and then outright ageing. The *Del Norte* ran the last passenger sailing, leaving New Orleans on

19 December 1967. Thereafter, the ships were downgraded to pure cargo vessels and their respective gross tonnages relisted at 8638 from 10,073. Several years later, in early 1972, they left on their final sailings: one-way passages across the Pacific to breakers at Kaohsiung, Taiwan.

In 1977, however, long after the Delta Line had suspended its deep-sea passenger services, the Company bought out the Prudential Lines, another American shipper, and inherited the four former Grace Line combination container-passenger sister ships, the *Santa Magdalena, Santa Maria, Santa Mariana* and *Santa Mercedes*, and ran them on an around-South America cruise service until 1984. There is more information on these ships in the following section.

GRACE LINE

SANTA CLARA, SANTA MONICA AND SANTA SOFIA, AND SANTA BARBARA, SANTA CECILIA, SANTA ISABEL, SANTA LUISA, SANTA MARGARITA AND SANTA MARIA

The American-flag Grace Line, by the mid-1950s well-established as the foremost steamship firm sailing to the west coast of South America as well as one of the earliest pioneers in Caribbean cruising, had suffered particularly heavy losses during the Second World War. Consequently, soon after the hostilities ended, one of their first acts in resuming commercial operations was to order new tonnage. At the time combination passenger-cargo designs were seen very much as the way of the future. They were extremely functional, deriving profit not only from passenger traffic, but from substantial amounts of freight. Furthermore, the Grace directors could not fail to be impressed by the exceptionally high standard of accommodation then being fitted in American-built vessels. Well ahead of most foreign-flag competition and, in some cases, even before the legendary transatlantic super-ships, passenger quarters were given full air-conditioning (still a rare feature for the immediate postwar years), and all staterooms were given either windows or portholes and had private bathroom facilities (again, offered at the time by only a handful of foreign ships). The American Export, American President, Alcoa, Delta and Panama lines either already had such 'combo' ships in service, at the builder's yard or on the drawing boards. Grace Line's enthusiasm, and projected needs on their Latin American routes, consequently resulted in no

During the 1950s and early 1960s the Grace Line tended to have at least three passenger sailings from New York on Friday afternoons. In this view, the fifty-two-passenger *Santa Isabel* is bound for a six-week voyage to the west coast of South America. Also sailing on Friday afternoons would have been a Grace Line 300-passenger cruise liner on a thirteen-day itinerary and another of their fifty-two-passenger combination ships on an eighteen-day round-trip.

Jeff Blinn, Moran Towing & Transportation Co

management would have preferred somewhat larger ships, the possibility of very favourable terms for the six ships plus a fast delivery by a shipyard known for quality work was too good a deal to pass up.

At about the same time, more partially completed C-2 type hulls were on the ways of the Federal Shipbuilding & Drydock Co, also builders of earlier Grace ships, including the *Santa Rosa* type flagships. These hulls, like those at Wilmington, had been laid down as US Navy attack transports, but with the earlier-than-expected end of the war, the Navy had no further use for the new vessels and the contracts were cancelled. Three combination ships, identical in almost all respects to the six under construction in North Carolina, were ordered.

The set of three sister ships, ordered from the Federal Shipyards, were built at Kearny, New Jersey, some five miles west of New York City, and soon afterwards converted from a shipbuilding to a ship-breaking facility. In rapid succession, these sisters were christened the *Santa Clara*, *Santa Monica* and *Santa Sofia*. They were (again, practically identical to the other six near-sisters) 8600 gross tons, 459 feet long and 63 feet wide. Their machinery consisted of steam turbines linked to a single screw, with a maximum service speed listed as 16 knots, making them among the fastest merchant ships of their day.

The series of six sister ships, completed at a Wilmington, North Carolina shipbuilding yard that was soon to close, were named, again with Grace's customary Latin flavour, the *Santa Barbara*, *Santa Cecilia*, *Santa Isabel*, *Santa Luisa*, *Santa Margarita* and *Santa Maria*. By late 1947, all nine ships of this group were in service, assisting the larger *Santa Rosa* and *Santa Paula* as well as a string of twelve-passenger freighters. At its postwar peak, in the mid-1950s, Grace could boast of no less than two dozen *Santa*s 'trading between the Americas'.

Each of the *Santa Clara* and *Santa Barbara* class vessels could carry fifty-two first class passengers. Accommodation was arranged on three decks: Boat, A and B. The Boat Deck was limited to open-air deck space. There was a verandah facing aft on A deck and the dining room was forward on B Deck. All cabins were on either A or B Decks, and each had a private bathroom, telephone and window or porthole. Just aft of the superstructure, on B Deck, there was a play deck area over a hatch covering and a small swimming pool just below the mast. On that same aft mast, a large white square was attached between the goal posts. On star-filled evenings in tropical waters, feature films were projected onto this outdoor screen for

less than two sets of ships: three of one class and six of the other, but with only the slightest differences between them.

According to William Kooiman, a former member of staff aboard Grace passenger ships, who has written a history of the firm and its ships:

A fleet of modern passenger-cargo vessels to augment the freighters, which were slowly being returned by the US Government, was an immediate need in the early postwar period. No firm plans had been formulated, but a size somewhat larger than the existing twelve-passenger freighters, but smaller than the 300-passenger *Santa Rosa* [built in 1932] class was contemplated. Coincidentally, the North Carolina Shipbuilding Co, a wartime subsidiary of the giant Newport News Shipbuilding & Drydock Co (and builder of a number of Grace freighters), was in the process of winding down their operations preparatory to closure. A number of partially completed C-2 type hulls were on the ways. Would Grace be interested? A deal was struck for the completion of six combination type vessels utilizing the standardized C-2 hulls and engine rooms. They would be modified to carry a maximum of fifty-two passengers in air-conditioned accommodations. While Grace

Howard Whitford

In their latter Grace years, in the mid 1960s, the *Santa Luisa* and her sisters were repainted with grey hulls and often downgraded for all-freight service.

after-dinner entertainment – Doris Day and Gary Cooper by moonlight!

Because cargo was always their priority, these ships' voyages were advertised as 'Casual Cruises'. Ports of call, arrival and departure times, and subsequent return to the US were always subject to change. The *Santa Clara* and her two sisters worked the seventeen- to nineteen-day Caribbean run, with sailings from New York every Friday afternoon, usually at 5 am. Ports of call were generally as follows: Maracaibo, Puerto Cabello, La Guaira and Guanta (all in Venezuela), Cartagena (in Colombia) and then homeward via Kingston (particularly in order to load Jamaican bananas). Minimum fares in 1960 for these round-trip sailings began at $535.

The six sisters of the *Santa Barbara* group normally traded on the forty-day west coast of South America run, sailing from New York (again, usually on Friday afternoons) for Cristobal and passage through the Panama Canal, then southward to Buenaventura in Colombia, Callao and Salaverry in Peru, Antofagasta and Valparaiso in Chile, and then northward via Guayaquil in Ecuador (for bananas and coffee), Buenaventura (for still more coffee) and finally a second transit of the Panama Canal. Of course, because of varying cargo commitments schedules were often changed. Frequently, these ships called at Philadelphia and Baltimore (and in later years at Savannah, Jacksonville and/or Miami) for special cargo calls. Occasionally, they would also put into Perth Amboy, New Jersey, to deliver nitrates from Chile for the giant Anaconda Corporation and, on at least one occasion, went to Bridgeport, Connecticut for similar freight purposes. The forty-day round voyage as far south as Valparaiso was offered for $800 in 1960.

By the late fifties, however, the opportunities for

these ships to make a high profit began, slowly, to disappear. Stiff competition began to appear, namely in the form of the nationally-owned Grancolombiana and Venezuelan lines, which were luring precious and revenue-producing cargos into their ships. Furthermore, Grace was faced with the increasing cost of hiring American crew (which had always been more expensive than foreign labour). Schedules were altered again and again in order to try and achieve better results. The extra (and expensive) passenger-carrying service was dropped from many sailings. In the end, a new series of six twelve-passenger freighters were designed as replacements. This was the *Santa Lucia* class which finally came into service in 1966–67.

The original fifty-two-passenger *Santa*s began to go through a rather tangled series of name and ownership changes, their careers often resembling characters in some long-running soap opera. The *Santa Clara* was the first of the group to leave service, in 1959, and was sent to the US Government 'mothball fleet' near Bear Mountain, New York. Over a decade later, in September 1970, she was sold for $171,000 to Spanish shipbreakers and towed across the Atlantic to Castellon. The *Santa Monica* was sold off to an American holding company in 1963 and became the *Maximus* for general tramping. According to William Kooiman,

The former *Santa Monica* gained a special place for herself when she obtained a charter to carry Red Cross supplies to Cuba in exchange for prisoners held by that nation since the Bay of Pigs invasion. She discharged 5000 tons of cargo at Havana and embarked 900 passengers. She arrived at Port Everglades, Florida after a mercifully short voyage.

Fred Rodriguez Collection

Grace Line's brand new *Santa Rosa*, commissioned in June 1958, approaches New York Harbor on her maiden voyage.

A year later, in 1964, her name reverted to *Santa Monica*, but in 1966 she was bought by the Cosmos Navigation Corporation, a virtually unknown American carrier and rechristened *Cosmos Trader* just in time to be assigned to the Vietnam military supply run. This latter service occupied a considerable amount of time during the final years of most of these remaining *Santa*s. Far from the tranquil Caribbean or coffee ports of South America they were now often seen, under new names and in different colouring, in such ports as Saigon, Da Nang, Cam Rah Bay and Qui Nhon. The former *Santa Monica* ended her days at a Taiwan scrapyard in August 1969.

The *Santa Sofia* followed a similar pattern: she was renamed *A & J Faith* in 1963, reverted to her original name a year later, then to *Cosmos Mariner*, from 1966 until scrapped on Taiwan in August 1970. The *Santa Barbara* remained with Grace, becoming the *Santa Monica* in 1966, before finally going for scrap at Baltimore in December 1968. Once at the breakers' yard, the final details were evidently changed and

instead she was towed across to Bilbao, Spain for scrapping. The *Santa Cecilia* was sold off in 1968 to the Anchor Shipping Corporation, another little known American tramp operator, and became their *Julia*. She too went to the Vietnamese run until immobilized in the Pacific, during a voyage from Mobile to Saigon, in February 1970. She limped to Honolulu, discharged her cargo and was estimated to be beyond economic repair. In April, she put into Kaohsiung on Taiwan, reportedly with a heavy list, and was promptly scrapped.

The *Santa Isabel* became the *Santa Cristina* in 1967. Only a year later she was sold to Anchor Shipping and renamed *Sofia*. She was scrapped on Taiwan in July 1970. The *Santa Luisa* was sold to the Central Gulf Steamship Company in 1969 and her name abbreviated to *Luisa*. After some Southeast Asian military sailings, she too was broken-up at Kaohsiung, in May 1970. After considerable time in lay-up, the *Santa Margarita* was towed to Bilbao, Spain, in November 1968 for breaking up. Finally, the *Santa Maria* was renamed as *Santa Elena* by Grace in 1962. Four years later, she became the *Santa Sofia*. In 1969, she also went to the Anchor Shipping Corporation, was rechristened the *Sun* and worked on the government supply service. Rusted and in poor mechanical condition (similar to the other sisters during the twilight years), she arrived at Kaohsiung in February 1970 and was soon broken-up.

SANTA ROSA AND SANTA PAULA

In 1957–58 Grace spent $50 million on two brand-new passenger-cargo cruise ships, the 15,000-ton sisters *Santa Rosa* and *Santa Paula*. They replaced two older passenger ships, the 9900-ton *Santa Rosa* and *Santa Paula* of 1932–33. The new ships, which had 300 all-first class berths in high standard accommodation (there was a high number of interconnecting suites, all cabins were very spacious and every room had private bathroom facilities), were used on Grace's premier service, weekly two-week Caribbean cruises, sailing from New York each Friday afternoon. In their early years, the itinerary was listed as Curacao, La Guaira, Kingston, Nassau and Port Everglades and return to New York. Minimum fares in 1960 were $595 for the round-trip sailing.

Commissioned in June and September 1958, the liners were built at the giant Newport News Shipyards in Virginia, builders of the earlier *America* and the speed champion *United States*. When the *Santa Rosa* was delivered, for several months she was teamed alongside the original *Santa Rosa* which had been renamed *Santa Paula*. The elder *Santa Paula* had to be retired first and, in consequence, when both earlier ships were retired, there were two *Santa Paula*s in lay-up reserve status. When the new *Santa Paula* was delivered, she made an unusual excursion, becoming the largest passenger liner to sail along the upper Hudson River, well beyond New York City, to Albany.

The new Grace 'twins' became exceptionally popular cruise ships. According to William Kooiman, who served in the purser's department aboard both ships,

Only twenty to thirty per cent of our passengers were one-way travellers; the remainder were full two-week cruise passengers. Although fitted with four large cargo holds, our freight in the early days was actually quite light. Southbound, we would carry refrigerated goods such as eggs, butter and cheese as well as manufactured goods, machinery and foodstuffs. The northbound sailings were extremely light, taking only small amounts of coffee and, in later years, tropical fruits from Jamaica.

The 'grand opening' of the *Kuwait Mariott Hotel*, the former *Santa Paula*.

Although their schedules were frequently disrupted by American seamen's and dockers' strikes, the only other event of note occurred when, on 26 March 1959, the inbound *Santa Rosa* collided in fog with the US-flag tanker *Valchem* off the New Jersey coast. This was a particularly serious collision: the tanker's aft deckhouse and funnel was lifted off by the sharp stem of the Grace liner and carried into New York Harbor on the smashed bow of the *Santa Rosa*.

In late 1969, the once powerful Grace Line fleet was bought out by an other American shipper, the Prudential Lines. The two combined to become the Prudential-Grace Lines (until 1975) and the funnels of the ships were repainted in Prudential colours. William Kooiman recalled,

The *Rosa* and the *Paula* had just had a record year in passenger service. The *Santa Magdalena* class ships were losing money, however, and strikes were frequent. Furthermore, the Grace Company was disturbed by frequent jurisdictional disputes, especially in Latin American ports. In the end, when the offer from Prudential was received, the Grace management decided simply to concentrate their assets in other areas. In little more than two years, the Prudential management decided to strengthen their cargo ship operations, especially with a new series of *Lash* barge-carrying freighters. With great regret, the *Rosa* and the *Paula* were abruptly withdrawn from service.

The two Grace liners were laid-up at Hampton Roads, Virginia, in early 1971 and have rarely sailed since. The *Santa Rosa* was sold off, after considerable rumour that she would be converted to a US Navy hospital ship, to the Vintero Sales Corporation, a New York-based shipowner with Venezuelan interests. She was renamed *Samos Sky* and used for cruises from

La Guaira to the Caribbean and Florida. In 1976 she was sent to a Baltimore shipyard for a refit. Little else seemed to have occured. Partially stripped and in neglected condition, she was later shifted to an un-used berth, also in Baltimore harbour, where she remains at the time of writing. At the last report, the former *Santa Rosa* was in very poor condition.

The *Santa Paula* fared better. After little more than a year in lay-up, she was cleared by the US Government for sale to the Ocean Special Shipping Co of Greece, a holding company for the Sun Line cruise ships. Although it was planned to rebuild her (with over 700 berths) for Aegean and Caribbean cruises as the *Stella Polaris*, she was laid-up for several years. In 1976, she was taken in hand by Greek dockyards and rebuilt for the Mariott Corporation as a stationary hotel and resort complex. The final alterations were completed at Rijeka before the for-mer liner was towed through the Suez Canal and Red Sea to her new home base in Kuwait. Now known as the *Kuwait Mariott Hotel*, her owners are listed as the National Hotel & Tourist Co of Kuwait. Such a Middle Eastern base is far removed from her once familiar North American trade.

SANTA MAGDALENA, SANTA MARIANA, SANTA MARIA AND SANTA MERCEDES

In the early 1960s, Grace decided to strengthen its west coast of South America service with a quartet of very modern combination liners. Ordered from the Bethlehem Steel Company yards at Sparrows Point, near Baltimore in Maryland, each of these ships was dedicated to a country served and was fitted with appropriate décor and artifacts: the *Santa Magdalena* for Colombia, the *Santa Mariana* for Ecuador, the *Santa Maria* for Panama and the *Santa Mercedes* for Peru. They were delivered to Grace in a period of fourteen months, beginning with the *Magdalena* in February 1963 and finishing with the *Mercedes* in April 1964.

They were rather unconventional in design, with the Grace colours painted along the uppermost decks and the exhausts worked through small stovepipes; the latter were replaced by actual funnels, which were lifted aboard the ships by helicopter while at their normal New York harbour berths. Specially designed to carry as many as 175 containers, each ship had four large gantry cranes, two forward and two aft, each one capable of lifting a 20-ton container. Several of the cargo holds included side doors and extendable underdeck cranes for handling palletized cargo and cars. There was a special capacity for 90,000 stems of bananas, 10 tanks for 100 tons of bulk liquid cargos and 20,000 cubic feet of refrigerator spaces. The superb passenger quarters were located on three decks and included a restaurant with a full sea view, several public lounges, a children's playroom, open-air pool, outdoor cinema and top-deck observatory with swivel chairs (added specifically for transits of the Panama Canal).

At first, the ships were scheduled for weekly departures on voyages of twenty-six day duration, from Port Newark, New Jersey (fifteen miles west of the customary New York City passenger ship piers) to Kingston, Cartagena, Cristobal, Balboa, Buenaventura (Colombia), Guayaquil and Callao, before reversing course for New York. Although

The *Santa Maria* and her three identical sister ships were especially designed for the embryonic container cargo shipping industry in Latin America. For this purpose, they were fitted with their own container cranes for loading.

Roger Sherlock

initially popular as cruise ships as well, William Kooiman recalled that cargo was an important element of their operation. 'Southbound, we took mostly manufactured goods, but the biggest and most profitable cargos came on the northbound runs. These were bananas and coffee.'

Soon after their hulls were repainted in black in 1968 (they later reverted to the original grey), the scheduled operations of these four ships began a continuous series of changes. In spring 1969, the *Santa Magdalena*, *Santa Maria* and *Santa Mercedes* were reassigned to a nineteen-day round-trip schedule as far south as Guayaquil while the *Santa Mariana* ran a separate thirty-nine-day itinerary as far south as Valparaiso. Beginning in January 1970, the three former ships began outbound calls at Bermuda while the *Mariana* added a southbound stop at Port Everglades and homewards to Jacksonville. At about the same time, these ships passed into Prudential Line's ownership, were given new funnel colours and their operations listed under Prudential-Grace Lines' operations. According to William Kooiman, their services slumped considerably at this time.

'Their overall operating certificates were actually in jeopardy. They were terribly neglected and, despite being less than ten years old, were thought by some to be ready for scrapping. With much of their cargo trade gone to less expensive South American-flag ships and the passenger trade seriously rivalled by other cruise companies, the four sisters known as the 'Santa Ms' were run like 'tramps' in the late sixties and early seventies.

In a large Prudential reorganization in 1972, the *Santa*s *Maria*, *Mariana* and *Mercedes* were refitted and redecorated for a new passenger service around continental South America, sixty-four-day round-trip voyages that departed from Vancouver, Tacoma, San Francisco and Los Angeles and sailed to Manzanillo, Balboa, the Panama Canal, Cartagena, Puerto Cabello, La Guaira, Rio de Janeiro, Santos, Buenos Aires, the Straits of Magellan, Valparaiso, Callao, Buenaventura and then returned to the West Coast ports. Minimum fares in 1980 began at $7500. The *Santa Magdalena*, which had been left on the New York–South America 'banana run' with her passenger quarters closed-off, was transferred to the West Coast in 1975, refitted, and then joined her three other sisters. In later years, after Prudential-Grace changed its name to Prudential and was bought out by the Delta Lines of New Orleans (in 1977), the continuation of passenger services for the four ships was

frequently re-evaluated. They had very serious competition from less expensive foreign-flag cargo ships and all their passenger cruise sailings only appealed to the upper-market of the US travel industry. When, in 1983, the Delta Line itself changed owners, the fate of the four ships was sealed. A year later, the vessels, in rather poor and neglected condition, were decommissioned at San Francisco. The *Santa Mercedes* was transferred to the US Maritime Commission, who have had her rebuilt as the merchant marine cadet training ship *Patriot State*. With a capacity for 600 students, she sails for the Massachusetts State Maritime Academy. The other three ships are laid-up near San Francisco harbour at the time of writing.

MOORE McCORMACK LINES

BRASIL AND ARGENTINA

At the same time as the Grace Line built two new passenger cruise ships in the mid-fifties, another US shipper, the Moore McCormack Lines, also based at New York, ordered a large pair of liners for its east coast of South America run. Replacing two veteran liners, the 20,000-ton *Brazil* and *Argentina* of the late 1920s, the new liners, at some 23,000 tons, would be more compatible with the ever-increasing cruise trades. Apart from providing regular service for one-way as well as interport passengers between New York, Rio and Buenos Aires, both ships would be ideally suited for both long and short cruise sailings, either for one or two weeks to the Caribbean, or six weeks to the Mediterranean or Scandinavia, or eight weeks around continental Africa.

Built in the American deep south, at the Ingalls Shipyards at Pascagoula, Mississippi, the *Brasil* (using the Portuguese spelling) was commissioned in September 1958. The *Argentina* followed three months later, in December. Each cost an expensive $25 million and were planned as part of a forty-ship replacement programme for Moore-McCormack, America's most important shipper to the South American east coast. They had all-white hulls, sharply raked bows and a very modern silhouette created by having a dummy funnel contraption that was actually a glass-covered solarium and observatory (both of which were removed during their 1963 refits). Their exhaust was released through twin uptakes that were positioned aft. There were two cargo holds forward, a tall mast placed above the bridge and a mast with booms

The funnel on Moore McCormack's *Brasil* and her sister ship, the *Argentina*, was a dummy and used as a solarium. Smoke was dispensed through the twin uptakes placed aft.

on an aft deck for one further hatch. The accommodation was of a very high standard, described by a commentator as 'comfortable modern', and included twin outdoor pools, several fine public rooms, four deluxe suites and 182 large staterooms, all of which had private bathroom facilities. The ships were primarily routed on a thirty-one-day schedule that left New York and went to Barbados, Rio de Janeiro, Santos, Montevideo, Buenos Aires and then returned via the same ports with the exception of the call at Trinidad which was replaced by Barbados.

Unfortunately, these sister ships were not successful. During the 1960s, their operations became more and more deficit-ridden, primarily because of the high costs of American-flag ship operations and also as more and more passengers travelled in less expensively priced foreign-flag competitors. These ships were also frequent victims of strikes, disruptive periods that caused cancelled sailings and periods of idleness lingering at backwater shipyard berths. In the late sixties, their operations were coordinated with the Grace Line in an effort to trim expenses. In fact, this was of little help. While new cruise itineraries were being prepared, in the late summer of 1969, both ships were abruptly withdrawn from service and

placed together at a Baltimore shipyard. Moore McCormack no longer was interested in passenger liner operations. In fact, just prior to their retirement, the Company chairman commented, 'Why they were built in the first place remains a mystery of corporate decision-making.'

Untouched for nearly three years, they were finally cleared by US Government regulations, sold to the Holland-America Line and registered at Curacao. Sent to Bremerhaven, they were refitted for further cruise service. The *Argentina* became the *Veendam* and the *Brasil* the *Volendam*. Further details on their careers are given in the Holland-America Line section on page 109.

MATSON LINE

LURLINE AND MATSONIA/LURLINE

The Matson Navigation Company of San Francisco had the best known name in Hawaiian islands shipping. Along with freight and regular passenger services to and from Honolulu, the Company began the first round voyage cruise services to this area in the late 1920s. These all proved to be a great boon to Hawaiian tourism, and in fact provided the very groundwork for its enormous popularity today. The first cruise sailings were run by the 17,200-ton *Malolo*, which appears in a subsequent section of this book as the Greek *Queen Frederica*. Her great success led, by the early thirties, to a trio of even larger, more luxurious ships – the *Mariposa* and *Monterey* for an extended run to the South Pacific and to Australia and New Zealand, and the third sister, the *Lurline*, for assistance on the busy Honolulu route.

Built by the Bethlehem Steel Company at Quincy, Massachusetts, the new ships were among the most beautiful and highly praised of their time. They also became three of the most long-lived passenger ships. The *Mariposa*'s career lasted for over forty years and the *Monterey* and *Lurline* remained afloat well past their fiftieth years. Each of these ships originally had two evenly slanted funnels (the familiar, large blue 'Ms' were not added, however, until after the Second World War), and well proportioned superstrutures offset by two tall masts. The accommodation was nothing if not handsomely modern, often considered to be among the very finest at sea in the thirties. It was originally arranged for 475 in first

class and 240 in cabin class (onboard the *Lurline*). They were all called to war duties just after the attack on Pearl Harbor in December 1941, and thereafter undertook successful, accident-free work as high-capacity troopers. However, once the war was over, because the costs of ship repairs and refits had risen dramatically, only one of the ships, the *Lurline*, was selected for reactivation. She returned to Honolulu on her first commercial visit, on 20 April 1948, to a gala reception of 200 escort craft and the Governor's special proclamation of 'Lurline Day'. Once again, she became a highly popular passenger vessel.

The original *Mariposa* and *Monterey* were kept in lay-up quite near San Francisco, at the old Bethlehem Shipyards at Alameda. Some years later, in late 1953, when it was realized that the former would not be brought into service again for Matson, she was sold to the Home Lines and became their *Homeric* under

Docked at San Francisco's Pier 35 between voyages to Honolulu, the original *Lurline* was among the most popular and successful of all Pacific liners. She was retired in 1963 and replaced by her near-sister, the *Matsonia*. The *Lurline* became the *Ellinis* for the Greek Chandris Group.

Matson Line

Panamanian colours. She too appears later, in the Home Lines section on page 113.

Out-of-work and laid-up, the converted cruise ships *Mariposa* (left) and *Monterey* were moored together for a time in San Francisco Bay.

Panamanian colours. She too appears later, in the Home Lines section on page 113.

The *Monterey* was later moved to the Federal Government's 'mothball' defence fleet in Suisan Bay (also near San Francisco), until she was reacquired by Matson in February 1956. Trading prospects, at least for the immediate future, were encouraging for the Honolulu service out of both San Francisco and Los Angeles. Furthermore, Matson directors saw some possibilities in other types of cruising and also planned to reopen their prewar South Seas passenger service by rebuilding two large cargo ships as the 'new' *Mariposa* and *Monterey*.

The original *Monterey* had not been in use since her final military sailings in 1946 so was towed through the Panama Canal to the big Newport News Shipyards in Virginia for complete refurbishing. A year or so later, she reappeared as the *Matsonia* in her gleaming white colours with modernized quarters for 760 all-first class passengers. Her first sailing was a special cruise from New York to California, which began on 22 May 1957, National Maritime Day. Thereafter, for some years, there were two large Matson liners trading on the five-day run to Honolulu, the *Lurline* and the *Matsonia*.

Fred Stindt, in his very fine *Matson's Century of Ships* covered the Company's entry into other cruise services.

In the winter of 1957, a Christmas cruise to Acapulco was inaugurated by the *Lurline* and the same followed at Christmas time in the years 1958 through 1961. The *Lurline* also made a spectacular 73-day South Pacific-Orient cruise, sailing from San Francisco, on January 7 1958 and returning on March 19. The ports visited were Tahiti, Pago Pago, Suva, Auckland, Wellington, Sydney, Port Moresby and such exotic stops as Bali, Singapore, Bangkok, Manila, Hong Kong, Kobe and Yokohama before returning to San Francisco. The *Lurline* also participated in a Tahiti–Acapulco cruise in January 1960.

Mr Stindt added,

To give the liners added public exposure, scheduling was arranged to include stops at San Diego, Seattle and Hilo where 'open house' hours were posted. A unique idea – a 'cruise to nowhere' – gained much publicity when the Peninsular Volunteers Inc chartered the *Lurline* for a one-day overnight trip outside the Golden Gate for a fundraising event.

Unfortunately, by the early sixties, passenger sales began to sag, a problem that was compounded by frequent American labour strikes, escalating operational costs and the age of the two Hawaiian liners (they would be thirty by 1962–63). Losses in the Matson passenger department reached $2.2 million by 1962. Fred Stindt recalled this period.

To improve declining passenger sales, a new concept was launched in December 1961. The liners were advertised as floating 'resort hotels'. Top entertainers were

Author's collection

engaged for each voyage with different party and dining themes scheduled each evening, such as 'Night in Paris', 'Night in Venice', 'Barbary Coast', etc, featuring décor, dress and foods of the theme countries. The ships' cruise staffs were expanded. And, a Mariner Club was started to honour repeat passengers on the Matson liners. As passenger lists came in from each voyage, each passenger was sent a membership card and henceforth received information on all future cruises. By 1965, the membership totalled 20,000.

After a strike [for seventy-one days in the spring of 1962], the *Matsonia* was sent on a special promotional visit to Seattle where the 1962 World's Fair was being held. In Seattle, on April 25th, 26th and 27th, the liner served as a hotel for the passengers while they took in such Fair attractions as the Space Needle and Monorail. The *Matsonia* then sailed for Hawaii. However, five voyages were later cancelled [due to strikes], and the decline of passenger reservations, due to the uncertainty of sailings, forced the Company to lay-up the *Matsonia* at the Bethlehem Shipyards when she arrived in San Francisco on September 5th.

On the morning of February 3rd 1963, the *Lurline*'s port turbine failed to respond while the ship was arriving at Los Angeles from Honolulu. It was found that the high and intermediate pressure turbines were badly damaged. Hundreds of blades on the rotor rings had somehow either melted or were sheared off. The repair costs would be high and so it was decided to lay-up the *Lurline* in San Francisco and 'steam up' the *Matsonia* to replace her. The *Lurline* arrived in San Francisco on one engine on February 5th; it was her last trip under the Matson flag. The ship was placed in lay-up and subsequently offered for sale 'as is,

where is'. She was sold to Marfuerza Cia Maritima S/A [the Chandris Lines] on September 3rd 1963, repaired and renamed *Ellinis* and began operating from Europe to Australia.

The *Matsonia* was renamed *Lurline*, the fourth Matson vessel by that name [and generally considered their most popular name], in christening ceremonies at Pier 35 in San Francisco on December 6th 1963. The author of this book had been the master of ceremonies.

The *Lurline*, ex-*Matsonia*, continued in service to Honolulu and frequently ran cruises as well. In 1969–70, three quite special trips were planned. On 5 November, she departed on a twenty-eight-day sailing from San Francisco to Los Angeles, San Diego, the Panama Canal, Curacao, La Guaira, Trinidad, Barbados, Martinique, St Thomas, San Juan, Port au Prince, Kingston, Balboa and Acapulco. On 11 January she set off on a fifty-three-day voyage around continental South America, calling at Mazatlan, Lima, Valparaiso, Puerto Montt, Puerto Arenas, Montevideo, Buenos Aires, Santos, Rio de Janeiro, Bahia, Trinidad, Curacao, Balboa and Acapulco. A third long cruise was scheduled for 29 March, for forty-five-days to Honolulu, Yokohama, Kobe, Keelung, Hong Kong, Manila, Guam and Honolulu. Fred Stindt added,

The *Lurline* had also inaugurated the 15-day Makahiki Cruise to the islands of Oahu, Kauai, Maui and Hawaii. To publicize it, the Company revived the 'boat train', which had been a colourful feature of the *Malolo* sailings in the late twenties and early thirties. The special train operated from Los Angeles, stopping at main cities along the Southern Pacific's coastline tracks. At San Francisco, the train was shunted by the San Francisco Belt Line to Matson's Pier 35, where passengers boarded the *Lurline* for a 10pm sailing.

The *Lurline* finished her Matson career on 25 June 1970, when she steamed, dressed in flags overall, into San Francisco harbour for the last time. Her sailings had become far too expensive and there also was the problem of her age, nearly forty. Within days, she was sold to the Ajax Navigation Corporation, another subsidiary of the Chandris Lines, for use in the Australian migrant and tourist trades as the *Britanis*.

MARIPOSA AND MONTEREY

When the Matson Company decided to resume its South Pacific passenger service in the mid-fifties under a subsidiary firm known as the Oceanic Navigation

When commissioned in the late 1930s, the Panama Line's *Ancon* and her two sisters were among the most modern of combination passenger-cargo liners. Their accommodation, for 216 first class passengers only, was in sleek art deco style and included an extensive use of stainless steel and tubular furniture.

Company, they were, similar to many other American passenger companies, unable to build brand-new passenger liners, at least not without very strong government financial assistance. As they wanted combination ships, with limited passenger accommodation (365 first class berths was the final figure) and considerable cargo space as well, the conversion of two large freighters seemed the ideal solution. The 9600-ton, 563-foot long *Pine Tree Mariner* and *Free State Mariner* were bought from the US Maritime Commission in 1955. Both were members of the specially designed *Mariner* class of freighters, built in the early fifties and considered to be among the finest and fastest cargo vessels of their time. Steam turbined and fitted with a single screw, they had service speeds of over 20 knots.

The two ships were partially gutted and then rebuilt to Matson designs by the Willamette Iron & Steel Company of Portland, Oregon, at an expensive $20 million each. The *Pine Tree Mariner* was renamed *Mariposa* and entered service in October 1956; the *Free State Mariner* became the *Monterey* and began sailing in January 1957. They were routed on forty-two-day round-trip sailings, outbound from San Francisco and Los Angeles to Moorea, Papeete, Auckland,

Opua Bay of Islands (in New Zealand), Sydney, Suva, Niuafo'ou, Pago Pago, Honolulu and then a return to San Francisco. In later years, particularly after the withdrawal of the *Lurline* in the spring of 1970, both ships frequently made Hawaiian cruises as well, sometimes direct to Honolulu and return, but also on eighteen-day round-trips to Hilo, Kona, Lahaina, Nawiliwili and Honolulu.

Their accommodation was arranged on five passenger decks and the amenities included full air-conditioning, stabilizers, an outdoor pool, a theatre, gift shop, beauty salon and barbers shop. There were two Lanai Suites, both three-berth, that were located on the Promenade Deck and consisted of a bedroom, sitting room and bathroom. Six Deluxe Cabins, all two- or three-berth, comprised a sleeping area, a sitting or dressing area and a private bathroom. All of the other staterooms, with from one to four berths, had private facilities. The public rooms included the Pool Terrace, Outrigger Bar, Polynesian Club, Card Room, Southern Cross Lounge, library, writing room and the dining room.

Increasingly, however, both the *Mariposa* and *Monterey* were serving as passenger ships and, more specifically, as round-trip cruise liners. Fred Stindt wrote of this period in the late sixties.

Matson cruises to new ports in the Pacific and elsewhere were gaining in popularity. The passenger ships were still not profitable in the face of high operating costs, but at least they were breaking even. The *Mariposa* made three summer cruises in 1968 and three more in 1969 to Alaska via British Columbia. In the South Pacific, Melbourne was included on two trips, one each by the *Mariposa* and *Monterey*, as well as a stop at New Hebrides Island. In May–June 1969, the *Monterey* sailed on a South American Spring Cruise with a stop at Galapagos Islands. The July Australian trip included a visit to the Great Barrier Reef. The *Lurline* continued with its named Island Cruises and, in 1969, inaugurated several twenty-day 'super cruises' to Hawaii, which included ten days of Island cruising with three nights in Honolulu, two in Nawiliwili, two at Maui, one in Hilo and two at Kona. During this period, the price of a moderate outside room with bath averaged $55 a day or, for a 42-day cruise, $2310.

In April 1970, the *Monterey* continued with two 11-day cruises to Mexico, a 20-day Hawaii cruise, a South American cruise in May and June plus a voyage to Alaska before resuming the South Pacific run. The *Mariposa* also made three voyages to Alaska in 1970. In the middle of that year, Matson announced its most ambitious cruise – the Grand Premier, as it was advertised – a 56-day Mediterranean cruise on the *Monterey*, to start from San Francisco, on April 16th 1971 and from Los Angeles and San Diego on the following day. The ship was sold out before the travel folders were mailed. But, the cruise under the Matson flag was never to be made.

The directors of the Matson Lines decided to terminate their interests in passenger shipping and so, in early 1971, sold the *Mariposa* and *Monterey* (along with two freighters) to another American-flag Pacific coast shipper, the Pacific Far East Lines. The liners were transferred at a cost of $5½ million each and with little further alteration, except the repainting of their funnels in Pacific Far East colours, continued sailing. The ships had about seven years further trading under the US flag.

When their desperately needed government subsidies expired in 1977–78, the *Mariposa* and *Monterey* were unable to earn their keep. Even when full to the last upper berths, expenses far exceeded their income. The *Monterey* was laid-up at San Francisco, in January 1978; the *Mariposa* followed her at the same port, in April. For a time, in a forlorn state and in complete darkness by night, they sat together along the San Francisco and later the Oakland waterfronts. The *Mariposa* was placed on the sales lists and has since found new life. She was sold first to the president of World Airways for $2.7 million and later resold, in October 1980, to the C Y Tung Group. She departed from San Francisco on 7 November of that year, escorted by the ocean-going tug *Smit New York*, for

delivery to a shipyard at Mihara, Japan. Gradually restored, she was sold in 1983 to the Chinese, who renamed her the *Jin Jiang* for short-sea services between Hong Kong and Shanghai. She remains in this service at the time of writing. The *Monterey* remained in lay-up until 1986, when she was sold to new owners, Aloha Pacific Cruises, who intend her to re-enter Hawaiian inter-island cruise service out of Honolulu. She has been refitted extensively, first at Portland, Oregon and then at Helsinki. She was expected to resume sailing in summer 1987.

PANAMA LINE

ANCON, CRISTOBAL AND PANAMA

These were three of the most outstanding combination passenger-cargo liners of all time. Built especially, by the Bethelehem Steel Company of Quincy, Massachusetts, for the 'supply run' to the Panama Canal Zone from New York, they were given exceptionally high standard accommodation. Every cabin had private bathroom facilities, some had private verandahs and all of the public rooms were in very contemporary décor with emphasis on the use of sleek metals and spatial efficiency. Raymond Loewy, noted for his superb abilities in creating streamlined style, designed the 'Panama trio'. With accommodation for 216 first class passengers only, the three sisters were known to be among the finest combination passenger-cargo liners of their time.

Delivered in the otherwise tense summer of 1939, the three ships saw rather brief commercial service before being called to wartime duties by the US Government. They were all refitted as army transports, given extended troop quarters and the *Panama* was temporarily renamed the USS *James Parker*. They were not returned to their original owners until 1946, then restored to their original status and resumed sailing to the Caribbean.

Successful ships, their revenue was balanced between their passenger operation and the freight carried in their five holds. Their fourteen-day round-trip sailings to Cristobal, with a call at Port-au-Prince in Haiti in each direction, were offered as cruises. However, once in port, their passengers had to stay ashore in hotels rather than live aboard the ships.

When their trade finally began to wane, particularly in comparison to the fortunes of the rival Grace Line, the *Panama* was the first to be selected for

Built in the early 1930s, especially for the Miami–Key West–Havana run, the cruise ship *Florida* spent her final years on the overnight trade to Nassau for the P&O Steamship Lines. After being retired, she served as a floating hotel at Montreal during Expo 67.

disposal. Withdrawn and offered for sale, she passed to the ownership of the American President Lines, in January 1957, and became their *President Hoover* for transpacific service between California and the Far East. She remained under American colours until 1964, and then was sold to the Greek-flag Chandris Group, becoming their *Regina* and later *Regina Prima* until scrapped in 1985.

The *Ancon* and *Cristobal*, long familiar sights in New York, with their regular Tuesday and Friday afternoon sailings, remained in service until the spring of 1961. They had become expensive ships to operate and though there was a rumour that they might be transferred to a long-time competitor, the Grace Line, their commercial passenger-carrying days were, in fact, over. The *Ancon* was transferred to the Maine Maritime Academy at Castine and became their training ship *State of Maine*. She remained in service until broken-up in 1973. The *Cristobal*, while still operated by the Panama Canal Company, was downgraded to a twelve-passenger cargo vessel and was rerouted to New Orleans for further 'government only' service to the Canal Zone. She was scrapped in 1981.

PENINSULAR & OCCIDENTAL STEAMSHIP COMPANY

FLORIDA

This company should not be confused with Britain's far larger, better known and more historic Peninsular & Oriental Steamship Company, the P&O Line. It was an American-flag firm based at Miami and engaged in short-sea, overnight cruise trades. Their last

and only vessel falling into the scope of this book was the 4956-ton *Florida*.

Built at the giant Newport News Shipyards in 1931, and originally designed for the Miami–Havana overnight service, she retained the same owners for almost all her life. Used as a troop transport during the Second World War, she was refitted and then returned to her Cuban sailings in February 1947, with approximately 500 all-first class berths.

In September 1955, in an effort to reduce her costly American labour problems, the *Florida* was placed under Liberian colours and registered to a newly created P&O subsidiary, the Blue Steamship Company of Monrovia. Later, as political troubles under the then new Castro regime began to surface, the Havana service was dropped entirely and replaced by twice-weekly cruises between Miami and Nassau. Minimum fares for the three-day voyages began at $54 in 1960.

By the mid-sixties, however, the P&O Company was rapidly losing interest in the cruise trades, especially as costs continued to rise, competition increased and the ageing *Florida* neared the end of her economic life. While this older ship was retired in 1966 and then laid-up at Jacksonville to await disposal, P&O briefly chartered the Zim Lines' *Jerusalem*, a 9920-tonner that had been built in West Germany in 1957 as reparations to Israel, which was renamed as *Miami*. The charter was cancelled within two years and the ship sold to another Miami firm, the Eastern Steamship Lines, for whom she was refitted as the *New Bahama Star*. The *Florida* was finally bought by Canadian interests, who renamed her *Le Palais Flottant* and sent her to Montreal for use as a floating hotel during that city's Expo 67. Thereafter, she was sold to scrappers and, in June 1968, was towed across the Atlantic and broken-up at Valencia in Spain.

three

THE
VIKINGS

BERGEN LINE

VENUS

John Havers, the noted ship historian from Southampton, fondly remembered her as the 'rolling *Venus*', a small 6269-ton passenger ship that cruised in the winter months from Southampton to Madeira and the Canary Islands. Completed in May 1931, by the Elsinore Shipbuilding & Engine Company of Denmark, she was then the world's fastest motor ship, with her Burmeister & Wain diesels giving a 19 knot service speed. She was also the largest passenger ship trading on the North Sea, sailing in regular service between Newcastle and Bergen with periodic calls at Stavanger and Haugesund.

She was seized by the Germans during the occupation of Norway, and later, in spring 1945, found sunk at Hamburg. Promptly salvaged, she was sent to her builder's yard and then underwent a three-year overhaul and modernization that included considerable changes to her hull and superstructure, and even a new bow. The accommodation was

arranged for 133 in first class and 278 in tourist class, later adjusted to 259 all-first class for her winter 'sunshine sailings'. For her off-season service, the ship's black hull was repainted in a cooler white. Noted British passenger ship author C M Squarey wrote at some length about the 420-foot long *Venus*.

Since Southampton is in England and Madeira a part of Portugal, anybody might be pardoned for thinking that either the British or the Portuguese provide the connecting link. It is true that the Union-Castle Line call at Madeira bound south and north for some of the year, but the shipowner who came to the rescue of several thousand Britons and, in the process, substantially saved the side for Madeira, is Norwegian. Looking through the business telescope for new pastures for the winter months, the Bergen Line spied that the UK–Madeira run was not overloaded with tonnage, and so with most commendable enterprise, they put the *Venus* on a scheduled service. There must now be many hundred British who thank their lucky stars that the *Venus* came their way.

This dauntless, hard-working, well-maintained ship makes the run in a little over 72 hrs. Everyone knows that if the Bay of Biscay is in a turbulent mood, it likely enough means a frisky ride, but very few mind that because of the compensation that follows. Willing and considerate service is a feature of this ship, as is also her famous Smorgasbord lunches. The main lounge is attractively and comfortably furnished and has about it an inviting air of relaxation. The aft lounge draws the younger people, and fun and laughter abounds there, particularly in the evenings. Her owners very wisely confess in their well put together publicity that their cabins are small. I was glad to try one of the smallest ones myself on the voyage to Madeira because, while it is true you cannot swing the proverbial cat in them they are cunningly equipped and you can get along in them quite all right; seldom have I seen better public bathrooms and lavatories than on this ship – many people remarked on this good point.

Considering she was built for the overnight North Sea run, this ship adapts herself wonderfully well to her present most enterprising role. All on board deserve much credit for the way they really do try to 'please the customer'. The name *Venus* will long be remembered in Madeira; there is only one thing about her I deplore – the age-old custom of keeping time at sea by striking the ship's bell is not observed.

The *Venus* survived until 1968, by which time she was thirty-seven years old. The Madeira–Canaries winter trade had been taken over by two new Norwegian cruise ship-ferries, Fred Olsen Line's *Black Prince* and *Black Watch*, and a third, even larger ship, the *Blenheim* was on order from the old John Brown

Listing slightly, the fire-damaged *Meteor* is shown here in a Vancouver shipyard where she had been brought for inspection and repairs. Her Norwegian owners lost interest in her but she found new life with the Greeks, sailing as the *Neptune* for the Epirotiki Lines.

Vancouver Sun

yards on the Clyde. The Bergen Line had a partnership interest in a new, very deluxe international cruise firm, the Royal Viking Line, which was planning a trio of liners to go into service in the early seventies. The *Venus* was laid-up for a time amongst rumours she might be sold for further trading, but was finally sold to shipbreakers at Faslane in Scotland.

METEOR

Prior to the Second World War, the Bergen Line operated a very well known cruise liner, the 3610-ton *Meteor*, built originally in 1904 for the Hamburg American Line. The Company acquired her in 1921 and eventually regarded her as the best purchase they ever made. She was so popular and well run, and had such a devoted following, her voyages became bywords in between-the-wars leisure travel. She was seized by the invading Germans in the spring of 1940, later used as a hospital ship and finally found sunk at Pillau, in March 1945.

Following the Second World War the Bergen Line took an active interest in rebuilding Norway's coastal passenger and mail service, known as the Hurtigruta. The basic hull design for one of these later vessels was like that of a small cruise ship. She was completed, by the Aalborg Vaerft Shipyards of Denmark, in January 1955, as the 'new' *Meteor*. Her reputation would be almost as well known and exacting as her predecessor's.

Veteran cruise traveller Gordon Dalzell remembered the 'little *Meteor*', as she was often called.

She was a lovely little ship [2856 tons, 297 feet long], a little club ship in fact [there was a maximum of 146 first class berths only], on which we sailed to the North Cape in the intimate setting of only 100 other passengers. She wasn't a ship trying to be exceptional, but instead was just a very good, very solid and typically Norwegian vessel. She was also a good little sea boat.

The accommodation was arranged on five passenger decks: Boat, Promenade, Upper, Main and A. The public areas consisted of an Observation Lounge, Veranda Bar, the Bergen Lounge, the

Viking Bar and the Dining Room, which included a centrally placed dance floor. On deck, in addition to open-air seating areas, there were salt water showers. Nearly seventy-five per cent of her staterooms were equipped with private bathroom facilities.

The *Meteor*'s yearly operational pattern was well established. From December to March, she cruised in the Caribbean, usually sailing from San Juan, Puerto Rico. She would then cross the mid Atlantic, customarily on a two-week 'positioning voyage' from San Juan to Monte Carlo. A Mediterranean cruise would follow, often similar to the twenty-four-day run schedules in the spring of 1965, which took her from Monte Carlo to Civitavecchia (for Rome), Katakolon, Alexandria, Port Said, Beirut, Patmos, Istanbul, Piraeus, the Corinth Canal, Palermo, Motril, Lisbon and terminated at Southampton. Several short voyages to ports in the British Isles would follow and then, by early June, she would be stationed at Bergen, her home port, for as many as six North Cape cruises, two cruises to Spitzbergen and one or two voyages to the northern cities of the Baltic. In September, she might run a charter cruise to the Western Isles of Scotland for the National Trust and, by mid-September, set off from Harwich on a Mediterranean cruise that would terminate at either Monte Carlo or Venice. By December, she was sent again to the Caribbean, to resume her island voyages.

In the summer of 1970, with shifts in the cruise trades, the *Meteor* was reassigned to a different summer service, sailing from Vancouver on increasingly popular cruises to Alaska and British Columbia ports. Most unfortunately, on 22 May 1971 during one of these northern cruises, near Vancouver, she caught fire and was badly damaged. Although she was declared a total loss and was expected to be sold for scrapping, she was bought by the Greek company Epirotiki Lines. She was refitted, renamed *Neptune* and used for Mediterranean cruising.

NORWEGIAN AMERICA LINE

OSLOFJORD AND BERGENSFJORD

Prior to the Second World War the Norwegian America Line had established a very fine reputation on the North Atlantic trade, sailing between Oslo, Stavanger, Kristiansand, Copenhagen and New York, and then, after the war, with increasing interest in cruising,

Norwegian America's *Bergensfjord* of 1956 was designed to divide her time between service on the North Atlantic and luxury cruises to the tropics. Though similar in appearance to *Oslofjord* of 1949, she had more extensive passenger accommodation.

Roger Sherlock

S Weirauch

The scorched and wrecked remains of the *Rasa Sayang*, the former *Bergensfjord*, capsized in Greece's Kynosoura Bay.

their beat. I predict for her a good future. She makes the most of her 16,800 gross tons; there is a notable sense of spaciousness about her; all of her public rooms are of fine proportions, and in common with the drift in the same direction to be found in other ships, it is hard to discern where first class ends and tourist class begins. When cruising she will be operated as a one-class ship, when these undiscernible differences may have their advantages. But when carrying two classes, the increasing tendency to make the difference between the two scarcely perceptible to the eye is not actually going to be good in the long run for first class sales.

In the mid-fifties, with the *Oslofjord* regarded a considerable success, the Norwegian America Line decided to build a modified version of her, but with a far larger transatlantic capacity (878 berths in all). Although this new liner would come from a British yard, Swan, Hunter & Wigham Richardson Ltd at Wallsend-on-Tyne, the two ships would be quite similar: the same tapered funnels, identical light grey hull colouring and similarly sized hulls (both being approximately 577 feet long). This later ship, the new flagship of the Norwegian merchant marine, was delivered in May 1956 as the *Bergensfjord*. She, like the *Oslofjord*, was intended to ply the seasonal North Atlantic run, though mostly in the peak season months between May and October and, in addition, to cruise, both on long as well as short voyages, varying from five-day New York to Bermuda sailings to three-month voyages around the world. Her cruising capacity was limited to 420 passengers, or slightly less than half her transatlantic complement. For the off-season period in 1959–60, Norwegian America offered cruises from New York as shown below.

as a noted luxury cruise company. Their first new postwar liner was the 16,844-ton *Oslofjord*, built by the Netherlands Shipbuilding & Drydock Company at Amsterdam and first commissioned in November 1949. With a transatlantic capacity for 640 passengers in first and tourist class quarters, her cruise capacity was limited to 360 passengers, all of them in first class. C M Squarey was impressed with his visit to the *Oslofjord* in January 1950, just after her entry into service.

In the war, I lived for some months with a naval constructor whose habit it was to describe anything good or anybody good as a 'lovely job'. The *Oslofjord* is certainly a 'lovely job' – lovely to look at, delightful within and furthermore a first class advertisement for the excellent craftsmanship of her Dutch builders. About six months before her completion, her Dutch builders told her owners that the ship would be completed on a given date; she put to sea on that very day, not with twenty-four plumbers and thirty-six carpenters and a dozen polishers trying to finish off their respective jobs, but instead with every tap working properly and even every ashtray in its right place – a fine achievement, and all done in what must probably be a record time of 6½ months [since launching in April 1949].

In a sense, it is perhaps fortunate for her rivals on the more southerly routes that this noble ship keeps away from

These two ships remained a well-matched, highly popular and superbly reputed team until the mid-sixties. Soon after the maiden arrival of the 24,000-ton *Sagafjord* however, the older *Oslofjord*'s future fell into question. She was given an extensive overhaul and refit at Amsterdam during the winter of 1966–67, with the intention that she would spend most of the

Bergensfjord	October 2	West Indies, 17 days, 9 ports, from $390
Bergensfjord	November 20	West Indies, 17 days, 9 ports, from $390
Oslofjord	December 22	West Indies, 13 days, 5 ports, from $295
Oslofjord	January 8	West Indies, 24 days, 15 ports, from $550
Bergensfjord	January 15	Around the World, 87 days, 22 ports, from $2450
Oslofjord	February 3	Mediterranean, 49 days, 19 ports, from $1125
Oslofjord	March 25	West Indies, 13 days, 5 ports, from $290
Oslofjord	April 8	West Indies, 10 days, 3 ports, from $225

One of the finest cruise ships ever built, the *Sagafjord*, is shown berthed at Hamilton, Bermuda, an unusual call for her. Just behind her is Moore McCormack's *Argentina* and the Incres Line's *Victoria*.

time in cruising. In fact, she remained on the Norwegian America schedules for less than a year afterwards. In December 1967 a charter was arranged with the Greek-flag Goulandris Group for their Greek Line passenger operations. She retained her Norwegian name, registry and staff and cruised on a year-round basis from Southampton as a replacement for an earlier Greek liner, the *Arkadia*. Her sailings ranged from a three-day mini cruise to Amsterdam to a fortnight to the Canaries, Madeira and Portugal, to three weeks in the Caribbean. This charter lasted for about ten months and, while there were rumours that the *Oslofjord* would be returned to North Atlantic service for the newly formed Ensco Shipping Company's intended service between Liverpool and Montreal, she was in fact chartered for three years to the Italian-flag Costa Line. She was placed in summertime service from Genoa to either the Mediterranean or to West Africa and the Atlantic Isles and then in a winter programme from San Juan on seven-day Caribbean voyages. She sailed under her original name until December 1969, when, more appropriately for an Italian cruise company, the name *Fulvia* was painted across her bow and stern. Her days thereafter were sadly numbered. On 20 July 1970, with over 700 passengers on board, she caught fire following an engine room explosion while at sea some hundred miles north of the Canaries. The French liner *Ancerville* was among the ships that sped to her rescue. All passengers and crew were saved. However, the badly burned *Fulvia* was unable to withstand the attempted tow into Tenerife. She sank later on the same day.

Ironically, fire would also spell the end for the

George Devol

Anchored in Norway's Geirangerfjord, the *Vistafjord* (in the foreground), on a cruise from Hamburg and the Soviet *Maxim Gorky* which departed from Bremerhaven.

Bergensfjord. When the French Line lost their Caribbean liner *Antilles* in January 1971, they were rather desperate to find a replacement liner. Although the *Bergensfjord* was not scheduled for replacement until the arrival of the brand-new *Vistafjord* in the spring of 1973, the French made an offer for the older ship that the Norwegians could hardly refuse – she was sold in April 1971 and delivered six months later. The French Line renamed her the *De Grasse* (the name *Louisianne* had originally been considered), refitted her with 580 first class berths and sailed her under the tricolor. Though it was intended that she would make some Atlantic voyages between Le Havre, Southampton and the Caribbean (with the important calls being the French islands of Guadeloupe and Martinique), her mainstay thereafter was mostly in cruising, from Le Havre to Scandinavia, from Cannes within the Mediterranean, and from San Juan to other Caribbean ports. However, soon after the dramatic increases in fuel costs in 1973, the *De Grasse* was back on

the sales lists. She had been less than a financial success to the French Line, a Company then wanting to terminate their costly deep-sea luxury liner trades. The fabled *France*, the last of their transatlantic liners on the New York run, was withdrawn the following year – another victim of incurable economic woes.

Though it was thought at various stages that *De Grasse* might be sold to the Home Lines for their North American cruise operations (as a replacement for their fire-damaged *Homeric*) or to Israeli interests who wanted her for a floating hotel at Tel Aviv, she was, ironically, resold to the Norwegian, Thoreson & Co Ltd, who placed her under the Singapore flag as the *Rasa Sayang*. Her new operations were quite unusual for the time: two-week cruises from Singapore to Indonesia. Her reputation was scarred in June 1977, following a fire at sea during which she was abandoned by her passengers and crew. Withdrawn within a year, she was sold to Cypriot-flag Greeks, who renamed her the *Golden Moon*, supposedly for Aegean and eastern Mediterranean cruising. In fact, she never left her moorings at Perama, near Piraeus. In 1979, it was reported that she was to be chartered to a Dutch travel firm at Rotterdam, who wanted to sail her as the *Prins van Oranje*. This, too, never came to pass. Another year went by and in the summer of 1980, her Greek owners arranged for a charter to the Soviet-controlled CTC Lines for cruising from Australia out of Sydney. Renamed *Rasa Sayang*, she was undergoing an extensive overhaul at Perama when, on 27 August 1980, she was swept by fire, towed into the shallow reaches of the harbour and then allowed to capsize. Her remains are still visible and lie quite near to another former cruise ship, the *Reina del Mar*, previously Furness-Bermuda Line's *Ocean Monarch*.

SAGAFJORD AND VISTAFJORD

Though they are both over 24,000 tons and look rather similar, with single funnels, masts placed above the bridge and sleek grey hulls, there is in fact eight years difference in age between the *Sagafjord* and her fleet mate *Vistafjord*. The former was built in the south of France, at Société des Forges et Chantiers de la Méditerranée at Toulon, in 1965; the latter came from Swan Hunter Shipbuilders Ltd at Newcastle and was delivered in 1973. However, they are similar in one respect – they are considered by many to be amongst the most luxurious, best run cruise liners afloat. In recent editions of *Fielding's Worldwide Cruises* by Antoinette DeLand, the *Sagafjord* was the only liner to be surveyed that was given a 5½ star rating. Ms DeLand wrote in her 1985 edition,

The *Sagafjord* has been voted 'Cruise Ship of the Year' for two successive years by the members of the prestigious World Ocean & Cruise Liner Society, who report annually on their findings afloat. It is not surprising that the *Sagafjord* was chosen the favourite ship twice recently for she is a great lady of the sea and without equal for a vessel of her size. There is a lovely spirit on board the *Sagafjord* that I have not found elsewhere, and it seems to be infectious because so many passengers return again and again. This is a vessel on which passengers' faces are as familiar as the crew!

Cruise voyager Gordon Dalzell was aboard a *Sagafjord* Mediterranean cruise in 1980, just after Norwegian America's merger talks with Norway's Royal Viking Line had broken down. (These talks might have resulted in the *Sagafjord* and *Vistafjord* being integrated into their fleet as the *Royal Viking Saga* and *Royal Viking Vista*.)

Norwegian America Cruises [to which their name was changed from Norwegian America Line] all around had the slight edge over all other cruise companies. They offered an excellent mix of German, British and American passengers, and all of it done in an atmosphere of warmth and a positive attitude. Their recognition of past passengers was outstanding, however. Aboard the *Sagafjord*, just after we had arrived in Athens [at Piraeus], we were taken for an evening reception at the Norwegian ambassador's residence for drinks and a buffet and then to a posh restaurant for dinner. There were special menu cards, wines for each course and brandies afterward. We were even given special photo albums as a keepsake. Later, when I realized that I needed some film, but that it was after hours, the photographer kindly had it delivered on a silver tray! Norwegian America always did it up well – and because we were members of the Fjord Club [an organization of repeat passengers].

In the January 1986 edition of *Ocean & Cruise News*, editor-publisher George Devol wrote,

After the announcement that the Cunard Line had purchased the company [in 1983], rumours and misconceptions about forthcoming changes circulated widely [including one that insisted the ships would be renamed *Aquitania* and *Mauretania*], all exclaiming how the changes would 'ruin' the ships. As we stated in a report on the *Vistafjord* last year [written by the author of this book], not a single one of these rumours was true, and our most recent trip on the *Sagafjord* reconfirmed this. At last, all the misconceptions can be put in their final resting place. Our experience shows that the minor changes Cunard made were all positive changes, and that both the *Sagafjord* and *Vistafjord* are far better ships than they have been at any time in the past. It is always nice when making a return to a quality ship to find that nothing has changed, but when you return to a ship such as the *Sagafjord*, which has always had an impeccable reputation and you find that it has actually improved, this, we think, is a most commendable achievement. One expects an Ultra-Deluxe ship such as the *Sagafjord* to not only offer the best, but to also come at a higher price than others. While the cost of a cruise on the *Sagafjord* is slightly more, we think if you compare prices you will find that it is no more costly, and, in some instances, even less than many ships in the Deluxe and Superior categories of cruise ships. The *Sagafjord* remains the one ship by which all others are judged, and while some are able to approach some of her aspects and at the same level, we haven't found one yet that exceeds it. Long live the *Sagafjord*!

Alvin Grant, who worked in Norwegian America's reservations department, had similar sentiments about these two ships.

Both the *Sagafjord* and *Vistafjord* are dream ships. Both are beautifully designed and superbly decorated. The *Sagafjord* does reflect something of a North Atlantic design [she was intended, in the mid sixties, to make several crossings each summer between Oslo and New York]. Placing the dining room, for example, on a lower deck and without windows reflected concern over the effects of a turbulent Atlantic. She was always the more favoured of the two, the more home-like and had an exceptional 50–70 per cent repeat passenger following. The *Vistafjord* was also exceptionally pleasant and was praiseworthy for her upper-deck dining room with windows overlooking the sea. However, there was one rather noted design error. All of her stateroom closets were too small, in fact smaller than the average telephone booth. Consequently, the ship made very few long cruises on which passengers carried large amounts of clothing. On her few long-distance trips, special racks had to be fitted to the cabin walls for extra clothing, but which, in fact, made the entire setting look quite messy. Also, and most unfortunately, the *Vistafjord* never quite recovered from one of her earliest long cruises, a fifty-day voyage around continental South America. Just prior to sailing, there was a revolution in one of the countries on the itinerary. The passenger list slumped dramatically. This, compounded with the closet problem, gave the ship something of a reputation for long cruises. The sale to Cunard, in 1983, was the result of a slump in the cruise industry and so our Oslo owners lost interest in passenger shipping. The two liners and the Norwegian America name changed hands for about $73 million. One of our reservations officers, who had worked for Cunard for twenty years, suddenly found himself again in their employ.

Lennart Hakanson, Cunard-Norwegian America's senior vice president for Fleet Passenger Services, attempted to explain the great success of both the *Sagafjord* and the *Vistafjord*.

Both ships are staffed by an international crew, representing as many as thirty different nations, but despite the obvious differences, it actually creates very few problems. Therefore, we have a very happy crew on-board. All of the hotel staff members are European trained and come to us ready to serve, particularly in the manner of the great hotels. Our ratio between passengers and crew is quite exceptional, especially in these cost-conscious times. On board the *Sagafjord* for example, we carry 500 passengers that are looked after by 350 crew members. This is a yacht-like quality. The friendliness of our crew is another great asset and we believe our staff is the friendliest of all the luxury cruise ships. For our passengers, we emphasize tender loving care – no request is too great. The attention to details is very important such as those little touches in the cabins – the fruit baskets, nuts, champagne, a plate of strawberries and the gifts of robes and tote bags. We also give great care to the ships, to their maintenance and upkeep, and both are visited often by our shoreside personnel.

With the *Sagafjord* and *Vistafjord*, we are not attempting to create a fun-fun-fun image, but instead one that is somewhat more formal, more of the grander and the traditional. Consequently, our passengers tend to be older, richer and better travelled. Our repeat clientele averages 60 per cent and, for the annual world cruises, this is as high as 80 per cent. We, of course, cater to the special requests of our passengers such as favourite cigarettes and cigars, diets, even full pages of advance hair appointments. The repeat passengers are actually the easiest of all to please, no doubt because they are the most familiar with the ships and sea travel. The long cruise passengers are less complicated and have less specialized demands then, say, those passengers of earlier days on the likes of the *Caronia* and the Swedish American liners.

While so many cruise industry observers have said that the long, expensive cruise will gradually disappear, Lennart Hakanson disagrees.

Such trips are here to stay. There are more and more passengers who want very good if not exceptional travel, even at as much as $300 per day. The average world cruise passenger, for example, continues to remain the same. The most changing aspect will be, however, for more and more new ports of call and new itineraries. This is where the biggest changes will occur in the long cruise trades.

The *Sagafjord* and *Vistafjord* rarely meet. The *Sagafjord* tends to be based in the Pacific, sailing in summer alternately to Alaska and on Far Eastern voyages. She occasionally puts into the Caribbean or even on a more distant course to South America. Her winters are spent on her annual three-month cruise around the world. In contrast the *Vistafjord* operates primarily as a European cruise ship, sailing in summer from Hamburg to such areas as the Norwegian fjords, the Baltic cities, the British Isles and even to more remote Iceland and Greenland. In spring and autumn, she is based at Genoa for one- and two-week cruises within the Mediterranean, the Aegean and occasionally to the Black Sea. In deepest winter, she is stationed at Port Everglades in Florida for Caribbean cruises. Peter Hagmann, the cruise director on board the *Vistafjord* in 1985, gave some insight into her European operations.

The slump in cruise travel prompted by the oil price increases in 1973 led to our European services. Furthermore, the *Vistafjord* had had a rather unsuccessful cruise around South America with a scant 180 passengers aboard. She needed to be used in new areas. Since we had used the *Sagafjord* in European cruising in 1974 and since our chief competitor was the ageing German liner *Europa* [the former *Kungsholm* of 1953], it seemed the ideal alternative. The *Vistafjord* has been cruising from Hamburg as well as Genoa ever since [1975].

However, the European cruise market does not have the boom-like quality of the Caribbean. There is a limited market for luxury ships such as ours. Only a few can continue. Instead, it is the less expensive European-based ships, such as those of the Soviet Union, that actually increase. The Russians have in fact taken almost everything, but not on traditional luxury cruise ships.

When we first began cruising in Europe with the *Vistafjord*, as many as 80 per cent of our passengers were Germans. Now, this is more evenly divided: 60 per cent German-speaking and 40 per cent others. On this cruise [a two-week trip from Hamburg around the British Isles, in August 1985], we have 290 German-speaking passengers onboard [Germans, Swiss or Austrian], 220 Americans and 60 British. It makes a very interesting mix and the staff enjoy the obvious differences.

FRED OLSEN LINE

BLACK PRINCE, BLACK WATCH AND BLENHEIM

The Fred Olsen Line had a well-known name in North Sea passenger shipping. The result of their decision in the mid-sixties to replace their existing passenger tonnage with a pair of new ferry-cruise ships was rather novel. In order to economize, the identical sisters *Black Prince* and *Black Watch* shared operations. Fred Olsen would operate the ships in the off-season, from September until May, on the passenger and cargo run from London and/or Rotterdam to Madeira, Las Palmas, Tenerife and Lanzarote in the Canaries and occasionally to either Lisbon, Cadiz, or Agadir in Morocco. In the peak summer months, the ships would ply the North Sea routes for the Bergen Line, sailing to Bergen and occasionally Kristiansand from Newcastle and periodically from Amsterdam or Cuxhaven. For these voyages, the ships were renamed the *Venus* and the *Jupiter* respectively.

Built by the West Germans, at the Lubecker-Flenderwerke yards at Lubeck, the 9500-ton pair first sailed in 1966. Their summer-time capacity of 591 passengers was reduced to approximately 350 for the

Roger Sherlock

Built on the Clyde, at the former John Brown yards, the *Blenheim* was the largest and last of the Fred Olsen liners designed especially for the winter-time cruise trade to the Canaries. She later became the *Scandinavian Sea*, then the *Venus Venturer*, and now sails as the *Discovery I.*

off-season cruise voyages. The success of this pair led to a larger, improved version, the 10,700-ton *Blenheim*, which was built by the Upper Clyde Shipbuilders (formerly the John Brown yards) in 1970. Her passenger capacity alternated too, from 1100 in summer to 370 for cruises. She sailed for the Fred Olsen Line for just over a decade until, in 1981, she was sold to the Danish Lauritzen Group for the new North American cruise operation known as Scandinavian World Cruises. Refitted and renamed the *Scandinavian Sea*, with her passenger capacity altered to 1107 berths, she was used on short-sea services from Port Canaveral, Florida, on trips to Freeport in the Bahamas or on 'cruises to nowhere'. On 3 September during one of these voyages, she caught fire and was seriously damaged. Laid-up for a time, she was placed on the sales lists and finally went to little known buyers called the Venus Cruise Lines. They renamed her the *Venus Venturer* and she was towed to Spain for thorough reconditioning. The ship resumed cruise sailings in November 1986, as the *Discovery I*, mostly from Port Everglades to the Bahamas.

The sisters, *Black Prince* and *Black Watch*, have remained in service and are very popular ships. During 1986, the *Black Prince* was converted to a full time cruise ship, for Scandinavian and Mediterranean as well as Atlantic Isles cruises, and was relisted as having capacity for 487 passengers. Frank Braynard, the noted maritime author and curator of the Museum of the American Merchant Marine, has cruised aboard the *Black Prince* and was delighted with her.

Did you know that the design of the stack on this superb little liner is an imitation of a Viking's helmet? Fred Olsen, her owner, has always been very proud of his Norse ancestry. One of the most attractive art objects aboard is a statue made of various metals of the famed British *Black Prince* himself. We loved our cruise on this grand vessel, this spotless Nordic queen. A real ship, with very fine food, courtesy everywhere and style. We sat at the Chief Officer's table, Captain Lars Nedland, a most cordial and jolly Viking himself. I made a dozen sketches aboard of the stack, the bow, the stern, the interiors, and now wish I could find a place to use them for all to see. There are two other highpoints – each time going and coming when we passed our sister ship, the equally gallant *Black Watch*, everyone on both ships lined the rails and shouted, waved and clapped their hands. What moments, what memories!

NORWEGIAN CARIBBEAN LINES

SUNWARD, STARWARD, SKYWARD AND SOUTHWARD

Christian Kloster, based at Oslo was the managing director of Klosters Rederi A/S, the parent of the Norwegian Caribbean Lines of Miami, one of the largest and most successful cruise companies in the world. In 1986, the Company controlled eight liners including the 70,202-ton *Norway*, the former transatlantic *France* and at the time the world's largest passenger ship.

Mr Kloster was one of the two family cousins who ran and virtually controlled this shipping operation, along with several other family members and private stockholders. His equal partner was his cousin Knut, who was listed as chairman of the board. Both operated from the Kloster headquarters in Oslo, thereby leaving the operation of NCL, as Norwegian Caribbean is best known, to a separate management team in Miami.

The earliest decades of the Kloster Company had been spent in cargo shipping. Begun by Christian Kloster's grandfather, the business started with a single ship, an old tramp. But steady growth followed, despite heavy losses in both World Wars and the severity of the Depression.

Christian Kloster, who had been groomed from childhood for his position as managing director, recalled the decision to diversify into passenger shipping.

By the early sixties, we had a strong fleet of tankers and bulk carriers, with many in the 60,000-ton class. However, our findings were that there was a need for a ship to transport passengers and their cars between England and sunny Spain. Also, the tourist image of Spain was a substantial incentive. It was just the beginning of the huge British tourist bonanza to the sun. We felt encouraged. We ordered an 11,000-ton car ferry from a local shipyard at Bergen [Bergens Mekaniske Verksteder A/S]. Named *Sunward*, she was capable of carrying 558 passengers, all of them in a single class, in very comfortable accommodations. She was placed on the Southampton–Spain run, but then encountered serious problems almost from the start. First, the British Government had imposed crucial currency restrictions on overseas travel. Then, there was the unpleasant political situation between the two countries

Built especially for a new ferry service between England and Spain, the *Sunward* of 1966 was soon rerouted to an experimental cruise service from Miami to the Bahamas and later the Caribbean. *Sunward*'s instant success led to the building of three other larger cruise ships.

Roger Sherlock

over Gibraltar. We had to find an immediate alternative service for the *Sunward*. We had had some contact with the Arison shipping people [who today own the rival Carnival Cruise Lines], who had just lost their charter of the Israeli car ferry *Nili*, which they'd been running as a cruise ship. The Florida cruise trade was then very, very new. We decided to gamble. At the end of 1966, we put the *Sunward* on the Caribbean run out of Miami, under the banner of our newly created Norwegian Caribbean Lines. It was an instant success. When Klosters Rederi of Oslo was formed in 1906, no one could have ever anticipated that they would some day own a passenger company, one of the world's most popular cruise firms as well as owner of the world's largest liner.

Quickly, we ordered a second, larger ship – the 12,940-ton *Starward* – from the Weser Shipyards at Bremerhaven. She had a larger capacity, 747 in all, than the *Sunward*. However, we also included a stern-loading garage since trailer traffic, particularly to Jamaica, was then a part of the trade. [This service has since been terminated and the garage on the *Starward* has been converted to cabins.] After the *Starward* had been commissioned at the end of 1968, we promptly ordered a near-sister, the *Skyward*, with 740 berths and also from the Weser yards, which was delivered in late 1969.

The prospects of Caribbean cruising steadily grew, and we were steadily encouraged. Next, we ordered a pair of 17,000-ton sister ships, the *Southward* and the *Seaward*, from the Cantieri Navali del Tirreno shipyards at La Spezia, near Genoa in Italy. The *Southward*, an enlarged version of the earlier ships and with a capacity of 770 passengers, entered service in December 1971. However, the *Seaward* project was abandoned just after the Italian shipyards were nationalized and the building costs suddenly jumped by 50 per cent. We were very disappointed not to get her. The ship was, however, completed but with modifications as the *Spirit of London* [later renamed *Sun Princess*] for the P&O Lines. There were also some subsequent changes within the fleet. The original *Sunward*, which was no longer conducive to the cruise trades, was sold off – first to the French [for the French Line as the *Ile de Beaute*, on the Corsican and Sardinian trades out of Marseilles], then to the Middle Eastern interests who presently sail her as the Moslem pilgrim ship *Saudi Moon*.

With our steady growth, we turned to a variety of ideas by the mid-seventies. We seriously considered the world's first catamaran cruise ship, a 600-footer with something like a 175-foot beam. She would have had a double hull that would have included a glass bottom concept. We even talked of such amenities as an underwater bar. However, while we still needed the increased capacity within our cruise fleet, the high cost of building such a large, unusual hull caused us to postpone the idea. However, the plans are still close at hand and we still look them over periodically [1983].

At the time of writing, in 1986, the *Starward*, *Skyward* and *Southward* are still employed in the seven-day cruise trades out of Miami. The *Starward* is routed to a Bahamian outer island, Ochos Rios in Jamaica, Grand Cayman in the West Indies and Cozumel in Mexico; the *Skyward* sails to Cancun, Cozumel, Grand Cayman and a Bahamian outer island; and the *Southward* runs to Puerto Plata in the Dominican Republic, St Thomas, San Juan and Nassau. Minimum fares for a week's voyage begin at $895.

SUNWARD II

The fourth member of Norwegian Caribbean's 'white ships' is the *Sunward II*, named after the Company's first passenger ship, which was sold in 1973. This vessel, added to the fleet four years later, had been built originally for Cunard at the Rotterdam Drydock Company in Holland. As the *Cunard Adventurer*, she and her twin sister, the *Cunard Ambassador* (which became an Australian sheep carrier following a subsequent fire), were actually ordered in the late sixties. Their owners were to have been Overseas National Airways, then attempting to create a companion cruise division for their charter air fleet. Soon after the keels were laid, however, money problems set-in and Cunard took a fifty per cent share. Then, there were more financial woes. Cunard finally took full ownership. However, in the first of a supposed 'new generation' of tropical cruise ships, the style and tone of the earlier Cunarders was blatantly missing, and in its place the new pre-fab, formica, mass-market approach. Many Cunard loyalists were not impressed. The *Adventurer* went on the Caribbean circuit, mostly out of San Juan. But even the Cunard Company was less than pleased and soon had the pair replaced by a new, larger team, the present *Cunard Countess* and *Cunard Princess*. The *Adventurer* was taken off Cunard's trade and, in autumn 1976, she joined Norwegian Caribbean.

She was renamed the *Sunward II* and was given a radical refit, first at Rotterdam and then at Jacksonville. She was greatly improved, becoming a far more comfortable and charming ship. Everything was changed, from the curtains and carpets to the sun decks and even the smoke stacks. When she was recommissioned in the spring of 1977, she was a very worthy addition to the already well-run NCL fleet. Currently, she plies the increasingly-popular three-and four-day cruise trades out of Miami. On Friday

Freshly outfitted as the world's largest cruise ship, the *Norway* made a special transatlantic crossing, in May 1980, from Oslo to New York and Miami. She also made a brief call at Southampton. The 1035-foot liner is shown berthed at the Ocean Terminal, used by her when she sailed as the *France*.

afternoons, she sets off on three-day weekend trips to Nassau and a Bahamas outer island; on Mondays, she departs for a four-day run to Nassau, the outer island and Freeport.

NORWAY

The 70,202-ton, 1035-foot long *Norway* is, at the time of writing, the world's largest passenger liner. The record was previously held by the original *Queen Elizabeth*, a giant Cunarder of 83,673 tons, which was destroyed by fire at Hong Kong in 1972 and later scrapped. Even her successor, the *Queen Elizabeth 2*, which is placed at 67,107 gross tons, has to be content with second place when compared to the *Norway*, the former French Line *France*, her previous rival on the North Atlantic trade. Not surprisingly, Norwegian Caribbean rarely misses an opportunity to promote the special status of their flagship.

In the mid-seventies, cruising worldwide fell into a slump, caused particularly by the vast increases in

the cost of fuel. Some pessimists said that the trade would never recover and that the last new cruise ships had been built. Certainly, there seemed to be very little hope for large liners, particularly the last remaining superships. By 1978–79, however, there was something of a recovery and cruise operations began once again to show some promise. Christian Kloster recalled,

By the late seventies, we began searching for new tonnage. We looked at the *Michelangelo* and *Raffaello* [laid up near Genoa], and even the *United States* [idle at Norfolk], but the most impressive by far was the *France*, then moored at a backwater at Le Havre. She was of absolutely impeccable quality. Everything about her – from the hull plating to the engines – was top quality. After all, she had been a personal project of De Gaulle himself and therefore cost [during construction in the late fifties] was incidental. According to our inspection teams, she was built to last for fifty years.

We bought the *France* for $18 million [in 1979] and, realizing that she must have a special identity, decided almost immediately to rename her as *Norway*. I seem to recall some brief suggestions like *Queen of Norway* or *Ocean Queen*, but simple *Norway* was perfect.

The French Line was very cooperative from the start.

Roger Sherlock ◁

Southern Newspapers ▷

In July 1984, the *Norway* revisited Southampton as part of a series of North European and Scandinavian cruises. To the right, far off in the misty distance, is the *Queen Elizabeth 2.*

We hired several of their personnel, including the former staff captain, who knew the 1035-foot long liner intimately. They stayed with her during the refit at the Hapag-Lloyd Shipyards at Bremerhaven and then through her maiden voyage.

At present, we have spent about $130 million on the *Norway* project. Considering that a brand-new liner of half her size costs upwards of $125 million, we are quite pleased. To us, the *Norway* is now a 'new ship', with at least twenty-five years of service ahead. Blended with her very high quality, we believe in an equally high standard of maintenance and consistent improvement.

In January 1981, I was aboard the *Norway* for a week-long Caribbean cruise. She had been in Norwegian service just some six months. My diary entries were quite extensive and exuberant.

On this day [25 January], far bigger than any floating object in sight, the *Norway* looms over the sheds and, in fact, dominates the entire harbor. She's enormous. She'll be our ship for the week ahead, a luxuriant seven-day run in the Caribbean. I was immediately thrilled, that sense of excitement that grows as you approach the pier and prepare to set sail.

The *Norway* is the 'place to be' these days in the cruise trades. There are so many reasons, not the least of which is her near-flabbergasting size. I felt an immediate rapport with the ship – knowing that it was going to be not just a good, but absolutely grand voyage. It was. On a scale of ten, the *Norway* rated a nineteen. She's wondrous.

The great ship had been the famous French flagship *France* in earlier days. She was Charles De Gaulle's dreamboat, first begun in 1956 and looked upon as a technological tonic to a nation that was about to lose yet another colony: Algeria. She was to represent all of the glories of modern France and was, in fact, a clearly designed late example of the 'ship of state', that concept of the floating palace showing off the very best in art, decoration and mechanics. The French Government poured millions into the art alone. Picasso, Monet and dozens of other national artists were represented on board. She had incredible suites, some so large as to have their own warming kitchens and private dining salons. Even the dogs went in high style, with an authentic New York City fire hydrant and special menu cards sent ahead to their masters and mistresses. The circular first class restaurant, known as the Chambord, was nominated as the best decorated room aboard a liner since the glorious thirties. It all had such elegance, such chic, a floating overture to a lost era. At the launching in 1960, President de Gaulle beamed with pride as his wife named the new ship.

The *France* sped across to New York in the early winter of 1962, and was received with all of the hoopla and applause that the French had hoped for. She was magnificent and, even if some of the lounges, ballrooms and bars weren't all that stunning, the French Line still had impeccable powers. That old line about 'more seagulls following the French liners' was still true: the cooking was flawless. Four and five stars throughout. Even well into the sixties, the French managed to maintain that lofty and fantastic image of red-jacketed bellboys, Rolls Royces and Cadillacs below in the garage and mountains of Vuitton trunks stacked along the Promenade Deck. One brochure of the time euphorically described days aboard the *France* as having '. . . lemon-meringue skies, cinnamon sunsets and liquorice nights'.

Well, if the jet had made remarkable and devastating inroads since 1958, and then sent hordes of liners scrambling off to the cruise trades or, more likely to the boneyards, the *France* settled down to a life of astonishing success. She never averaged less than 90 per cent capacity for a year's sailings and all of this while only detouring to the tropics once or twice in January and February. To the French Government and the French Line – as partners in the ship – she was well worth the $70 million she had cost.

However, goddesses – even French ones – were not totally immune to sweeping change. By 1972, ten years after her maiden trip, the *France* was slipping further into the red, even when completely filled. The Government, while no longer completely convinced of her prestige, continued to subsidize her operations. Onboard, cost-cutting was in full swing, however. The free wines disappeared from the restaurants, the flow of caviar all but crept to a halt and rust spots began to appear on that once gleaming hull.

Another two years passed before the axe finally fell [September 1974]. The d'Estaing Government killed off the desperately needed subsidy, without which the French Line could no longer operate the ship. The political forces felt, in whatever wisdom, that the monies would be better spent on the Concorde. Suddenly, the *France* was finished – out of service, laid-up, discarded.

The twelve-year-old liner was for sale. Rumour abounded. Would the Soviets really take her for cruising as a prime source of still more Western currencies? Could some Arabians really be thinking of her as a pilgrim ship to Mecca? Could she become a flamboyant floating Club Med? How would she perform as a roving ambassador [a trade display ship] for the People's Republic of China? And finally, as at least one newspaper wildly suggested, could Aristotle Onassis really be thinking of it as a 'super yacht' for his wife Jackie [the former Mrs John F Kennedy].

In 1976, an Arab businessman named Akram Ojjeh bought the ship for $22 million. His plan was as bizarre as balloon rides over the desert or the revival of travel by Zeppelin. He wanted to turn the *France* into a combination centre of French culture and lavish gambling casino, and all while anchored off – of all far-removed locations – Daytona Beach in Florida. Ojjeh even bought the famed Wildenstein collection of antiques, but how would Louis XV, all gilt and polish, go with the original French Line formica and stainless? The project foundered quickly.

The *France* sat, rusting and still unwanted. She was a white elephant – a dinosaur from a lost age – that could hardly pay her way in a time of rocketing fuel costs and inflated labor rates. There were even faint whispers about the scrapyard.

Then, the Klosters Company of Norway saw hope in the exiled liner. After all, they owned 'the first fleet of the Caribbean', the Norwegian Caribbean Lines, which then owned four sparkling, curved and raked cruisers. They worked the tropic Caribbean trades on three- to seven-day trips and were turning away as many passengers as they could accommodate. At first, thought was given to a big, new liner, but inflated shipyard costs and distant delivery dates were troubling. The *France*, after a major rejuvenation for cruising, was the perfect answer. The Norwegians bought her for $18 million, and then moved her to a West German shipyard for the necessary cosmetic surgery.

The dog kennels and those lavish suites – dated remnants of the transatlantic era – were pulled out. In their place, a whole new entertainment, fun-in-the-sun complex was created: two outdoor pools, vast sunning and strolling decks, lido bars, an open-air restaurant, two decks of shops, a disco (with a plexiglass floor covering a multi-colored array of flashing neon), a theatre redesigned for Las Vegas-style shows, a gambling casino and even an ice cream parlour. The *France*'s more restrained colors were brightened with miles of patterned carpets, other coverings such as imitation slate and $1 million worth of art, including an abundance of posters and Scandinavian tapestries. In a flash, the *France*, renamed as the *Norway*, went from first class Atlantic liner to a first class cruise ship. A basically indoor ship became an outdoor ship. And, as if just for good measure, she became the biggest liner in the world [increasing from 66,348 tons to 70,202 tons].

But what about those worrisome economic problems which paralyzed the French? How could the former *France* be expected to pay?

The Norwegian Caribbean directors and designers were not just resourceful, but sharply inventive. First, one entire engine room (of the two on board) was closed down. This initial saving came in the form of far less fuel oil. After all, in the Caribbean, her purpose is to seductively glide about at a very moderate 15–16 knots, instead of the 30 or so when she swept across the North Atlantic. Second, more passenger cabins were added – increasing her capacity from 2044 to over 2100. Her chances at profitability were greater.

Finally, the crew was reduced from over 1100 to 800, and became multinational. There are well over 25 different nations represented onboard (Jamaicans, Koreans, Austrians, Colombians, Chinese, Bahamians, English and, among yet others, a full roster of Norwegian officers). In reflection of this diversity, she is the first liner to fly the flag of the United Nations as well as her Norwegian colors. The third source of cost saving therein came in both staff reduction as well as less expensive labor.

A second maiden voyage, a new life – the *Norway* was back in service in June of 1980. Now, seven months later, most of her 'teething problems' have been worked out. She's nearly total perfection. We set sail from Miami at 5pm, amidst the sounds of thunderous whistles and as a yellow-haired Norwegian band pressed out ethnic marches. It seemed as though all 1372 passengers were on deck, but then one's never crowded or cramped on the *Norway*. There wasn't a tug-boat in sight as she rather smartly undid herself from the dock and aimed her stem for the open sea. The flag-bedecked *Carnivale* and *Mardi Gras*, the former Atlantic liners *Empress of Britain* and *Empress of Canada*, were outbound just ahead of us. Then, the 13,000-ton *Mermoz*, the last French cruise ship in American waters, was patiently awaiting her turn to cast off.

My love affair with the *Norway* was fervent from the start. During that first evening, all of my thoughts were turned into better ones still. After dinner, from the stern decks, the magical sight of a liner with long rows of lighted decks was about a mile off. Even the silhouette was shrouded in the deepest black. I thought of her passengers dancing in the lounges, languishing at the bars, peering out from the top deck rail. Only later did an officer near the bridge tell us that it was the *Mardi Gras*, giving off an allusion of far greater dimensions than her 650 feet and 27,000 tons.

The *Norway* has now settled down to a prescribed pattern: weekend sailings through the year on seven-day cruises to Nassau, St Thomas, St Maarten and a Bahamian outer island. In 1986, minimum fares were listed at $1195. Earlier, during the summer of 1984, *Norway* ran a series of Scandinavian cruises from Hamburg (where she had a major overhaul) as well as Amsterdam and Southampton. There were also two transatlantic 'positioning' cruises, both of which were somewhat reminiscent of the ship's earlier days as a French liner.

Very often, the *Norway* has sailed at close to full capacity. In the summer of 1985 there were two unexpected passengers on board. Two young men aged nineteen and twenty-two stowed away. When apprehended, on the last day of their cruise, their enthusiasm for the ship was close to awe, particularly for the glamour and luxury of the vessel. One said 'It's the most beautiful thing I've ever done. There's nothing like a cruise!' Both boarded the ship at Miami, mingling unnoticed with a large group of visiting travel agents. Sleeping on deck and in odd corners, they used public toilets and showers in the gymnasium, but otherwise joined the other passengers and participated in the activities. They did not go ashore, however, fearing that they would have difficulties re-boarding the liner. Without table reservations for dinner, they 'stuffed' themselves at the nightly midnight buffet. They were finally detected during the last day at sea – several officers had noticed that the pair was always in the same clothes. Norwegian Caribbean did not file official charges, but the two were forced to reimburse the Company with monthly installments. An official added, 'The publicity might be worth many times the costs to the Line, but we want to avoid encouraging stowaways'.

The *Norway* has been used in prime time American television advertising, which has often been timed to coincide with a showing of the popular 'Love Boat' series and she was also used, in May 1986, for a week-long live broadcast of another highly popular programme, the morning news and talk show 'Today'. She was taken off her normal Caribbean itinerary and kept off the US south-east coast. On several days, she was anchored offshore, at Wilmington, North Carolina; Savannah, Georgia; Jacksonville and then Miami, Florida; and finally a visit to Freeport in the Bahamas. Two-hour daily broadcasts were run from the ship which required the assistance of over a hundred technicians, writers, editors and producers, all of whom were aboard. The executive producer added, 'The technical planning and logistics involved in airing a two-hour show live each day from an offshore liner was as complex as we have ever faced.'

Soon after the *Norway*'s initial entry into service and the noted success of the Caribbean's 'first super-cruiser', Norwegian Caribbean began studies for even larger cruise tonnage. The most ambitious was the 200,000-ton 'Phoenix project', assuredly the largest passenger ship design ever contemplated. It was said this would cost some $500 million, require the assistance of over seventy-five banks and other financial institutions, and she would carry as many as 5000 passengers. Although it was often rumoured that by 1985–86 construction had begun, in a West German yard, plans had in fact been modified. In view of the slump in US cruise operations, Norwegian

Royal Caribbean Cruise Lines

The Royal Caribbean Cruise Lines described it as a 'once in a lifetime occasion' when their three cruise ships lay together at St Thomas. From left to right is the *Sun Viking*, *Nordic Prince* and *Song of Norway*.

Caribbean revised its plans and then made preliminary announcements of a new 70,000-tonner (with 2200 berths) and then, in another revision, for a 90,000-tonner (with 3000 berths). Negotiations were said to be underway with several European shipyards, but no firm decision had been reached at the time of writing (winter 1986).In summer 1986, the Company placed an order, at the Wartsila yards in Finland, for one 40,000-tonner.

With the acquisition of the Royal Viking Line and its three deluxe cruise ships (in 1984), the Norwegian Caribbean fleet of five liners remains one of the biggest and busiest cruise operations of all. No doubt, there will be further expansion ahead for the 'first fleet of the Caribbean'.

ROYAL CARIBBEAN CRUISE LINES

SONG OF NORWAY, NORDIC PRINCE AND SUN VIKING

In the late 1960s, in the first great flourish of interest in the North American cruise trades and with very promising forecasts for as much as a decade ahead, two other Norwegian shippers followed the Kloster Company's creation of their Norwegian Caribbean Lines. Isak M Skaugen and Anders Wilhelmsen, both large and well-known cargo shippers, formed the Royal Caribbean Cruise Lines (which should not be confused with the Greek-flag Royal Cruise Lines, which was formed a few years later). This new Norwegian firm would be headquartered at Oslo, but (again similar to Norwegian Caribbean) operationally based at Miami, then fast becoming the largest cruise port in the world.

From the Wartsila Shipyards at Helsinki in Finland, the virtual masters of cruise ship design and construction in the 1970s, the new company ordered three near-identical 18,500-ton sisters. They were given musical themes in their planning and decoration, and were later commissioned as the *Song of Norway*, in November 1970; the *Nordic Prince*, in July 1971; and the *Sun Viking*, in December 1972. With berthing for approximately 725 passengers each, they were designed especially for Caribbean sunshine cruising with spacious upper decks, an open-air pool and lido area and, most notably, a cocktail bar attached to the aft side of the funnel. This popular amenity provided passengers with a 180 degree view of the stern section and the sea below. In the larger and improved *Song of America*, added to the fleet a decade or so later, in November 1982, the bar was extended so it completely encircled the funnel.

These three liners quickly became highly popular, well-reputed ships and were often booked to full capacity. Originally used mostly on seven- and fourteen-day cruise itineraries out of Miami, in more recent years their scheduling has been varied to include eight-, ten- and eleven-day voyages, special calls at such ports as New Orleans and Savannah and, beginning in the spring of 1985, a seasonal weekly cruise run between New York and Bermuda using the *Nordic Prince*. A European cruise schedule is being considered for the summer of 1989.

Another Norwegian shipper, Gotaas-Larsen, joined the partnership of Royal Caribbean's owners in the Company's first decade, a time of success best emphasized by the 97.5 per cent occupancy rate on all three liners. In response, in 1978, the *Song of Norway* was returned to her builder's yard at Helsinki, cut in half and fitted with a new 85-foot midsection. This increased her capacity from 724 to a much needed 1040 berths, extended her open deck areas, the public rooms and her restaurant. This rather unusual extension of a major passenger vessel, which temporarily avoided the need to construct a costly additional liner, was completed in less than three months, between late August and late November 1978. As time was a prime consideration, the final outfitting of the *Song of Norway*'s interiors was actually done at sea as the ship sailed homeward to Miami. The *Nordic Prince* was similarly treated and taken in hand by Wartsila between March and June of 1980. Though it was thought that the *Sun Viking* would follow as well, she has, in fact, retained her original design. Vincent Messina, a former member of staff with Royal Caribbean and an ocean liner historian, said

The *Sun Viking* was not lengthened because of a change, a sudden downward swing, in market projections. There was a temporary slump. Instead, she became the Company's 'experimental ship' for sailings to the western Caribbean, to Bermuda and for the eight- to eleven-day itineraries.

The great success of Royal Caribbean has been said to lie with its uniformity of high standard operations. Vincent Messina added,

They were a very demanding company to work for. The passengers were always 1000 per cent in the right. They are, however, a very conservative firm, even despite their trendy 'state of the art' image. They are not trailblazers. The entire operation is standardized and this creates the consistent high standard. It all follows an 'Operations Manual,' which prescibes every detail – 'If it's Tuesday, it must be Island Night!' The highest maintenance is, of course, another very important factor. The ships are always impeccable and, as an alternative to costly drydock overhauls, they each have 'wet dock' repairs, improvements and modifications at their regular Miami berths.

Wartsila Shipyards

Between March and June 1980, the *Nordic Prince* was 'jumboized' at her builder's yard at Helsinki. An 85-foot midsection was added to the vessel which increased her passenger capacity from 724 to 1040.

The *Sun Viking* (in the foreground) meets with the enlarged *Nordic Prince* at Ocho Rios on Jamaica. Both ships were on cruises from Miami: the *Sun Viking* on a fourteen-day voyage and the *Nordic Prince* on an eight-day sailing.

Royal Caribbean Cruise Lines

Royal Caribbean Cruise Lines

Arriving in Miami for the first time, in November 1982, the 1414-passenger *Song of America* was a larger, more contemporary version of the earlier *Song of Norway* trio.

Twin pools are part of the vast Lido Deck aboard the *Song of America* and the Viking Crown Lounge completely encircles her funnel device.

Royal Caribbean Cruise Lines

Brenton Jenkins, after over twenty years with the Cunard transatlantic liners, joined Royal Caribbean in 1978 and has since served as hotel manager aboard all of their ships.

At Royal Caribbean, we have a wonderful sense of uniformity aboard our ships and in all areas, which is something we didn't have with the old *Queen Mary* and *Queen Elizabeth* or any of the other Cunarders. They were all different ships. These RCCL liners all maintain the same exceptional standard. The only difference is in their itineraries, from seven- to fourteen-days. They have continuity, which from an operational standpoint is excellent. Of course, we do not have complete continuity. For example, all of our officers rotate between ships. There's never a sense of monotony. In fact, I'm up for a change myself [December 1981].

George Devol, editor of *Ocean & Cruise News*, wrote in 1981,

The *Song of Norway* is a ship that people of all ages can enjoy. By having a well balanced choice of activities, there is a little something for everyone. One aspect that we particularly like about RCCL is the way they present their product in their brochures. It is easy for the people who write these brochures to get carried away and over glamorize what they are actually offering. It is only after you board a ship that discrepancies show up and you find out that many things which you read about in the brochure are either not offered or were 'pumped up' out of proportion. It was a pleasant surprise to find that the *Song of Norway* delivers 100 per cent exactly what is in print in their brochures and sales material. No doubt one of the prime reasons for the success and excellent reputation that Royal Caribbean enjoys is that they offer an excellent product without any disappointments or letdowns.

SONG OF AMERICA

Even after the 'jumboizing' of the earlier *Song of Norway* and *Nordic Prince*, the Royal Caribbean directors could not ignore the obvious: they needed still another liner, a fourth, even larger ship. They returned to the acclaimed Wartsila yards at Helsinki and agreed upon a 37,584-ton vessel with a maximum capacity for 1575 passengers (1414 berths would be considered standard cruise capacity, however). Launched in November 1981, she was delivered exactly a year later and has since been used on the Company's busiest cruise itinerary, seven-day runs between Miami, Nassau, San Juan and St Thomas. Soon after she was commissioned, George Devol wrote,

1982 was an exciting year for the cruise enthusiast with the introduction of five brand-new liners in the US market: the *Tropicale, Atlantic, Scandinavia, Astor* and the *Song of America*. The final entry for the year, the *Song of America* is also the largest of the new vessels. Our first look at the ship came during the christening ceremonies, which took place in Miami during the first week of December. It was a festive and exciting few days, which included an overnight cruise, dinners and the actual christening of the ship by opera star Beverly Sills, who was chosen to be the ship's godmother. [Earlier, in 1970, film star Ingrid Bergman had christened the Company's *Song of Norway*.] The ceremonies culminated

Comparative scale models of the 74,000-ton *Sovereign of the Seas*, which is to be delivered in early 1988, and the 18,500-ton *Sun Viking*, which was commissioned in 1972.

with a Gala Dinner onboard and a fireworks display. Needless to say, the introduction just began to wet our appetite and we looked forward to making our first full voyage on the ship, which is exactly what we did a few weeks later.

Following his week-long cruise in the Caribbean, Mr Devol wrote,

The design of this new ship incorporates over ten years of experience [with the earlier trio of cruise ships] and with added refinements. One of the most notable features aboard the *Song of America* is the exceptional layout of her public rooms. Nearly all main public rooms are located amidship and aft on two decks, and all are convenient and easy to reach. A case in point are the dining rooms. Located one deck below the other public rooms and aft, they are a few short steps away while at the same time out of the way of normal passenger traffic. The main lounges are mostly on the Cabaret Deck. The Can-Can Lounge and the Oklahoma Lounge are the two largest on the ship. Also found on the same deck is the America's Cup Bar, the Gaming Room, Card Room and the cinema.

Because the ship was built to operate year round in the warm sunny areas of the Caribbean, the maximum use was made of the open deck areas. With no need for sliding roofs, the entire top deck of the ship can be used for sunning and outdoor activities. Although we cannot say for sure, we would have to imagine that the pool area (which has two large swimming pools) has to be one of the largest, if not the largest, single open deck area afloat. This area alone can accommodate over 1000 deck-chairs, and there is still additional seating in other areas.

Vincent Messina recalled the first appearance of the new *Song of America*.

It was a considerable adjustment for Royal Caribbean to add this ship, which was much larger than the *Song of Norway* trio. It was an experience similar to Norwegian Caribbean's, who had added the giant *Norway* after owning nothing larger than the 17,000-ton *Southward*. The *Song of America* was an improvement over the earlier ships and assuredly one of the new generation 'state of the art' designs. She had a full theatre, a separate disco and far greater deck space. However, the one disappointment seems to have been that her cabins proved to be slightly too small.

SOVEREIGN OF THE SEAS

In the summer of 1985, in another promising review of the future of the North American cruise industry, Royal Caribbean ordered a new cruise ship that will be double the size of the *Song of America* and, in fact, the largest cruise ship in the world. Contracted from Chantiers de L'Atlantique at St Nazaire, France, the builders of most of the great French transatlantic liners and more recently of Holland-America's new *Nieuw Amsterdam* and *Noordam*, this 74,000-ton liner, due for delivery in early 1988, will accommodate 2500

passengers and cost some $175 million. Intended for the weekly Caribbean trade out of Miami, her design is to follow the style of the highly successful *Song of America*. There is an option for an identical sister ship, which would be added in 1989. It was rumoured that the first of these cruise super-ships would be called *Song of the World*. Later, names proposed included: *Viking Dawn*, *Serenade*, *Nordic Empress*, *Song of Normandy*, *Song of Brittany*, *Song of Florida*, *Caribbean Song*, *Enchantress*, *Majestic Dawn* and *Nordic Isle*. The formal selection, *Sovereign of the Seas* was announced in March 1986.

ROYAL VIKING LINE

ROYAL VIKING STAR, ROYAL VIKING SKY AND ROYAL VIKING SEA

Yet more enterprising and farsighted Norwegian shippers decided to diversify into the North American cruise trades in the early seventies. Three well-established firms, the Bergen Line and the Nordenfjeldske and Klaveness companies formed the Royal Viking Line. (The Klaveness Company has since left the partnership.) Their intentions, however, went beyond the Caribbean area, to deluxe international cruising. Their itineraries, which are published in an annual booklet known as the *Atlas*, range from two-day trips out to sea to hundred-day circumnavigations of the globe.

Three 21,800-ton sister ships were ordered from the ever-busy Finns, again from the Wartsila yards at Helsinki. Each vessel's berth capacity was limited to as few as 536 passengers. The *Royal Viking Star* was commissioned in June 1972; the *Royal Viking Sky* in July 1973; and finally the *Royal Viking Sea* in November 1973. They were immediately appraised as three of the most beautifully decorated ships of their time. Stephen Parker, then a promising young chief steward, was aboard the *Royal Viking Star*'s maiden cruise in September 1972, which was the inaugural voyage for the Royal Viking operation.

It was a unique, very deluxe company that wanted to capture the lucrative, highly loyalist markets enjoyed by the likes of the Norwegian America and Swedish American lines. The *Royal Viking Star*, being my first ship, was so beautifully decorated and designed that it gave me the feeling of a floating hotel. One of our challenges was to

The *Royal Viking Sea*, during a Northern Cities cruise, is moored alongside Hamburg's Overseas Landing Stage.

Hamburg Information GmbH

Frank Duffy

provide almost any service, fulfill any need. We had 320 staffmembers, representing twenty-eight nationalities, that catered to a very distinctive, very demanding, but often very delightful complement of 500 or so passengers. Personally, my Royal Viking days (until 1977) offered an enormous education and tremendous sense of exposure.

David de Havilland, who later sailed with the Holland-America Line, recalled the first Royal Viking cruises as well.

I began on board the *Royal Viking Star*, on her maiden sailing. I started as cruise director with a sixty-six-day sailing around the Pacific and finished seven world cruises later, in 1979. I especially remember travelling for an entire year without repeating a port. They were a marvellous firm to work for and well deserve their high reputation.

The economics of passenger ship operations became more difficult, so Royal Viking decided to improve the profitability of their three ships by sending them to the Hapag-Lloyd shipyards at Bremerhaven to be lengthened (with 90-foot insertions) in order to increase their capacities to 758 passengers. The *Royal Viking Star* was altered between August and December 1981, the *Royal Viking Sky* in the following year, between September and November, and finally the *Royal Viking Sea* in 1983, between March and June.

Well known from New York to the North Cape

Cruise ships at New York on 7 September 1985 – a scene reminiscent of the gatherings of transatlantic liners there in the 1950s and 1960s. At the top, berthed together in the same slip are the *Bermuda Star* and the *Britanis*, then the *Nordic Prince*, *Queen Elizabeth 2*, *Atlantic*, *Oceanic* and *Royal Viking Sea*.

The *Royal Viking Sea* at the Hapag-Lloyd Shipyards at Bremerhaven in March 1983 being prepared for lengthening. A new 90-foot section was inserted in the liner's midships area.

Hapag-Lloyd Shipyards

and from Southampton to Sydney, the trio (owned since 1984 by the Norwegian Caribbean Line, but still sailing under a separate Royal Viking banner) have a very loyal following. Frank Braynard recalls,

Since 1973, my wife Doris and I have made nine cruises on Royal Viking ships, almost everywhere under the sun and loved every minute. Few ships have lived up to the hopes and claims of their owners as these three great white, clipper-stemmed beauties have done! On our last trip [across the North Atlantic, from Venice to Port Everglades], 80 per cent of the passengers were repeaters, which is quite a record. They are excellent sea boats, their decorations are classic and their tone quietly sophisticated. My own sketchbook *Search for the Tall Ships* has a chapter on each of these three lady liners, with ten to twenty sketches made of vistas onboard each of them. I dedicated this book to the Company. Later, I was delighted to have them buy several thousand copies to give away to passengers. Living-up to the highest of Norse seagoing traditions, their officers and crew give everyone aboard a feeling of confidence. Their pretty cabin stewardesses never seem to stop smiling, do their job beautifully and when it comes to crew entertainment what a show they put on. Praises to Royal Viking!

SEA GODDESS CRUISES

SEA GODDESS I AND SEA GODDESS II

Prompted by the deluxe, luxury type of cruises offered by the Norwegian America and Royal Viking lines,

still more Norwegians decided to enter the cruise trades. In the early 1980s K/S A/S Norske Cruises, itself a newly formed company which had entered the cruise trades, created Sea Goddess Cruises, with the intention of building as many as eight 4200-gross ton deluxe cruising yachts. Though this $2½ billion plan was later modified and the number of sister ships reduced to two, the original concept remained: great luxury, intimacy and speciality. This company and its ships are unlike most others.

Commissioned respectively in March 1984 and in April 1985, the *Sea Goddess I* and *Sea Goddess II* were built at the Wartsila yards in Helsinki, each with an overall length of 344 feet. They represent the new (and increasingly popular) generation of smaller cruise vessels that can offer a select, very personalized atmosphere as well as the ability to visit more remote ports of call. The ships each have a maximum capacity of 116 passengers, berthed in 58 suites or double-berth rooms. In her first season, the *Sea Goddess I* was based in the Mediterranean, with departures from such ports as Malaga, Monte Carlo, Civitavecchia (for Rome) and Piraeus (for Athens). Ports of call included marinas, coves and select beach areas on the Costa Del Sol, the French and Italian Rivieras, the Balearic Islands, the Greek isles and along the Turkish and Yugoslavian coasts. A sample itinerary for

During her special maiden cruise, the *Sea Goddess I* sailed to the Pool of London. She is shown passing the Tower of London.

Alex Duncan

the *Sea Goddess II*, departing from Monte Carlo in April 1986, was an eleven-day voyage that called at Sorrento, Capri, Bonifacio, Ibiza, Barcelona, Collura, St Tropez and Portofino. Minimum fares began at $6900. Other itineraries have included winters in the Caribbean from St Croix in the Virgin Islands, along the South American coast between Rio de Janeiro and Buenos Aires, and in Southeast Asian and Pacific waters. The *Sea Goddess I* was, in fact, chartered for nearly five months, beginning in October 1986, to serve as a review and hotel ship for the America's Cup Races at Perth, Australia.

Being among the most expensively priced cruise ships ever to sail, their accommodation is said to be among the most luxurious afloat. All the cabins have sitting areas, for example, that can easily be converted to private dining areas. Each stateroom has its own well-stocked library, stereo system, television and video systems, an individual snack-filled refrigerator, a bar stocked with passengers' favourite drinks, and very ample wardrobes. The general amenities include a sauna, swimming pool, beauty salon, casino, gift shop, outdoor cafe (for breakfasts and lunches), several bars and a main salon. A lift connects the four passenger decks. A unique 'tailgate' platform is fitted to the stern and can be lowered to make it easy to enter the water access for swimming, water skiing, windsurfing and snorkelling. All equipment is provided, including two speedboats. The aft end of the funnel serves as a decorative waterfall. With all wines and champagnes included in the fares, passengers can dine at any time they wish, either in the ship's restaurant, where there is no assigned seating, or course-by-course in their staterooms. Almost all items are prepared to order. Because of their restricted nature, the ships have also been chartered for private parties, for an estimated $500,000 for a one-week cruise. Soon after she was commissioned one man from Palm Springs, Florida celebrated his seventieth birthday by taking seventy friends on a Sea Goddess cruise.

An advertisement for Sea Goddess Cruises, in January 1986, read,

Let the Sea Goddess life carry you away to Europe this spring or this summer. In the spirit of a yachtsman, 12 uncommon Mediterranean itineraries offer you selections of exclusive marinas and resorts with sophisticated shops and night life, unspoiled villages that lead you to scenic and historic sights, and secluded anchorages where you can enjoy water sports from the ship's unique platform astern.

Wartsila Shipyards

Resembling a great luxury yacht, the dining room aboard the *Sea Goddess I* is both decoratively stunning and invitingly spacious.

Wartsila Shipyards

A typical cabin aboard the *Sea Goddess I*, which includes a sitting area, bedroom, full-sized bath, television, stereo system and private bar.

From spacious suites and superior dining to complimentary wines and spirits, the Sea Goddess life is reserved for only 58 couples. The 1986 Mediterranean double-occupancy rates per person are $4400 for 7 nights, $6300 for 10 nights and $6900 for 11 nights.

Though the bookings were not quite as good as expected and the two ships were, in fact, close to being returned to their builders, in summer 1986 a twelve-year charter agreement was made with Cunard. These unique vessels have now joined the ranks of the *QE2*, *Sagafjord*, *Vistafjord*, and the *Cunard Countess* and *Cunard Princess*.

four

FROM
NORTHERN
PORTS

HAPAG-LLOYD

EUROPA (1953)

The Hamburg American Line and North German Lloyd had two of the best known names in passenger shipping; they were assuredly the very finest companies within the German merchant fleet. However, after the devastation caused by the Second World War neither company was in a position to rebuild its liner operations. Instead, they began by operating a few small coasters and harbour tugs, then gradually added some freighters and reopened many of their overseas services. It was not until 1953–54, that both firms were able to add passenger tonnage, in the form of six brand-new sisters of the *Hamburg* class (the *Frankfurt*, *Hamburg* and *Hannover* for the Hamburg American Line and the *Bayernstein*, *Hessenstein* and *Schwabenstein* for North German Lloyd). However, these were combination passenger-cargo ships, which, although given high standard accommodation for eighty-six first class passengers, were assigned to the long-haul run out to the Far East via Suez.

Thereafter, Hamburg American seemed barely interested in the passenger trades. In 1957, they bought the Swedish Lloyd liner *Patricia*, a 6600-tonner that had divided her service between the London–Gothenburg route and some winter cruising, and had her refitted for longer, more expensive, year-round cruise operations as the *Ariadne*. This was, in fact, a short-lived venture. She was sold in 1961, for Caribbean service out of Miami for Liberian flag owners.

In contrast the North German Lloyd was keen to re-establish its transatlantic passenger service to New York. In a joint effort with the Swedish American Line in 1954, they reopened part of this service with sailings from Bremerhaven. The motor liner *Gripsholm*, then a thirty-year-old veteran, undertook this service, but a year later was fully transferred to the Lloyd and renamed *Berlin*. Her popularity and success led, within four years, to the purchase of another second-hand, but far larger ship, the 32,200-ton *Bremen*, which had been the French *Pasteur* of 1939. She ran a two-class service on the traditional Atlantic run, and, in her first winter season of 1959–60, reopened the Company's Caribbean cruise trade, which had last been offered in the fateful year, 1939.

Some years later, in 1965–66, in particular because the veteran *Berlin* was nearing retirement (she went to Italian scrappers in autumn 1966) the Lloyd added yet another liner, a ship that could be used to expand its growing cruise services. Because the Swedish American Line was about to add yet another brand-new liner, named *Kungsholm*, the previous ship of the same name, which had been completed in Holland in 1953, was placed on the sales lists. Her beautiful design and decoration, and impeccable maintenance, certainly left a strong impression when the first team of Lloyd engineers had a look over her in the autumn of 1964. A sale was arranged, a short refit was scheduled and the ship was introduced in early 1966 as the *Europa*.

Although planned to run some transatlantic voyages, she was soon relegated to year-round cruising. She was 21,500 tons, exactly 600 feet long had capacity for 769 passengers and had seven passenger decks: Sun, Verandah, Upper, Main, A, B and D. Completely air-conditioned and stabilizer-equipped, her special amenities included both indoor and outdoor pools, a gymnasium, theatre, children's facilities, gift shop, beauty salon and barber's shop. Her cabins, with one to four berths, were all outside and all had private bathroom facilities. The public rooms

Luis Miguel Correia

The *Europa*, one of the most beautifully decorated and popular cruise ships of her time, sailed for the West Germans from 1966 until 1981. Previously, she had been the renowned *Kungsholm* of 1953 owned by the Swedish American Line.

consisted of the Smoking Room, Lounge, Cocktail Lounge, Writing Room-Library, twin Verandahs, the Europa Lounge and the Restaurant.

Captain Heinz-Dieter Schmidt transferred from the North German Lloyd's freighter division to its highly praised passenger ships in 1967, and gained his master's license three years later.

I was second officer in our flagship, the 697ft *Bremen*, which was an excellent 'sea boat' and where the service was impeccable. Unfortunately, with the possible exception of the current *Europa* (of 1981), that kind of highly disciplined, skilled hotel service has vanished. Our captain aboard the *Bremen* would often tell us stories of the old *Berlin*, the former *Gripsholm* of 1925, which became West Germany's first postwar liner in 1955. In the end, in November 1966, he had to deliberately run her aground at 'half ahead' on the beach of the scrapyards at La Spezia in Italy. Most interesting, however, all of the artwork had been removed. It seemed that the original sale contract stipulated that the paintings must be returned to the Swedes, who in turn placed them in museums and in Gripsholm Castle.

North German Lloyd merged with the Hamburg American Line in 1971 and soon after, in view of the devastating affect of jet competition, it was decided to discontinue the historic Atlantic passenger service and concentrate instead on high-standard cruising. Captain Schmidt vividly recalled this transitional period.

The *Bremen* was burning 420 tons of fuel a day and was

Hapag-Lloyd

Hapag-Lloyd's *Europa* of 1981 has been called one of the most handsomely decorated cruise ships of the past decade.

therefore becoming increasingly expensive, a problem further complicated by frequent breakdowns with her ageing French-built turbines [from 1938–39]. Regrettably, soon after the final transatlantic sailing in December 1971, we had to sell her [to the Chandris Group, who sailed her thereafter as the *Regina Magna*]. We wanted to continue in North American cruising with the beautiful *Europa*, but then ran head-on into new, very strict codes with the US Coast Guard. Another disappointment, but we had to withdraw from American service entirely.

In 1973, we very much wanted to buy the financially-ailing *Hamburg*, a luxurious 24,900-tonner built in 1969, to resume New York cruising and then sell off the *Europa*. Unfortunately, there was a last minute disagreement over the price with the German Atlantic Line and the ship went instead to the Soviets, becoming their *Maxim Gorki*. Ironically, she has been used ever since in the German luxury cruise market, on year-round charters to the immense Neckermann Travel Co of Frankfurt. To this day [1984], she remains a very luxurious, superbly maintained ship.

The *Europa* was eventually retired in the autumn of 1981 and sold to Italy's Costa Line for further service under the Panamanian flag. She was renamed the *Columbus C.*, a choice inspired by the well-known prewar North German Lloyd liner *Columbus*, which sailed from 1922 until 1939. Germans would continue to be part of the ship's clientele. In summer, she would sail from Bremerhaven to Scandinavia and for much of the remainder of the year, from Genoa. There would also be cruises from South American ports. Unfortunately, during one of her summer voyages, in July 1984, she rammed a harbour break-water at Cadiz in Spain and then later capsized at her berth. Finally salvaged, she was beyond economic repair and was later sold to Spanish shipbreakers.

EUROPA (1981)

Captain Schmidt recalled the creation of Hapag-Lloyd's first brand-new liner.

In looking to the future, in the mid-1970s, Hapag Lloyd began a series of studies and design tests for a new deluxe liner. At the time, we had a 70 per cent repeat market in Germany, with a club-like atmosphere and even a loyal inner circle of German millionaires. Finally, this new ship was approved, becoming the 33,800-ton *Europa* of 1981. She was built with a subsidy from Bonn and, in an effort to balance shipyard employment, the original plan was to construct the forward half of the ship at the Weser Shipyards and the aft section at the Bremer-Vulcan yards. However, this rather novel scheme never came to pass. She was built completely at the Vulcan works.

The 758-passenger *Europa*, delivered in December 1981, has been called one of the most beautifully decorated liners of her day. In every sense, she has been intended for the upper end of the cruising market. In the October 1985 issue of the *Ocean & Cruise News*, Philip S Dawson wrote,

In the highly competitive cruise market of today, West Germany's new *Europa* stands as one of the few major Western ships with a national identity of her own – a 'ship of state' to be sure. In the bygone era of the green ocean liners, passenger ships were floating microcosms of the nations which operated them. One could sample the language,

cuisine, culture and lifestyle of these countries on the high seas and without necessarily ever touching their home shores. Unfortunately, the homogenized nature of most of the modern travel and leisure industry has eroded such individuality into a single, bland 'international' stereotype.

When Hapag-Lloyd planned the new *Europa* in the late seventies, they did so with the confidence that the German-speaking luxury market would alone support such a ship for the coming 25 or 35 years. Accordingly, the new *Europa* was specifically planned to provide this market with worldwide travel in superlative luxury with the security and home comforts of the best German resorts and urban hotels to be found ashore.

The *Europa* divides most of her cruising between Bremerhaven and Genoa. Her schedule for 1986 read:

January 19	19-day cruise from Singapore to Indonesia
February 7	19-day cruise from Singapore to Hong Kong
February 27	16-day cruise from Hong Kong to Colombo
March 19	20-day cruise from Colombo to Genoa
April 6	44-day cruise from Genoa to Alaska
May 19	49-day cruise from Alaska to Bremerhaven
July 9	18-day Polar cruise from Bremerhaven
July 27	13-day British Isles cruise from Bremerhaven
August 9	14-day Fjords cruise from Bremerhaven
August 23	20-day Fjords–Baltic Cities cruise from Bremerhaven
September 13	21-day Mediterranean cruise from Bremerhaven
October 4	20-day Greek Isles cruise from Genoa
October 24	15-day Black Sea cruise from Genoa
November 8	60-day Amazon–Caribbean cruise from Genoa

PETER DEILMANN COMPANY

REGINA MARIS

According to Captain Schmidt, who joined the Peter Deilmann Company after serving with the aforementioned Hapag-Lloyd,

She had been built for previous German owners, the Lubeck Line, in 1966, and had established a very high reputation for cruises to Scandinavia, the British Isles and to the Atlantic Isles.

The 5800-ton *Regina Maris* was then sold, in 1976, to Canadian interests, but flying a Bermudian flag. Renamed *Mercator One*, she was plagued with union and regulatory problems, and consequently spent most of her time in lay-up, first at Bermuda and then at Halifax. The Deilmann Co bought her in 1979, and renamed her *Frankfurt One*. Given a full refit, she then had the most unique balance of West German registry, but with Singapore as her homeport. [Full Singapore registry came a year later.] She reverted to her well-known name of *Regina Maris* in the autumn of 1980.

Her career was thereafter quite chequered. Captain Schmidt added,

The Deilmann Co wanted to use the ship for older, richer Germans, the upper end of the market. In summer, we sailed to Spitzbergen, the Fjords, the Baltic and even around Britain. In autumn, she would sail on Mediterranean cruises out of Genoa and, in winter, to West African ports out of Las Palmas. Later, she was given out to charter and began sailing in Southeast Asian waters, mostly between Manila and Singapore. She was often chartered to Neckermann, Travel Dynamics and specialty museum groups, and tended to visit very exotic, very unusual ports like Nias and Pare Pare. In 1982, she was chartered to a newly formed, but short-lived American firm, the Sun World Cruise Lines of St Louis, who wanted a gambling ship for weekly cruises in the Caribbean out of Santo Domingo. It all failed to materialize and instead we did some seven-day St Lawrence River cruises from Montreal. Then, quite suddenly, we were without a charter. I recall remaining with the ship for eight months, laid-up at St George, Bermuda.

However, Captain Schmidt saw the little *Regina Maris* return to cruise service under Deilmann banner.

In the spring of 1983, we began a series of seven-day cruises from Bremerhaven to the Geirangerfjord, Bergen, Vik and Flaam. This was the first weekly cruise service ever offered from Germany. We then moved the ship to the Mediterranean for charter and, for a time, sat out a slack period in lay-up at La Spezia. I recall that we were moored just across from the salvaged former *Gripsholm* [of 1957], which had been moved to Italy after capsizing in a Greek drydock. Known later as the *Navarino* she was then renamed as the *Samantha*. Then, much to our surprise, our little *Regina Maris* was sold to the Greek-flag Latsis Line. Renamed *Alexander*, after tycoon John S Latsis's first grandson, she was at first placed under the British flag, with London as her homeport and the Channel Island of Sark as her operational base. Soon afterward, however, she was placed under the Greek flag. Mr Latsis – who is extremely rich, has Swiss headquarters and who owned over 100 tankers at one point – has strong links to the Saudi Arabians. Two of his passenger ships, the former British liners *Windsor Castle* [Union-Castle Line, 1960] and *Aureol*

The Lubeck Line's *Regina Maris* was built in 1966 especially for cruising to remote areas. She was rebuilt in 1985 as a Saudi Arabian yacht.

Schiffsfotos Jansen

[Elder Dempster Lines, 1951], currently serve as accommodation ships in Arabian ports. His plan was to convert the former *Regina Maris* into a pleasure yacht and present it to the King of Arabia.

Extensively refitted at Bremerhaven, the ship sailed off to her new life in the summer of 1985. Arnold Kludas, the well-known German maritime author and historian, recalled the departure of this former German cruise ship.

Unfortunately, very little was known of the conversion of the former *Regina Maris*. Her Greek owners did not allow the Lloyd Werft shipyards to publish the details of the conversion and consequently no photographs were published of her new interiors. The ship arrived as the *Alexander* at Bremerhaven, on 15 December 1984, and was delivered back to Latsis on 7 August 1985. She is now a luxury 'guest ship' for only twelve passengers for the Royal House of Saudi Arabia.

BERLIN

According to Captain Harry Biehl, the master of this yacht-like cruise vessel,

Built at Kiel [at the HDW Shipyards] and christened as the *Berlin*, this 7800-tonner was designed deliberately for 330 passengers or the equivalent of one charter jetload of passengers and even a few seats for changeover staff. Taking exactly ten months to build, she was schemed and decorated for intimacy and the then increasing German cruise market. After her maiden trip, in June 1980, we kept her in the Baltic for a time. Initially, we marketed the *Berlin* only to German regional groups, such as a trip mostly with Bavarians. We were therefore better able to improve our

Blue Funnel Cruises

In 1983–84, the German cruise ship *Berlin* was chartered to Blue Funnel Cruises of Singapore and temporarily renamed *Princess Mahsuri*. She was used mostly on two-week voyages and sailed from Singapore as well as Sydney.

Luis Miguel Correia

West Germany's Hadag Company's first and only deep-sea cruise ship, the *Astor* of 1981, was designed especially for luxury service, particularly on fly and sail voyages. Unsuccessful, she was sold in 1984, to the South Africans, but retained her original name. Sold again a year later, she became the *Arkona* for the East Germans.

product and then appeal to a more sophisticated cruise clientele. Afterward, we ventured out on longer, far more diverse cruises: the Mediterranean and Black Sea, West Africa, South America and a special visit to the American East Coast in May 1982, with calls at Miami, Port Canaveral, Savannah and New York.

In autumn 1982, the Deilmann Company received a lucrative charter offer from Blue Funnel Cruises of Singapore and, having considered the effects of the worldwide travel recession at that time, the agreements were promptly signed. According to Captain Biehl,

The charter was to run for three years [it was abruptly cancelled in two years, in December 1984] with renewal options. The *Berlin* was renamed as the *Princess Mahsuri*, after a well-known figure of Southeast Asian folklore. About 29 of the 150 crewmembers remained from Deilmann; the others were employed directly by Blue Funnel. Mostly, they were Filipinos, who had sailed previously on the Manila-based cruise ship *Dona Montserrat* [ex-*West Star*, ex-*Cabo Izarra*]. That ship had been suddenly sold to the Chinese, but since Germans knew and liked her [from air-sea charter tours], we hired most of her crew. We maintained the same friendly standard on the *Princess Mahsuri*.

Though she offered cruises from Sydney to the South Pacific islands and to New Zealand, and from Singapore to Indonesia, other Southeast Asian ports and the Far East, she suffered from a major ailment known to some new cruise ventures: lack of passengers. There were few Europeans willing to make the long, often expensive flight to the East, a limited demand for her services in the United States and even the nearby Australians sought a slightly less formal, less expensive ship for their holiday voyages. The *Princess Mahsuri* was returned to her German owners, reverted to her original name, and has since been cruising for them in many areas. In autumn 1986, the Berlin was lengthened with a 90-foot insertion which substantially increased her cruising capacity.

The Deilmann Company, based at Neustadt in Holstein in northern Germany, has two other cruise ship interests: the *Danube Princess*, which sails on the Danube River from Passau (near Munich) from March until November and the little forty-seven-passenger *Nordbrise*, which runs highly unusual Greenland coastal cruises during the summer.

HADAG

ASTOR

The buoyant enthusiasm of luxury, up-market cruising in Europe and overseas air-sea tours using European ships increased substantially in the early 1980s, thus the Hadag Company, based at Hamburg and best known for its harbour excursion craft and dayboats to the island of Heligoland, decided to enter deep-sea cruising. Together with the government of the city-state of Hamburg, which was interested in initiating employment in local shipyards, a contract was signed with the HDW Shipyards (at Hamburg) for an 18,800-ton cruise ship. Designed with a maximum of 683 berths, which would be restricted to about 550, the new ship was intended to challenge

Hapag-Lloyd's position as the most select West German cruise firm. Hapag-Lloyd had been using the very popular *Europa*, a highly-acclaimed vessel that was then approaching her thirtieth year, but they too were planning a large, luxurious liner. Their 33,800-ton 'new' *Europa* was commissioned at the same time as the Hadag ship. Unfortunately for the Hamburg owners, the well-established, very historic Hapag-Lloyd had a more secure position and certainly a far greater and more loyal following – at best, Hadag would have to be content with Hapag-Lloyd's overflow.

It was initially planned to name her *Hammonia*, but she was christened *Astor* and delivered in December 1981 (she had, in fact, been delayed by a shipyard fire). Her name was selected for marketing reasons to link her with the famous Astor family. Considered one of the more luxurious liners of the 'new cruising generation', her accommodation was arranged on seven decks: Sun, Bridge, Boat, Promenade, A, B and C. Impressively and often impeccably decorated in fine German contemporary taste, there was a Conference Room on the Bridge Deck; the Lido Bar, Night Club and outdoor pool on the Boat Deck; the Main Lounge, Library, Card Room, Harry's Bar & Lounge, twin galleries, a full shopping centre and the Waldorf Astoria Restaurant on the Promenade Deck. The cruise office and passenger reception were located on A Deck, and the auditorium and the hairdressers on B Deck. The sauna, indoor pool and fitness centre were positioned on C Deck. Howard Franklin, a lecturer and cruise host aboard the *Astor*, was among those delighted with the ship.

The *Astor* has a quiet elegance, restrained taste and has reintroduced the use of dark woods, a feature which has been all but done away with in modern ships. She is, in fact, an attempt to recapture a lost era in ocean liner travel.

The *Astor* cruised, with a German staff and German passengers mostly, to Scandinavia, the Mediterranean, the Caribbean, the Amazon and even put into the east coast of America (New York, Philadelphia, etc) once, in October 1982. On the whole she was not a very successful cruise ship. The *Europa* continued to secure the better part of the trade. Because of consistent losses, the *Astor* was sold, in a move that rather surprised international shipping circles, to the South Africans, for their Safmarine Lines (Safleisure) cruise division. Her name was retained and in spring 1984 she reopened part of the old main run, between Southampton and the Cape. It had last been operative on a regular basis in 1977, using Union-Castle's *Windsor Castle* and Safmarine's *S. A. Vaal*. Between these sailings, the *Astor* was sent on more cruises, both in the South Atlantic (to South America, the Seychelles, etc) and European waters (the North Cape, Atlantic Isles, etc), with a special emphasis on 'adventure itineraries'. Once again, however, she was only a moderate success. In the winter of 1985, she was sold, in another surprising move, to the East German Government's Deutsche Seereederei. She became, after delivery in August 1985, the trade union cruise ship *Arkona*. She replaced the earlier *Volkerfreundschaft*, the former Swedish *Stockholm* of 1948, which had just been retired. The *Arkona* was registered at Rostock in East Germany.

As a replacement Safmarine Lines ordered a 'new' improved *Astor*, from the HDW Shipyards at Kiel, financed by the sale of the old *Astor* to the East Germans. At some 21,000 tons she will have accommodation for 650 passengers, the design of which will be considerably like that of her predecessor. However, she will be used mostly for cruising and will operate fewer 'line voyages' to the South African Cape, the latter may be restricted to 'positioning voyages' to fit in with her cruise schedules.

DEUTSCHE SEEREEDEREI

VOLKERFREUNDSCHAFT

When she was launched from the Gotaverken Shipyards at Gothenburg, Sweden, on 9 September 1946, the motor liner *Stockholm* was the first new passenger ship destined for transatlantic service to go down the ways since the end of the Second World War. Completed in the early winter of 1948, she was a sleek, almost yacht-like vessel that was more like a combination passenger-cargo ship than a liner. She was 11,700 tons, 525 feet long and her capacity was limited to a mere 395 passengers, 113 in first class and 282 in tourist class. Powered by Gotaverken-built diesels, she had a service speed of 19 knots. She worked for Swedish American until 1959, when she was sold to Deutsche Seereederei and renamed *Volkerfreundschaft*.

The Swedish American Line had two very fine and very popular prewar liners, the *Gripsholm* of 1925 and the *Kungsholm* of 1928, and then two successive *Stockholm*s (of 1938 and 1940, both destroyed before seeing commercial service). In the period immediately after the war the Company thought more in terms of more moderate tonnage, namely a new, smaller *Stockholm*. The Swedish directors seemed to be more interested in combining the revenues from both passengers and freight. The *Stockholm* traded between New York, Copenhagen and Gothenburg, and made occasional calls at Bremerhaven, at Aarhus in Denmark and westbound at Halifax. In later years, she also made periodic cruises, usually from New York to Bermuda, Nassau or the Caribbean. One special cruise, which departed from New York on 26 August 1959, called at Leith, Oslo, Gothenburg, Helsingor, Copenhagen, Keterminde, the Kiel Canal, Hamburg, Ijmuiden, Antwerp, Guernsey, Dun Laoghaire and Glengariff. The minimum fare for twenty-nine days was listed as $700.

Richard Sandstrom, a Swede by ancestry and Vice Chairman of the New York Branch of the World Ship Society, has special recollections of the *Stockholm*.

She was built to replace the aged *Drottningholm*, a classical ship that dated from 1905 and which continued in Swedish American service until 1948 (and then for the Home Lines until 1955). That older ship was infamous as a 'roller' and the *Stockholm*, built just before the age of stabilizers, took over that distinction. In her early years, Swedish American encouraged first class bookings by having the best chefs and quality service. Consequently, the *Stockholm*'s small first class read like *Who's Who* on most voyages.

In November 1953, as the new *Kungsholm* joined the fleet and a year later revived the Line's long-distance cruise programme, the *Stockholm* became available for cruise and charter programmes. A New York travel firm arranged cruises on the Caribbean and Bermuda out of North Carolina ports, Morehead City and Wilmington. I had the good fortune to join her, in 1955, for a 'deadheading' voyage to Wilmington. For Southern palates, the ship souped up the bars with bourbon and even laid on grits for breakfast. And in turn, many Southerners were introduced to Swedish fare.

The *Stockholm* joins the ranks of maritime immortality for what should have been an ordinary mid-summer transatlantic crossing. She left, eastbound from New York, on 25 July 1956. That night, in dense fog off Nantucket, she rammed the 29,000-ton *Andrea Doria*. The larger ship sank to the bottom in the first daylight hours of the next day, as the *Stockholm* limped back to New York minus her sleek bow. In all, there were fifty-one fatalities in this tragedy. The maritime historian and author Frank O Braynard recalled the arrival of the Swedish ship.

I was at the Italian Line offices, on the State Street in Lower Manhattan, as the little liner crept past. The Italians stood silently at their harbourview windows, just staring at the Swedish ship. They had 'daggers' in their eyes. To them, she was the villain.

In fact, the inquiry that followed was settled out of court and the blame never publicly announced. The *Stockholm* was sent to the Bethlehem Steel Shipyards at 56th Street in Brooklyn and given a new bow. She did not return to service until December, over four months after the collision.

Soon after she resumed her Atlantic sailings, aircraft were to secure an increasingly dominant position on the northern run. With two larger liners, the *Kungsholm* of 1953 and the brand-new *Gripsholm* of 1957, both of which were ideally suited for alternating to one-class luxury cruising, the little *Stockholm* began to appear less useful and profitable. Her last sailing for Swedish American was scheduled for December 1959, on a final run out of New York, and shortly thereafter she was sold to the East German Government's Deutsche Seereederei of Rostock.

Renamed *Volkerfreundschaft* (which translated means 'International Friendship'), she was converted to the world's first trade union cruise ship. Her accommodation was converted for 600 passengers, all in one class. She sailed mostly from Rostock, occasionally made sailings from Black Sea ports and also, was often chartered, for about a month each year, to the Swedish-flag Stena Line for Scandinavian cruising. For the most part, however, the *Volkerfreundschaft* was under the veils of secrecy and security so common to Eastern bloc shipping. Dr Wolfgang Vieweg, formerly a resident of East Germany, now living in the West, spent his honeymoon aboard the former Swedish liner.

It was a 2½-week cruise from Rostock to Danzig, Riga, Tallinn and Leningrad and return. It was an expensive voyage by East German standards and required great patience just in awaiting the tickets, but the opportunity of such a voyage – 'a little hole in the door' as we called it – was wonderful. There was full entertainment on board and I especially recall the balance of 60 per cent Eastern music and 40 per cent Western tunes.

My wife had previously cruised in the Black Sea aboard the *Volkerfreundschaft*, again a very expensive trip and then returned from Port Said to Rostock, a four-week voyage. Once again, the application for tickets required a long wait. In fact, she had learned only two weeks prior to sailing that permission had been granted for her to sail.

Ironically, on this voyage, quite a number of passengers jumped ship in foreign ports.

The booking procedures for the former *Stockholm* were now very different from her earlier years. As Dr Vieweg also recalled

You had to pass at least seven security checkpoints in East Germany even before the sailing, three of which were the workers' union, the party and the state security system. All had to give their approval, otherwise there was no trip. We all had dreams and such a voyage was a wonderful opportunity and well worth the effort. This ship was our only ship for overseas visits.

On the longer cruises to Havana, several passengers once jumped over the side to rendezvous with some small craft. Thereafter, security onboard became very tight. Special windows and gates were installed and the crew would guard the outer decks at critical areas and times. Some passengers remained quite clever, however. Under the guise of taking a photo at the rail, they chose the right moment and made their jump over the side. At Havana, there were restrictive tours and then an immediate air flight back to East Germany. Later, certain passengers were restricted only to Eastern ports, in either the Soviet-controlled Baltic or Black Sea areas.

The Deutsche Seereederei also ran three other passenger ships: the 8100-ton *Fritz Heckert*, built in 1961; the 10,900-ton *Georg Buchner*, the former Belgian Line's *Charlesville*; and the 11,900-ton *J G Fichte*, previously the French passenger ship *Claude Bernard*. All have been withdrawn from service in recent years. The *Fritz Heckert* was mechanically faulty and has been laid-up, the *Georg Buchner* is a permanently moored maritime training school and the *J G Fichte* was scrapped in Pakistan in 1981.

After thirty-seven years of service, the *Volkerfreundschaft*, the former *Stockholm*, was retired too, in spring 1985. Initial reports were that she would be sold to the city of Stockholm and refitted under her original name as a museum and accommodation ship but the arrangements failed to materialize. Instead, in that July, she was handed over to Norwegian buyers, who planned to use her as some sort of floating club. She was moved to an anchorage in the Oslofjord where she waited for plans to materialize. Renamed *Volker*, she was later moved to Southampton to await new buyers.

As the *Volkerfreundschaft* was being retired, the East Germans negotiated the purchase of the 18,500-ton *Astor* from the South African Marine Corporation of Capetown. It was rumoured that she would be

The *Volkerfreundschaft* berthed at Lisbon with the Portuguese liner *Funchal* just beyond her.

Luis Miguel Correia

renamed *Volkerfreundschaft* or *Our Happy Country*, but she was recommissioned in October 1985 as the *Arcona*. Dr Vieweg added,

The former *Astor* will be exceptional luxury for the East Germans: the bathroom tubs, the clever lighting, even the electrical switches. People in the DDR, the German Democratic Republic, are very short on luxury and comfort items. It will be a great treat.

SWEDISH AMERICAN LINE

KUNGSHOLM (1953)

When they began cruising in the early 1930s, the Swedish American Line soon established one of the best reputations in the business and one that became comparable to the Company's high standards on the North Atlantic run between Scandinavia and New York. Their cruise programmes included not only short trips from New York to Bermuda, Nassau and the Caribbean, but longer, more expensive voyages, such as around South America, around Africa, in the Mediterranean and to the North Cape. In the prewar years, there was even a cruise to South America from Britain and another long voyage that included New York as a port of call. However, after the Second World War the Company could only resume its transatlantic services, primarily due to the pressing need for postwar passages in both directions.

Commissioned in November 1953, the 21,000-ton *Kungsholm*, built at the De Schelde Shipyards at Flushing in Holland, was created as a dual-purpose

ship, for both the Atlantic service and for cruising. She was decorated in classically handsome décor. Every one of her passenger cabins was outside and included private bathroom facilities, both novelties in the early fifties on the Atlantic run. As well as her crossings between Gothenburg, Copenhagen, Bremerhaven and New York, she was soon used in the winter, off-season for one-class cruises, one- and two-week Caribbean voyages as well as longer trips including Swedish American's first around-the-world cruise, in January 1955.

Erik Frostenius was a chief steward with Swedish American for over two decades and remembered the beloved *Kungsholm*.

I was aboard for a very special short cruise in the autumn of 1953, from Stockholm to Gothenburg, when we had the Swedish Royal Family onboard. Crown Prince Carl Gustav [the present King of Sweden] was to occupy one of the suites, but in which the plumbing had just packed-up. We had to make a very quick clean-up! I shall always remember this *Kungsholm* as a very beautiful ship with a very friendly crew.

The *Kungsholm* remained with the White Viking Fleet, as the Swedish American liners were called, until October 1965. A brand-new *Kungsholm* was then

Three cruise ships at New York's Passenger Ship Terminal in the winter of 1974. The *Kungsholm* is at the bottom and shares a pier with the Italian *Leonardo da Vinci*. At the top, in Berth 4, is the Dutch *Rotterdam*.

Four cruise ships at the Yokohama Ocean Terminal, on 22 March 1973: on the outer berth China Navigation's *Coral Princess* (left) and Holland-America's *Rotterdam* (right) and on the inner berth, the *Kungsholm* (on a three-month around the world cruise) and the *Gripsholm* (on a long Pacific cruise).

R Izawa

nearing completion and so her predecessor was sold. She soon joined the North German Lloyd and raised the West German colours as the *Europa*. More of her history is included in the North German Lloyd section as well as in the Costa Line section (she sailed for Costa as the *Columbus C.*).

GRIPSHOLM

By the mid-fifties, the Swedish American reputation was again excellent. According to Erik Frostenius,

This great, well known reputation was made by the service, the exceptional discipline of the crew and the food. The strong discipline was a complement to the great friendliness. In 1957, we had heard that the *Caronia* was the best cruise ship in the world and so we decided to make Swedish American liners even better by increasing the good service, keeping a stronger eye on the kitchens and especially the chefs, and placed all of the assistant stewards in charge of special sections.

The brand-new *Gripsholm* [commissioned in the spring of 1957] was my 'dream ship'. She always kept her heart. I was stationed at the Ansaldo shipyards at Genoa, Italy during her construction and remained with her for many years thereafter. She was, of course, an improved version of the previous *Kungsholm*, but made even more beautiful and more appealing. She had Gustav III styling in the

restaurant, for example. Once again, however, she was a ship made by the crew, who were exceptional and with excellent spirit. We were always supported in our efforts by the home office and were always given whatever we requested.

The *Gripsholm* was especially well known for her longer, more deluxe cruises. She remained with Swedish American until August 1975, when the Company decided to withdraw completely from passenger shipping. Laid up for a short while, she was sold by the end of 1975 to a Greek interest, Karageorgis Cruises, who renamed her *Navarino* and began two-week cruises in the Mediterranean from Piraeus and Venice.

KUNGSHOLM (1966)

This, the last of the Swedish American liners was ordered from the John Brown yards on the Clyde and delivered in the spring of 1966. A 26,600 tonner with the classic Swedish American profile of two well-placed funnels, she actually ran very few two-class transatlantic crossings, and was used instead almost from the start in continuous cruising. Her voyages included an annual three-month trip around the world, a six-week summer cruise to Scandinavia, eight weeks around South America and other assorted voyages including two weeks each August to the St Lawrence and Canadian Maritimes and a five-or six-day cruise to Bermuda. Erik Frostenius recalls,

She was a very modern ship, the last of the gleaming Swedish American liners, a ship that I grew to like gradually. She was, however, the best operationally of our final liners.

Like Cunard's legendary *Caronia* and several other cruise ships, the *Kungsholm* had a very loyal, devoted following. According to Erik Frostenius,

On the world cruises especially, we had passengers that would come year after year, like some private club. Our passengers included Marjorie Meriweather-Post, the well known millionairess, who I would meet with each morning to check over her personalized menus for the following day. She mostly took her dinner in the privacy of her own suite and was accompanied on her travels by a private party of seven or eight and which usually included a Russian count. Her suite was always redecorated especially for her and on every subsequent voyage. She tended to take the longer cruises and was met at each port by a special limousine. Everyone in the staff was always correct with her and always gave precision service.

Other long-distance cruise passengers included actress

Merle Oberon, who was beautiful and polite; Mr and Mrs Howard Johnson, who could not have been sweeter; and Helen Hayes, who was exceptionally polite and who always joined with the other passengers. All of the special requests – such as for cereals, teas and desserts – were honoured and fulfilled. Many of these passengers did not, however, always go ashore. Those ports that were particular favourites included Copenhagen, Stockholm and Hong Kong. The purchases were quite fabulous such as aquamarines and emeralds in Rio, furs in Copenhagen, pearls in Hong Kong, and diamonds and gold in South Africa.

We carried a staff of additional gentlemen on these longer cruises, some of which were from Thomas Cook's or American Express. It was required that they be in the main lounge for dancing. We always had far more women among the passengers. Of course, these women travelled with the most fantastic jewelry. I shall always remember the sight of them sitting in the main foyer as they collected their best pieces for dinner from the safety deposit boxes. We had a programme of ever-changing entertainment so that these passengers would never, ever become bored. However, these same passengers – who paid some of the highest fares – were the least demanding.

In the early seventies, the Swedish American Line, which was owned by the large Brostrom Group, was faced with increasing operational costs, compounded by the sudden increase in fuel oil prices in 1973–74. There were rumours that the Company would change to a 'flag of convenience' such as Panama or the Bahamas and begin to employ more multi-national staff. Unfortunately, a satisfactory agreement could not be reached.

Erik Frostenius said

The all-powerful Swedish maritime unions killed the Swedish American Line. They simply did not want to see the ships under some foreign flag and so refused all further discussion on the matter. Compounded with their concern of finances, the Company's directors decided to terminate the passenger division. It was a very sad decision.

The *Kungsholm*, then barely ten years old, closed Swedish American's passenger services in December 1975. This impeccably maintained vessel with an exceptional reputation was sold to Norway's Oivind Lorentzen, who assigned her to their Flagship Cruises subsidiary under her original, well-known name. However, single-ship cruise operations are vulnerable at best and this phase of the *Kungsholm's* career lasted for little more than three years. In the autumn of 1978, she was sold to the P&O Group, renamed *Sea Princess* and refitted for British-flag cruising, first from Sydney and later from Southampton.

In the stye of a royal yacht, the *Stella Polaris* was one of the world's best known cruise ships. Retired in 1969, after over forty years of service, she is now used as a floating yacht club and hotel in Japan under the name *Scandinavia*.

World Ship Society Photo Library

CLIPPER LINE

STELLA POLARIS

Built in the classical tradition of a royal or millionaire's yacht, the 5200-ton *Stella Polaris* – with a clipper bow, single yellow funnel and intimate accommodation for a mere 165 'guests' – was considered one of the finest cruise ships ever built. She, like the *Kungsholm*, had a loyal, faithful following. She was constructed in 1927, at the Gotaverken shipyards of Gothenburg, Sweden, for the Bergen Line. Establishing a formidible reputation before the war for cruising, she was, in 1940, captured by the Germans and used as a troop ship and then a recreation ship for U-boat crews. She resumed Bergen Line cruising in the late forties, and was then sold to the newly formed Clipper Line in 1952. Retaining her well-known name, she hoisted the Swedish colours and began what would become her established annual pattern of cruise service: winters from New Orleans to the Caribbean, spring in the Mediterranean, then summers in Scandinavia and a return to the Mediterranean in autumn.

Though Clipper never added a second cruise ship to its early operation, it purchased the Liberian-flag Incres Line in 1964 and thus acquired the 14,900-ton *Victoria* (the radically converted former *Dunnottar Castle* of 1936) which was based at New York. Among the slight alterations resulting from this transaction was the addition of summer cruises to Scandinavia from Copenhagen by the *Victoria*. Five years later, in 1969, because the *Stella Polaris* was well past forty, there was talk of a new Clipper Line ship. Unfortunately, duplicating a vessel in the style of the popular *Stella* would be prohibitively expensive and the conversion of a second-hand passenger ship seemed unsuitable. Consequently, the Clipper Line closed out its own services and retained only its interest in Incres. This lasted until 1975, when the latter company was forced into bankruptcy; the *Victoria* was later auctioned-off.

The *Stella Polaris*, which might have gone for scrap, was instead bought by Japanese interests, renamed *Scandinavia* and moored off Mitohama Beach for use as a floating country club, where she remains at the time of writing.

THE DUTCH

HOLLAND-AMERICA LINE

NIEUW AMSTERDAM (1938)

The famed Holland-America Line, perhaps the best known Dutch passenger shipping company of all, operated two distinct services: transatlantic sailings between Rotterdam, the Channel ports and New York, with class-divided passengers, and cruises, mostly from New York in the earlier years, on specially converted one-class ships. The *Nieuw Amsterdam*, a 36,000-tonner built in the late thirties, was one of the great 'dreamboats' of all time and a beloved favourite in both services. Decorated with great charm and warmth, and one of the best examples of 'floating art déco', the *Nieuw Amsterdam* was designed from the very start of her career to spend her winters in warm waters, sailing from New York on voyages varying from five-day sailings to Bermuda to three-week cruises in the Caribbean.

The *Nieuw Amsterdam* did good service during the Second World War as an Allied trooper, sailing to ports around the world, carrying an average of 9000

The 'darling of the Dutch', the majestic *Nieuw Amsterdam* of 1938 arrives at the Wilton-Fijenoord shipyards at Schiedam in Holland for her annual overhaul.

Wilton-Fijenoord Shipyards

Florida, for a continuous series of ten- and eleven-day Caribbean cruises. Vincent Messina was among those still loyal to the ageing former flagship of the Dutch Merchant Marine.

She was a grand hangover from the past – with woods, brass, two-deck lounges – that seemed a world apart from the new generation of cruise ships, which seemed to be all plastic, metallic and velours. Of course, there were fewer conveniences on a ship such as the *Nieuw Amsterdam*. There were many cabins, for example, without private bathroom facilities. The rates, of course, reflected this: $350 per person for eleven days in the Caribbean without a private shower and toilet; $500 per person with private facilities.

The service was also of another age. It was strict French silver service. There were trays of meats, for example. On current ships, in this era of economies, it's either full plate service or quasi-plate service. It is less elegant, somewhat more like Horn & Hardart gone to sea. There was also less to do on ships such as the *Nieuw Amsterdam*. There were far fewer of the elaborate entertainment programmes now found on cruise liners. Most of the *Nieuw Amsterdam*'s passengers went for the time at sea, for the rest and relaxation. Cruising then meant time at sea. Today, it's all fast-paced, fly-to-the-sun and eight-ports-in-seven days. It seems to be time on the ship as a floating hotel and far more time in ports for shopping and swimming.

In December 1973, the *Nieuw Amsterdam*, at the age of thirty-six, was finally retired. Her fate was sealed by the sudden increases in fuel prices, recent Holland-America losses of over $12 million and sheer old age. Vincent Messina was among those on her final cruise, scheduled just before the Christmas holidays.

The majority of the passengers on that final cruise were 'old cruisers', loyalists to the ship and to the sea and to whom it didn't much matter where they went. Among them was Mrs Elinora de Lara Kates, who was on her 219th voyage with Holland-America. It was her sixtieth voyage in the *Nieuw Amsterdam*, which included the maiden voyage, in May 1938. A special cocktail party was given in her honour and the invitations were printed in pink silk. At the gathering, she announced that her wishes were to die on board this beloved liner.

The last cruise was a pre-Christmas trip, which was usually the most difficult to book. It was always a weak seller. Thereafter, the annual Christmas trip from Port Everglades would be aboard the smaller *Statendam*. Some of the great treasures remained on the *Nieuw Amsterdam*, such as her mermaid door handles in the Smoking Room and the silver model of Henry Hudson's *Half Moon*. Months later,

troops per voyage. She was decommissioned in the spring of 1946 and joyously welcomed home to Rotterdam (she was affectionately dubbed 'the Darling of the Dutch'), and restored to much of her prewar ambiance and splendour. She resumed her winter cruises at the end of 1947.

It was rather ironic that, in the face of the phenomenal success of jet aircraft, it was the *Nieuw Amsterdam*, then the oldest member of the Holland-America fleet, warmly regarded as 'the grand hotel of the North Atlantic', that finally terminated the Company's century-old service between Rotterdam and New York. Thereafter, she would be used, like all of the other Holland-America liners, in the cruise trades. At the end of 1971, the 758-foot liner was permanently assigned to a new base: Port Everglades,

Everett Viez Collection

Arriving in Grassy Bay off Hamilton, Bermuda, the *Rotterdam* (left) and *Statendam* (right) on a seven-day cruise out of New York.

however, there were crates at New York, at Holland-America's Pier 40, that were marked from the *Nieuw Amsterdam* and then bound for the Rotterdam home office. [The *Half Moon* model, for example, is today in the Company's Seattle home office.]

It was all very sad, and on the night before her last night at sea with passengers, the air conditioning went out. However, everyone stayed in the lounge just the same to see the final variety show performances. The ship became a steambath. The band played 'Sentimental Journey' and everyone cried. She was indeed a very special ship with a soul. In her final years, Holland-America did an excellent job promoting the age of the ship: 'In this age of chrome and instant coffee, this is a ship with soaring ceilings and inlaid woods and ebony staircases. No, they don't make ships like this any more and it's a shame!'

In the winter of 1974, with a greatly reduced crew of sixty, the *Nieuw Amsterdam* slowly sailed across the Pacific to the scrapyards of Taiwan.

STATENDAM

When the Holland-America Line added the twin sister ships *Ryndam* and *Maasdam* to its North Atlantic passenger fleet in the early fifties, they attracted considerable attention. They were the first passenger ships to offer 90 per cent of their accommodation and facilities to the lowest grade of travellers, those in tourist class. First class, with a mere thirty-nine berths, occupied a smaller, upper-deck section of the ships and was only included because a small first class was prescribed by the ruling Transatlantic Passenger Steamship Conference. Though the tourist sections in these 15,000-tonners were very comfortable, they had one design flaw which made them unsuitable for any service other than the North Atlantic, namely winter

cruising: there were too few private bathrooms. Consequently, neither the *Ryndam* or *Maasdam* was ideally suited to the demanding, bathroom-conscious American cruise market, so in their early years the best they could offer were some 'economy cruises'.

The great success of those two ships on the Atlantic was, however, the catalyst for Holland-America to build a larger, improved liner. While she too would offer predominantly tourist class berths in her transatlantic quarters, she would also be well suited for off-season cruising because almost all of her tourist-class cabins would have private toilets and showers. She was named *Statendam*, was just over 24,000 tons, and entered service in the winter of 1957.

Captain Cornelius van Herk was aboard one of the ship's earliest cruises.

The *Statendam* was used for Holland-America's first around-the-world cruise, which sailed from New York on 7th January 1958 and returned on 26th April. The voyage lasted 110 days, steamed 32,024 miles and had 368 passengers onboard. The shore excursions were run by the American Express Co, which had a staff of 11 men onboard and one lecturer. We called at twenty-seven different ports in Africa, Asia and America. The first day out after leaving New York, we experienced very bad weather and the two spare wooden cruise tenders on the foreship were practically smashed.

During the cruise, I wrote an extensive report about the conditions in each port of call and the routes taken. Now [1985], everything is routine and most ports are familiar, but in 1958, most of them were new to most of us. Nobody died during the cruise and fortunately we didn't need the six coffins I had ordered in Rotterdam. Previously, I had received the message that the *Caronia* had an average of six

Jeff Blinn, Moran Towing & Transportation Co

The *Rotterdam*, the flagship of the Holland-America Line, arriving at New York's Pier 40, in spring 1964. At berth to the right is the combination liner *Prinses Margriet*, owned by the Oranje Line until chartered to Holland-America. Also, just barely visible, is the aft mast of the Norwegian America liner *Stavangerfjord*.

deaths on her world cruises. Arrivals in most ports was a big show, usually with the likes of a brass band waiting on the quayside. In Penang, however, the agent had hired the only band available: Rob Roy's Dance Band. With only one piano and two guitars, we hardly could hear the music they played. In Bali, all those with a Dutch passport were refused shore leave. While I was inspecting the jetty where the cruise tenders came alongside, the Indonesian soldier pointed the bayonet of his rifle at my breast.

Fekko Ebbens, then a deck steward and bar-lounge steward, recalled a more recent *Statendam* cruise.

My favourite ship of all, the *Statendam* was cruising full-time by the late sixties. She sailed to the Caribbean, the North Cape and out to the Pacific. I especially remember the Around South America cruise in 1970. Just before sailing, the American ambassador in Rio was shot to death. There were so many sudden cancellations that we sailed with only 150 passengers looked after by 500 crewmembers.

Captain Frederik van Driel also served in the *Statendam*.

I sailed in her first on long Pacific cruises from California [from San Francisco and Los Angeles in the late sixties], then on long trips from New York [to the North Cape, Mediterranean, etc] and finally on weekly seven-day cruises between New York and Bermuda. She was a beautiful looking and generally good ship, but she suffered one infirmity: she had only two boilers when she needed at least three or maybe four. Consequently, there were never any shutdown possibilities or, when repairs were necessary, the entire ship had to be stopped. Actually she was ideal for the short Bermuda run, which required only a forty hour sailing in each direction and on which considerable fuel savings were made.

The *Statendam* was reassigned to summer season Vancouver–Alaska cruises in 1981, but her days with the Dutch were, in fact, numbered. Her sailing schedules were being disrupted by engine and other

mechanical problems, and extended repair times. A year later, she was sold to the French-owned Paquet Cruises, who placed her under the Bahamian flag as the *Rhapsody*. She was sold to the Greek-owned Regency Cruises in spring 1986, and rebuilt (as a diesel-driven liner) for North American cruising as the *Regent Star*.

ROTTERDAM

Cees Tensen, Holland-America's Vice President for Marketing, called the 37,783-ton *Rotterdam*,

One of the most outstanding ships of her time. In the late fifties, she was among the first major luxury liners to have enormous conversion possibilities. On the two-class Atlantic run, where the ship sailed for about eight months of the year, the first class public rooms were located on the upper and forward decks. These passengers used the top level of the ship's theatre, for example, and the Odyssey Dining Room. The tourist class passengers had the aft public rooms, the lower level of the theatre and the La Fontaine Restaurant. There were sliding panels built in the ship for partitioning between the two classes. Then, at the onset of the extended winter cruise season, we could remove these partitions and make the ship all one-class, all first class in fact.

The *Rotterdam* was ordered from the Rotterdam Drydock Company in 1956. Launched and named by Her Majesty Queen Juliana, on 13 September 1958, she was commissioned exactly one year later. As well as being exceptionally luxurious and the new flagship both of the Dutch Merchant Marine and the Holland-America Line, she had a revolutionary design: she was the first Atlantic liner to do away with the conventional funnel or funnel device, and instead have twin uptakes that were placed aft. Jacob van den Berg, who was involved directly with the building of the ship and who later became a senior vice president for Holland-America, recalled this unique design idea.

The 'no funnel' design of the innovative *Rotterdam* was intended from the start, although we actually thought at first of twin stacks that were to be side-by-side rather than the tubular uptakes. A crossbar was needed to bridge these uptakes, especially to serve as the aft mast light. These uptakes were placed farther aft and thereby created larger top deck spaces and, of course, we were able to move the engine areas father aft as well. Years later, in the late seventies, we actually studied the possibilities of converting the steam turbine *Rotterdam* to a more cost efficient diesel driven liner, but it was found to be impractical.

The *Rotterdam* was included in Holland-America's annual winter cruise programmes. A sample listing for the 1963–64 season is given below.

The *Rotterdam* was converted for year-round cruising in 1969. Not only was she a luxurious ship, a symbol of a bygone era of ocean liner design and construction, but she has since also achieved a unique position within the cruise industry: she is the grande dame of the North American and world cruise fleets.

She occupies a very special place in the hearts of many crew and passengers alike. One officer recently commented, 'I love her and I know that she loves me!' Captain van Driel added,

She is not only an excellent 'sea boat' and in superb and meticulous condition, but her career has now paralleled that of the beloved earlier *Nieuw Amsterdam*, which was not only one of the most favoured Dutch liners of all, but one of the most beautiful and successful ocean liners ever built. There was an increasing fondness and loyalty to that ship, especially as she grew older. Now [1985], the same process is being repeated with the current *Rotterdam*. Many of our repeat passengers love this older ship and often, wanting a sense of familiarity, ask for the same cabin, same table in the restaurant and even ask for the same waiter!

Nico van der Vorm, the chairman of the Holland-America Line, agrees that the 748-foot long *Rotterdam* had a unique status.

Our *Nieuw Amsterdam* of 1938 was a very special ship. The *Rotterdam* is now very much like her. Furthermore, we are most fortunate and satisfied that our newest liners, the present day *Nieuw Amsterdam* and *Noordam* [completed in 1983–84], are in a luxurious style that is much closer to the

Ship	From New York	Cruise
Statendam	Nov 6th	Caribbean, 12 days, from $330
Statendam	Nov 20th	Caribbean, 14 days, from $380
Nieuw Amsterdam	Dec 6th	Caribbean, 12½ days, from $355
Rotterdam	Dec 20th	Caribbean, 15 days, from $495
Nieuw Amsterdam	Dec 21st	Caribbean, 12 days, from $385
Maasdam	Dec 23rd	Caribbean, 11 days, from $280
Nieuw Amsterdam	Jan 3rd	Caribbean, 11½ days, from $325
Rotterdam	Jan 6th	Caribbean, 15 days, from $465
Nieuw Amsterdam	Jan 17th	Caribbean, 14 days, from $420
Statendam	Jan 24th	Caribbean, 16 days, from $435
Rotterdam	Jan 25th	Around the World, 80 days, from $2700
Nieuw Amsterdam	Feb 3rd	Caribbean, 15 days, from $475
Statendam	Feb 11th	Caribbean, 14 days, from $435
Nieuw Amsterdam	Feb 20th	Caribbean, 14 days, from $450
Statendam	Feb 28th	Caribbean, 12 days, from $360
Nieuw Amsterdam	Mar 7th	Caribbean, 11 days, from $325
Statendam	Mar 13th	Caribbean, 9½ days, from $275
Nieuw Amsterdam	Mar 20th	Caribbean, 13½ days, from $395
Statendam	Mar 26th	Caribbean, 12 days, from $350
Nieuw Amsterdam	Apr 6th	Caribbean, 9 days, from $260
Nieuw Amsterdam	Apr 16th	Bermuda, 5½ days, from $165
Maasdam	May 27th	Caribbean, 10 days, from $195

classical *Rotterdam* than we first expected. The three ships create a most agreeable and compatible trio.

PRINSES MARGRIET

This combination passenger-cargo liner, which had only 111 first class berths, was built for another Dutch shipper, the Oranje Line, for a specialized service between Rotterdam, Southampton, Montreal and then to the Great Lakes, to ports as far west as Chicago. Delivered in the summer of 1961, by the De Merwede Shipyards of Hardinxveld, she and her near-sister, the *Prinses Irene* of 1959, were, at best, only moderately successful. Within a matter of a few years, their trade, both in passengers and cargo, had declined to such an extent that they were offered for sale or charter. The *Prinses Irene* was eventually sold to the Indonesians to become a pilgrim ship; the *Prinses Margriet* was chartered and then sold outright to the Holland-America Line for use in the final seasons of the Company's monthly direct service between Rotterdam and New York.

After just a few seasons as a transatlantic passenger ship, the 456-foot *Prinses Margriet* was chartered to yet another Dutch shipper, the Royal Netherlands Steamship Company, retaining Holland-America's passenger management, for twelve-day Caribbean

The yacht-like 374-passenger *Prinsendam*, an experimental ship for the Holland-America Line fleet. She is sailing in Alaska's Inside Passage, during a summer cruise from Vancouver.

Holland-America Line

runs out of New York. This proved an ill-timed schedule for a combination ship that was being rapidly outmoded. Most cruise passengers sailed instead aboard larger ships and freight was often sent in ships with more flexible schedules. By June 1970, after less than three years, this service was terminated. With no other role within the Dutch fleet, she was sold to somewhat unknown purchasers, the phosphate-rich government of the Pacific island of Nauru. She was refitted and renamed *Enna G*, retained her rather handsome passenger accommodation and ran forty-two-day cruises from San Francisco to Honolulu, Majuro, Ponape, Truk and Saipan. In 1984 she was withdrawn from service and laid-up; it is not clear what happened to her thereafter.

PRINSENDAM

'The engines-aft *Prinsendam*, completed in the spring of 1973, was to have been the prototype of a possible Holland-America fleet of 8500-ton cruise ships that were to be positioned all over the world,' according to Cees Tensen, the Company's vice president for marketing. Built at the De Merwede yards, like the *Prinses Margriet*, she was a rather unusual design for Holland-America Line, who had previously preferred larger cruise ships. Her capacity was limited to 374 passengers and she was more club-like, more intimate and best suited for specialist cruising to the more unusual ports of call than their previous vessels. Although there were persistent rumours of at least a sister ship, the *Prinsendam* remained unique in her owners' fleet. She had a long delivery cruise from Rotterdam to Singapore, after which instead of Caribbean or even a European service, she ran a special, all-year-round service which consisted of two-week cruises from Singapore to Indonesia. In later years, these were run for only part of the year, when Holland-America's interests in the summertime Alaska cruise trades peaked. Each May, the *Prinsendam* would shift to Vancouver for a full season of seven-day voyages along the renowned Inside Passage.

It was, unfortunately, during one of these latter sailings, an end-of-season 'positioning cruise' from Vancouver homeward to the Far East and Singapore, that the accident occurred which spelled the end for the *Prinsendam*. On 4 October 1980, she caught fire, was abandoned by her 524 passengers and crew, and, though salvage efforts were attempted later sank some fifty miles west of Sitka, Alaska.

VEENDAM AND VOLENDAM

According to Jacob van den Berg,

After building the smaller *Prinsendam* for the Indonesian trade, we began looking over available second-hand passenger ships that could be converted for long, luxurious cruising. We closely examined the potential of three French combination passenger-cargo ships, the 13,200-ton *Cambodge*, *Laos* and *Pacifique* of the Messageries Maritimes. Instead, we were quite fortunate to have obtained the 23,400-ton Moore McCormack Line's sisters *Argentina* and *Brasil*, which had been out of work and laid up at Baltimore since the fall of 1969. We took delivery in the summer of 1972. Bought for $10 million apiece, they were went to the Hapag-Lloyd Shipyards at Bremerhaven for full refits, improvements and updating.

At first, we planned to use these ships only on long cruises, carrying only 500 passengers. In fact, we sent the *Veendam*, the former *Argentina* [the former *Brasil* became the *Volendam*] on an around-the-world cruise in January 1974, as a substitute for the *Rotterdam*, which had been traditionally sent on this voyage.

Captain van Driel also remembered *Veendam* and *Volendam*, known as the 'V ships'.

I recall them as especially heavy ships with extra plating on their hulls, but which, in fact, caused drag and therefore extra fuel consumption. Ideally, from the economic standpoint, they should have carried 850 passengers, but instead were limited to 650. Their use in long-distance cruise service was precluded by the sudden and very sharp increases in fuel costs in 1973–74. Briefly, we even had to withdraw the ships and place them in lay-up at Newport News in Virginia. Fortunately, we did manage to charter the *Veendam* to a Brazilian tour firm, who sailed her as the *Brasil*. This was quite ironic as she had originally been the *Argentina*. We had Dutch officers and engine crew, and Brazilians in the hotel department for the five month contract and sailed from Rio de Janeiro on coastal cruises, to Miami and to the Azores and Dakar.

Afterward, in 1975–76, both the *Veendam* and *Volendam* were chartered to Greek shipowners at Miami, who wanted to use the ships in the Caribbean. Under the banner of the newly formed Monarch Cruise Lines, flying the Panamanian colours [it had been Dutch], they became the *Monarch Star* and *Monarch Sun* respectively. I was the only Dutchman on board amongst the Greek officers and the multinational hotel staff representing thirty or forty nations. These ships were eventually [in January 1978] brought back under Holland-America control and reverted to their earlier Dutch names [although they continued with the Panama flag]. Holland-America cruise operations were again expanding and profitable.

Holland-America Line

The *Monarch Sun*, formerly Holland-America's *Volendam*, waits at anchor at Ketchikan, Alaska.

In their later years, they were used mostly on the seven-day New York–Bermuda cruise run, but also sailed to the Caribbean from Miami and Tampa in Florida, and during some summers on the Alaskan route from Vancouver. Replaced by the brand-new *Nieuw Amsterdam* and *Noordam*, they were bought, in 1983–84, by Taiwan's C Y Tung Group. The *Veendam* has been leased to the Bahama Cruise Lines and currently sails as their *Bermuda Star*; the *Volendam*, following an extensive refit in Japan, joined Tung's cruise subsidiary, American Hawaii Cruises, for South Pacific cruising out of Tahiti as the *Liberte*.

NIEUW AMSTERDAM (1983) AND NOORDAM

The 33,930-ton *Nieuw Amsterdam*, first commissioned in the summer of 1983, and her sister ship, the *Noordam*, introduced in the following spring, have been judged as two of the three or four most beautifully decorated liners of the past decade. They are floating treasure chests of art and antiques, all of which are housed and carefully blended in these most contemporary ships.

Ordered from the Chantiers de L'Atlantique Shipyards at St Nazaire (the illustrious French shipbuilders that had built such notable transatlantic luxury liners as the *Ile de France*, *Normandie* and the *France* of 1912 and the more recent *France* of 1962), the new Dutch liners were first planned and then designed in the late 1970s. They were Holland-America's considered response to the ever-growing, ever-expanding North American cruise industry, which had increased to a $4 billion annual level (cruise sales), with over sixty different cruise ships by the early 1980s. More than ever before in the history of passenger shipping, liners had to be increasingly efficient and competitive, appealing not only to loyal regular passengers, but to first-time cruise travellers.

Jacob van den Berg led the design team that produced these two handsome new Dutch vessels.

The overall plans for these new sisters were based to a considerable extent on the engines-aft style of our earlier *Prinsendam*, that 8500-tonner first commissioned in 1973. There were, of course, some design changes. Most obviously, the new ships would be far larger and with greater capacities and facilities [the *Prinsendam* had a capacity for 375 passengers whereas the new ships had a maximum capacity for 1214 guests]. Another difference, as an example, was a specific detail such as the colouring of the funnel, which would have been done in our customary orange. That colour looked 'too heavy' on the initial test models and so we decided to use white instead. Of course, there have been considerable technological advances as well. In the overall design, the stern section is squared-off for better space utilization onboard and for greater efficiency in construction. Also, these two ships do not have traditional sheer, that sense of 'drooping' in the hulls of earlier liners.

While we would have liked to have built the pair in Holland, shipbuilding costs, delivery dates and financing arrangements are such essentials in present day shipping operations that instead we had to 'shop around' to various European yards and even to Japan. The orders finally went to the French, to Chantiers de L'Atlantique. They have had, of course, very extensive and distinguished experience in building large, first rate ocean liners.

Mr van den Berg added,

Once the major designs were completed, we hired an historian that would assist in the general decoration that would give the *Nieuw Amsterdam* an 'early New York' and West Indian theme and the *Noordam* an Asian-East Indian style. Spending over $1 million for each ship and requiring 2½ years of effort, some prized antiques were purchased. These items included a 17th century Bible from Holland's Golden Age, maps, jewel boxes, tapestries and rare china. We also added ship models, vintage costumes and paintings. These artifacts were collected and then kept in vaults until the vessels were near to completion.

Even the vessels' names had an historical precedent. According to Holland-America Line chairman, Nico van der Vorm

The name *Nieuw Amsterdam* was an obvious, most ideal selection for the first ship, especially when considering the glorious heritage of the previous *Nieuw Amsterdam* [1938–73]. Since that earlier ship was christened by Her Majesty Queen Wilhelmina [on 10 April 1937], we decided once again to ask a member of the Dutch Royal Family. Her Royal Highness Princess Margriet, sister to the present Queen and Godmother to all Dutch ships, graciously accepted our invitation. She followed in her grandmother's footsteps and named the *Nieuw Amsterdam* at Le Havre in July 1983. In this grandmother-to-granddaughter tradition, my grandmother had christened the earlier *Noordam*, in April 1938, and so it seemed appropriate that her granddaughter, my daughter in fact, should name the present *Noordam*. This ceremony was held in April 1984.

Once in service, in North American waters, both the *Nieuw Amsterdam* and *Noordam* became highly popular, often glowingly praised ships. The *Nieuw Amsterdam*'s collection of works of art strongly reflects the early Dutch West Indian Company and its explorations in the New World, with paintings, maps and documents, murals, painted tiles, statues, china, weapons and armour, historic costumes and old navigational instruments. There are eighteenth-century nautical instruments on display in the Crow's Nest bar-lounge, a copy of the document confirming the original Dutch purchase of the island of Manhattan in the Minnewit Terrace, and a fully detailed model of the sailing ship *Half Moon*, Henry Hudson's ship, in the Haelve Maen Room. There are statues of Henry Hudson and Queen Beatrix, a mounted figurehead from an earlier sailing ship, and a wedding chest from 1650. Adorning the staircase on Main Deck is an enormous Venetian lantern made in 1580. Four documents from the original Dutch West Indies Company hang opposite and Ming Chinese plates decorate the ship's restaurant.

The *Noordam*'s collection is largely from the other side of the globe, with rare vases, statues and Buddhas from China, Japan and Indonesia, seventeenth- and eighteenth-century European paintings, early Dutch costumes, ships' instruments and some magnificently hand-carved ship models that were made by prisoners of war during the eighteenth century European conflicts. The ship's collection of early world maps and charts is especially rare. The pride of the collection are two large wood sculptures representing water and sky, by the Flemish artist Grupello (1644–1730).

On both ships, the collections are sensitively integrated with the overall décor. As a matter of policy, there are no labels or signatures on the art. Instead, during cruises, walking tours are conducted by a member of the ship's staff.

John Groothuizen, who served on some of the Company's earlier liners and who is presently hotel manager on the *Nieuw Amsterdam*, is delighted with the 'N ships', as they are often called.

The *Nieuw Amsterdam* and *Noordam* are exceptionally beautiful ships. The idea of giving historic themes to the décor of each vessel and then using art and antiques has been both very pleasing and very successful. Much thought and research has gone into their design and arrangements as well. For example, they have far more windows than most liners. They also have many quiet spots, ample spaces for passengers to read, dream or just get away from it all. They are so well planned that not one inch of space is wasted or misused. In consideration of very contemporary trends, we have, for example, full conference facilities that even include a small theatre for private presentations. Our multichannel television system is excellent and includes not only major motion pictures and film favourites from the past, but documentaries, travelogues, news and feature items as well. [Every cabin on board is fitted with a television.] They are, of course, similar to our earlier ships, true members of the 'Spotless Fleet'. They are meticulous.

They offer a very relaxed and comfortable yet very elegant atmosphere for ocean travellers.

Technologically, the ships are among the most sophisticated afloat. Travel writer Barry Anderson wrote:

The double-deck Admirals Lounge aboard the *Noordam*.

Holland-America's new $160 million *Noordam* arriving at Tampa, Florida in April 1984 on her transatlantic maiden voyage from Le Havre via the Azores and Bermuda.

If a sea captain from the 1950s was to step aboard either the *Nieuw Amsterdam* or *Noordam*, he might think that he landed on another planet. Not more than two decades ago, ocean liners relied on celestial navigation to determine their position, they docked with the aid of tugs and they employed telephone and telegraph to communicate changes in speed between the bridge and engine room.

Today, signals from three different satellites orbiting in space are beamed to receivers on the *Nieuw Amsterdam* and *Noordam*, instantly translated by computer to determine the exact position that is displayed on a bridge monitor of each of these new twins at sea. As a backup navigation system, the 'N ships' also use a Loran unit that receives signals from shore stations. Still, all deck officers must take celestial sights with a sextant from time to time, to keep in practice.

Each of these ship's main radar is tied into an automatic plotter that keeps track of any other vessel within range. Another short range radar aboard, used for manoeuvring in harbours and narrow waterways like Alaska's Inside Passage, has such high resolution it can pick up a rowboat on the surface. Virtually everything, including the ship's engines, is controlled from the bridge and, in an emergency, the entire ship could be operated by a single officer.

Holland-America's present 'Big Three', the *Rotterdam*, *Nieuw Amsterdam* and *Noordam*, sail during the summer season, from June to September, on the Alaska cruise run out of Vancouver. Within their seven-day itineraries, they call at Ketchikan, Juneau, Glacier Bay and Sitka. For the rest of the year, the *Noordam* is based at Port Everglades, Florida for seven-day Caribbean cruises. The *Rotterdam* spends the autumn, winter and spring on ten- and eleven-day Caribbean trips, also out of Port Everglades. The *Nieuw Amsterdam* cruises, from October through May, from Tampa on seven-day western Caribbean cruises. All three ships also make trans-Panama Canal cruises, sailing to and from Vancouver and various other West Coast ports such as Seattle, Portland, San Francisco, Los Angeles and/or San Diego, and then onwards to Cabo San Lucas, Acapulco, Balboa, the Panama Canal, Cristobal, then various ports in the Caribbean such as the San Blas Islands, Cartagena, Curacao and St Thomas, before terminating at either Port Everglades or Tampa.

Alaskan cruises, Mexican cruises, Caribbean cruises, trans-Canal cruises, even short coastal cruises – those have aptly been described as 'the world of Holland-America'.

six

THE
ITALIANS

HOME LINES

ITALIA AND HOMERIC

It is appropriate that this chapter on the Italians begins with the Home Lines, a firm founded in 1946. Although it is a multinational company that includes Swedish, Swiss, Greek, Italian and American financial holdings, its operational base is at Genoa which makes it suitable for inclusion in this section. After some very successful years trading on the North Atlantic, in 1963 the Home Lines turned to full-time year-round cruising, a rather bold and innovative step at the time. Most liner companies were then still engaged in diminishing liner runs. Sailing from New York mostly, the Home Lines soon became one of the most popular and financially successful firms to make this transition.

Though their ships had been used for winter cruising in the fifties, the Company's decision to employ the 21,532-ton *Italia* on all-the-year-round

A poetic photo taken on 20 December 1969 in the fading sunlight of late afternoon as the *Homeric* departs on her annual Christmas cruise.

weekly cruises between New York and Nassau was an important turning point. Few companies, with the exception of the Incres Line with their veteran *Nassau*, were yet willing to invest so heavily in leisure cruising and abandon their traditional, class-divided services. With minimum fares beginning at $170, the *Italia* (the former Swedish American *Kungsholm* of 1928 and later the American war-time troop transport USS *John Ericsson*), could not have been a greater success.

In 1964, the *Italia*, by then nearly thirty-six years old, was replaced by the slightly larger *Homeric*, the former Matson liner *Mariposa* of 1931, which had closed out the Home Lines' Atlantic service to Montreal in October. In the following April, the *Homeric* replaced the *Italia* on weekly seven-day cruises to Nassau. The latter was sold off to Bahamian interests, who wanted to establish a floating hotel and resort complex at Freeport on Grand Bahama Island. Clouded in mismanagement and financial scandals, the *Italia*, renamed as the *Imperial Bahama Hotel*, survived for little more than a year. In September 1965, she was delivered to Spanish breakers at Bilbao.

The *Homeric*, known as the 'fun ship' and a vessel of enormous popularity, was replaced within a year on the Nassau run by the largest liner yet built for cruising, the 39,200-ton *Oceanic*. The older ship was thereafter re-routed to Caribbean cruising, on eight- to eighteen-day voyages. Later, despite her increasing age, she was still sailing and might have continued to do so, had it not been for a galley and restaurant fire which broke out on 1 July 1973 whilst outbound from New York some 90 miles off the New Jersey coast. Badly damaged, she was returned to port and then brought to Genoa for further inspection. The cost of repairs and the extreme smell of smoke that had permeated the liner prompted her end. She was handed over to Taiwanese breakers in January 1974.

OCEANIC

Arriving in New York for the first time in April 1965, the magnificent 774-foot *Oceanic*, then the largest and finest liner to be used for full-time cruising, soon became the most successful passenger ship of her time. Her seven-day sailings were often booked as much as a year in advance which forecast the increasing market for leisure sailings and the need for specially built and outfitted cruise ships. The $40 million liner is reported to have paid for herself within five

Jeff Blinn, Moran Towing & Transportation Co

A maiden arrival at New York's Pier 84, in April 1965, of Home Lines' magnificent *Oceanic*. Also arriving on her maiden call is Norway's *Viking Princess*. At berth, in the left corner, is the American Export liner *Independence*.

years and maintained a very enviable 92 per cent occupancy rate.

Built by the Cantieri Riuniti dell'Adriatico yards at Monfalcone (alongside Italian Line's *Raffaello*), the *Oceanic* was first intended to cruise only in winter and to sail the North Atlantic in peak summer season between Cuxhaven (Hamburg), Le Havre, Southampton, Quebec City and Montreal. Her accommodation was to have been arranged as 400 in first class and 1200 in tourist. However, the Atlantic run was already in decline and was discontinued by Home Lines (in October 1963). Despite this decision very little alteration was needed to the original design of the 'ship of tomorrow', as the *Oceanic* was known. She was restyled for cruising with 1200 all-first class berths. Her accommodation was in a sleek Mediterranean modern style, every cabin had private bathroom facilities, there were large public rooms and two top-deck pools that were covered with a sliding glass top known as the Magrodome.

Vincent Messina, who served aboard the *Oceanic* as a member of her cruise staff, recalled her enormous success and popularity.

The crew played a very large part in her success. There was tremendous longevity of service and, since the repeat passengers were seemingly endless, the staff remembered their names and recalled their preferences. Although she did a weekly shuttle service to Nassau, many passengers came once a year, asking for the same cabin with the same steward and for the same table in the restaurant with the same waiter. There was even an exceptionally high percentage of repeat passengers for the ship's longer Caribbean cruises in winter. On one occasion, during a sixteen-day Caribbean cruise, there were 873 passengers onboard – 793 were repeaters! There was a cachet about the *Oceanic*, a certain prestige. Decoratively, she might have been a bit cool, but her best secrets were the staff and the cooking. In short, it was all rich, creamy Italian charm! Every woman felt like a queen! There was also great flair in the food preparation and in its presentation as well.

I think that the *Oceanic* was, in many ways, a throwback to the grander liners of the past, especially during her longer winter cruises. On these trips, passengers would organize many private parties. There were, in fact, great rivalries as passengers tried to outdo each other and lure more guests. The ship even carried its own winter news reporter, who wrote a passenger gossip column. The *Oceanic* had an intangible magic.

The *Oceanic* did, like many liners, have her occasional mishaps. Vincent Messina added,

There was once a rather bad engine room fire when the ship was nearly lost. An oil line broke, a fire started and the blaze spread underneath the plates. On another occasion, during a violent storm, two cranes were swept off the foredeck. At another occasion, she collided with a tanker in New York harbour and was forced to return to her berth. Once at sea, however, she was always something of a 'pitcher'. She did, of course, have enormous reserve speed. In the winter of 1978, I recall her doing 26 knots and travelling from St Maarten to New York in two days flat.

In 1985, after twenty years of highly successful

service, the *Oceanic* was sold off. With the development of more specialized and efficient cruise ships, her original steam turbine design had become less and less profitable. Vincent Messina believed,

That longevity of staff, the *Oceanic*'s prime secret, had also changed. In 1965, she had an all-Italian crew, but, in 1985, there were more and more Colombians. Quite simply, it had become increasingly more difficult to find Italian personnel.

In her final months, all of the ship's major artworks were removed, the passenger loads decreased and even the crew was reduced. The final cruise [on 9 November 1985] was, however, sold out. It was an 11-day trip to the Caribbean.

The *Oceanic* returned to New York to deposit her final Home Lines' passengers, and slipped off, almost un-noticed, to Newport News, Virginia in the dusk of an autumn afternoon. It seemed a sad departure for a ship that had been so familiar to New Yorkers. She is now working under her original name for the Premier Cruise Lines, sailing twice weekly between Port Canaveral, Florida and the Bahamas.

DORIC

Soon after the *Homeric*'s unexpected loss due to a fire in July 1973, the Company began to search for suitable replacement tonnage, an appropriate but temporary ship at best. There were rumours that they would buy the French Line's *De Grasse*, the former *Bergensfjord* of 1956, which had been less than a success under the tricolor. Instead, in August 1973, they found an even more suitable vessel, the 25,338-ton, 1012-berth *Hanseatic*, which had just been placed on the sales lists by the financially ailing German Atlantic Line. She had been under the West German flag for a little over five years and used mostly on long, expensive cruises. She had been built in 1964, by Chantiers de L'Atlantique at St Nazaire, as the *Shalom* for the Zim Lines – Israel's unsuccessful bid to have both a large transatlantic liner as well as winter cruise ship. Expensive Israeli labour, her all-kosher kitchens and the lack of a suitable running mate all cast contributing blows.

Renamed *Doric* and refitted with a maximum capacity for 945 cruise passengers, she entered Home Lines' service in January 1974, first from Port Everglades to the Caribbean and later on the weekly seven-day run between New York and Bermuda. Vincent Messina also served aboard this vessel and recalled,

Arriving in New York on her maiden visit in March 1974 is the Home Lines' *Doric*. In the foreground is the Italian liner *Michelangelo*.

Jeff Blinn, Moran Towing & Transportation Co

She was a very cosy ship and therefore the ideal replacement for the beloved *Homeric*. The *Doric* always had a warm charm about her whereas the *Oceanic* was always the big grand hotel. She was, however, always a temporary ship for Home Lines. They soon began to plan for a brand-new ship of their own specifications. I especially recall a Christmas cruise aboard the *Doric* with 300 Mexican passengers on board. They spent money in the wildest way and numbers. They literally cleared out the gift shops. One passenger's wine bill was $3000 and all of the Dom Perignon was gone.

As the new *Atlantic* was about to come into service, the *Doric* was sold (despite thoughts of placing her in European and then American West Coast cruise service) and was delivered to her new Greek owners, the Royal Cruise Lines. She was refitted and given a new funnel and sails at present as their *Royal Odyssey*.

ATLANTIC

It was rumoured she might be named *Homeric II*, in an attempt to capture some of the great popularity of the

New York's Passenger Ship Terminal on 2 October 1982, with (from left to right) the *Scandinavia*, *Veendam*, *Atlantic* and *Oceanic* at dock.

earlier ship of the same name. The new 1179-passenger vessel was launched as *Atlantic*, on 9 January 1981, at the CNIM yards at La Seyne sur Mer in the south of France. She was delivered in the spring of 1982 and placed on the weekly New York–Bermuda run as a complement to the larger *Oceanic*. In winter, she was sent to Port Everglades for extended sailings into the Caribbean. The *Atlantic* was intended to be something of a successor to the highly innovative *Oceanic* but seemed to lack the stylish lustre that so marked the earlier ship's success. Much of the internal decoration seemed to fall short of the *Oceanic*'s richly luxurious tone and the exterior was even more disappointing. To many, her appearance more closely resembled a large car ferry. According to Vincent Messina 'In the spring of 1985, a blue band was painted around her hull to make her look better.'

HOMERIC

Launched at the Meyer-Werft Shipyards at Papenburg in West Germany, on 28 September 1985, this $147 million liner was built as a replacement for the earlier *Oceanic*, which was retired two months later. Shipbuilding costs for the two liners can easily be compared – the slightly larger *Oceanic* had cost $40 million just two decades earlier.

Delivered in the spring of 1986, the 1050-berth *Homeric* has been assigned to weekly New York–Bermuda service, sailing each Saturday afternoon, prior to the *Atlantic*'s Sunday afternoon departures.

ITALIAN LINE

LEONARDO DA VINCI, MICHELANGELO AND RAFFAELLO

In 1965, the state-owned Italian Line (part of the Finmare Group) operated no fewer than nine liners: the sisters *Augustus* and *Giulio Cesare* to the east coast of South America; a trio, the *Donizetti*, *Rossini* and *Verdi*, to South America's west coast; and the *Cristoforo Colombo* on the prestigious Atlantic run to New York, which was joined by the nation's largest liners, the stunning *Leonardo da Vinci* and the superliner twins *Michelangelo* and *Raffaello*. The 33,300-ton *da Vinci* was built at Genoa in 1960 and the 45,900-ton *Michelangelo* and *Raffaello* built at Genoa and Trieste respectively and completed in 1965. However, these ships represented the final grand era for the Italian Line. Deficit-ridden, totally reliant on government subsidies and kept in service to appease the very powerful Italian maritime unions, in little more than a decade, they were either sold off or scrapped.

Supplementing their transatlantic sailings to New York, the three larger ships ran cruises, mostly seven- to fourteen-day voyages to the Caribbean, and also three-week round-trips to the Mediterranean, known as 'Mediterranean Go-Rounds'. A sample itinerary for the latter is: New York, Casablanca, Algeciras, Palermo, Naples, Genoa, Barcelona, Algeciras, Lisbon and then homeward to New York. There were also some special sailings, such as a long Mediterranean cruise that included calls at the Black Sea ports, a winter voyage to Rio de Janeiro for the annual carnival, and some short cruises from Genoa and summer-time runs, by the *Raffaello* and *Leonardo da Vinci*, from Italy to Scandinavian and North European ports.

In spring 1975, when the Italian Government cut its desperately needed financial support, the *Michelangelo* and *Raffaello* were withdrawn from service. They were laid up for a time at La Spezia and looked over by a steady stream of potential buyers, until they were sold, in February 1977, to the Shah of Iran's Government for use as naval accommodation ships. The *Michelangelo* went to Bandar Abbas and remained there until she was scrapped in Taiwan in 1987; the *Raffaello*, which went to Bushire, was bombed and sunk in an Iraqi air attack in February 1983.

Under pressure from the still insistent maritime unions, the *Leonardo da Vinci* (which made the final Italian Line transatlantic sailing in June 1976) was kept in service for a time, under the banner of the specially created Italian Line Cruises International with Costa Line management, on the overnight cruise trade between Florida and the Bahamas. Her cruise trade proved as unprofitable as the Atlantic trade so she was laid up in September 1978. Despite rumours of new buyers and projects to reactivate her she never again left her moorings and, sadly, on 3 July 1980, was swept by fire. She was totally destroyed and then deliberately capsized. Her remains were later salvaged and, by the spring of 1982, had been scrapped at La Spezia.

ADRIATICA LINE

AUSONIA AND VICTORIA

Also part of the state-owned Finmare Group, the Adriatica Line maintained Italy's Mediterranean passenger services, catering for both port-to-port passengers and round-trip travellers. The Company's largest ships by the mid-seventies were the 11,879-ton *Ausonia* and the 11,695-ton *Victoria*.

Schiffsfotos Jansen

Berthed at Genoa, two of the last of the large Italian Line passenger ships, the twin-funnelled *Michelangelo* and the *Leonardo da Vinci*.

Antonio Scrimali

Painted in the colours of Italian Line Cruises International, the *Ausonia* of 1957 remains in Italian-flag cruise service at the time of writing (1986).

The *Ausonia*, built at Monfalcone in 1957, was the Adriatica Line flagship and was used on the 'express route' which alternated sailings between Venice and Brindisi or Genoa, and Naples to Alexandria and Beirut. Her accommodation was then divided into three classes: 181 in first class, 118 in second class and 230 in third class. By the early seventies she was used increasingly for one-class cruising so, after a period of lay-up, she was refitted in 1978 and introduced as a full-time cruise ship with 690 first class berths. For a time she was marketed by the Siosa Lines and later by Italian Line Cruises International. She remains in service at the time of writing, mostly on weekly cruise sailings from Genoa to the western Mediterranean.

The *Victoria* joined the Adriatica fleet in October

Initially used for some twenty years on Lloyd Triestino's Far Eastern passenger run, the motor liner *Victoria* was later allocated within the Finmare Group to the Adriatica Line, for whom she sailed mostly as a cruise ship. She remains in service to date, as the floating missionary ship *Anastasis*.

1974, after having sailed between Genoa, Naples and the Far East for another member of the Finmare Group, Lloyd Triestino. She had been employed in that service, with her sister ship *Asia*, since completion in 1953. Retaining her original name for Adriatica service, she was partnered with the *Ausonia* and also cruised, not only in Mediterranean waters but out to the Atlantic Isles and West Africa. The Adriatica Line decided to eliminate its conventional passenger services and instead concentrate on large car ferries, so in June 1977, the *Victoria* was decommissioned and was laid up. She was later sold to the Youth-with-a-Mission Organization, registered under Cypriot colours and her home port listed at Piraeus. She was renamed *Anastasis* and sent on worldwide voyages as a religious missionary ship that visits mostly Third World and underdeveloped nations. I recall, during a visit to Suva in Fiji, in July 1984, that numerous photos of the ship adorned shop windows and walls. One large colour print of the former liner in Suva harbour was priced at $35. Since then there have been reports that she endured a lengthy lay-up at Honolulu and that she underwent a refit at Vancouver.

ENOTRIA AND MESSAPIA

The 5200-ton sisters *Enotria* and *Messapia*, part of Adriatica's once large Mediterranean passenger fleet, were built at Leghorn and Taranto in 1950 and 1952 respectively. They too carried three classes of passengers: 76 in first, 44 in second and 162 in third. Their

voyages, often round-trip cruises, were based on a three-week itinerary that sailed alternately from Genoa and Naples or from Trieste, Venice and Brindisi, to Limassol, Haifa, Larnaca and Piraeus. They remained in service until 1975. Antonio Scrimali, the noted Italian marine photographer and specialist on Mediterranean passenger shipping, completes the history of these ships:

The *Enotria* finished her Italian service on 5 May 1975, and a few months later was sold to the Zam Zam Shipping Co and renamed *Zam Zam*. Thereafter, she was used in Red Sea pilgrim service. The *Messapia* was retired on 29 April 1975, and sold some months later to Kawther Shipping Co of Cyprus. Managed by the Orri Navigation Lines and renamed *Kawther*, she too was used in the pilgrim trades. Laid-up in 1977, she was to have been towed to Spain, in October 1980, for demolition, but after only one hour outside Piraeus, she began to leak and take on water. Returned to Piraeus, she then went onto the rocks at the entrance to the harbour and thereafter was demolished on the spot.

SAN MARCO AND SAN GIORGIO

The twin 4700-ton sisters *San Marco* and *San Giorgio* were built at Trieste in 1956 especially for the Turkish trade (to Istanbul and Izmir, via Piraeus). Like all of the Adriatica passenger fleet of the time, they drew profits from both passengers and substantial amounts of cargo. They, too, carried passengers in three classes: ninety-two in first, forty-five in second and sixty-six in third class.

They were sold to a Greek company, Cycladic Cruises, in 1976, and renamed the *City of Mykonos* and *City of Andros*. The latter was refitted for Aegean cruising, and, since late 1984, has been sailing for another Greek firm, the Ocean Cruise Lines, as *Ocean Islander*. She sails in both Mediterranean as well as Caribbean waters.

BERNINA, BRENNERO AND STELVIO

These three vessels were the smallest members of the Adriatica passenger fleet and the only units to carry just first class passengers (with eighty-one berths each). They were built in 1958–59 for three-week round-trip sailings from Genoa, Naples, Leghorn and Catania or Trieste, Venice and Bari, to Alexandria, Port Said, Beirut, Latakia, Famagusta, Rhodes, Mersin, Izmir and Piraeus. They were possibly the most popular vessels for cruise-like sailings and the accommodation on board was of notably high standard.

In the reorganization of Adriatica's passenger services in the mid-seventies, these ships were sold off. The *Bernina* and *Brennero* went to Egypt's Arab Navigation Company and became *Abu el Kassem* and *El Hassen* respectively. I recall seeing them, both in quite a neglected state, at anchor in Alexandria Roads in July 1983 when I was sailing inbound on Costa's *Eugenio C.*. The *Stelvio* was acquired by Greek buyers, but seems not to have been used. She was laid up in Perama Bay, and it was reported in late 1985 that she would be rebuilt for luxury cruising as the *Ocean Ambassador* for the Ocean Cruise Lines and be teamed with a former fleetmate, the former *San Giorgio*, now sailing as the *Ocean Islander*. However, the idea never came to pass; *Stelvio* was scrapped in 1987.

ILLIRIA

The 3700-ton *Illiria*, built for the Adriatica Line at Naples in 1962, was designed primarily as a cruise ship with only 170 first class berths. She worked a twelve-day service, sailing from Venice to Dubrovnik, Itea, Piraeus, Delos, Mykonos, Kusadasi, Kos, Rhodes, Heraklion, Nauplia, Katakolon and then return to Venice. Sold to Greek interests in December 1975, she has retained her original name and is registered to the Blue Aegean Line, but sails mostly under charter and in Mediterranean waters for Travel Dynamics, a New York-based tour operator.

SIOSA LINES

IRPINIA

Her long and very busy career which lasted over fifty years, began as the French *Campana* in 1929. Siosa bought her in 1955 for the Caribbean migrant trade and she was renamed *Irpinia*. She began sailing purely as a cruise ship after March 1970. Though periodically detoured to northern waters, cruising to Scandinavia from Tilbury as well as Bremerhaven, her mainstay was weekly cruises from Genoa to the western Mediterranean (to Cannes, Barcelona, Palma de Majorca, Tunis, Capri and Naples). Finally retired in 1981, she sat at anchor at La Spezia for another two years before being taken in hand by local scrappers. David L Powers visited the ship as the dismantling was in progress and reported, in an article entitled 'Farewell to *Irpinia*', in the spring 1985 issue of *Steamboat Bill*,

Vincent Messina Collection

The *Bernina*, a handsome combination passenger-cargo vessel, steams inbound past the Campanile and St Mark's at Venice.

Antonio Scrimali

Partially stripped down, the Siosa Lines' *Irpinia* awaits the breakers at La Spezia during the summer of 1983.

Irpinia was moored offshore next to the bulk carrier *Tyne*, both undergoing demolition at Cantieri Navali Santa Maria in La Spezia. Destruction of the old Siosa liner had begun August 2nd 1983 and now, six months later, the entire superstructure down to most of A Deck had been removed. Various pieces of the *Irpinia* such as lifeboats, sections of the hull, assorted furniture and even the swimming pool slide lay around the yard in confusing disarray. Large portions of the ship were being brought to shore by a crane mounted on a barge, where they would then be cut into smaller pieces and loaded onto a nearby waiting railroad car.

After having received permission from the foreman, I was taken out to the *Irpinia* by the yard's motor launch and told that I had two hours to explore the ship and take photographs. I had begun to regret not having a deck plan for the *Irpinia* since I was unfamiliar with her layout and

A veteran of some forty years in Latin American passenger service the Siosa Lines' *Ascania* ended her days as a Mediterranean cruise ship, sailing mostly on seven-day voyages out of Genoa. She was sold to ship-breakers in 1968.

Roger Sherlock

envisioned the unlit interior of the ocean liner as an endless maze of corridors and cabins.

To my dismay, all the remaining A Deck cabins had already been gutted, now leaving a vast unobstructed vista through the dimly lit interior. The only light filtered through the open portholes and stairwells to illuminate cluttered piles of doors, panelling and cabin furniture. Large puddles of rusty water stained the carpeting, which revealed in coloured outlines the former layout of the accommodations. On the open deck above, I discovered more doors and rolls of tightly bound carpets waiting to be removed from the ship. A section of ornate cast iron railing from the Grand Staircase lay twisted nearby. I had been told that a local furniture builder had purchased the rights to all the *Irpinia*'s wood fittings and teak decking, which would eventually be recycled into imitation marine-style furniture.

ASCANIA

The 9536-ton *Ascania* had a long, very useful life, like the *Irpinia*, and had also been built for the French, in 1926, as the *Florida*. Bought by Siosa in 1955, she too served mostly on the West Indies migrant trades before being reassigned to full-time cruising in June 1966. She worked a popular air-sea programme known as the 'Seven Mediterranean Pearls', out of Palma de Majorca to six ports: Cannes, Genoa, Naples, Palermo, Tunis and Cagliari. She remained in this service for two years and, after being replaced by the far larger *Caribia*, was laid up at La Spezia. In April 1968, she was handed over to local scrappers.

CARIBIA

Built in 1928 as the *Vulcania*, this motor liner sailed for the Cosulich Line before being integrated with the Italian Line (in 1937) for their Mediterranean services across the mid-Atlantic to New York. She and her near-sister *Saturnia*'s service was interrupted by the war, after which they sailed for another twenty years before the *Saturnia* was scrapped in 1966. The *Vulcania* was just about to pass into the scrapper's hands when Siosa's engineers decided she was a good investment and so she was bought by the Company, initially for Caribbean migrant service. In 1968, she replaced the *Ascania* for cruising in the western Mediterranean, which was becoming increasingly popular with air-sea package tours. The *Caribia* was featured in Pan Am airline tours from the USA. She was, in fact, one of the few cruise ships to retain her class-divided accommodation which was organised as follows: 337 in first class, 368 in cabin class and 732 in tourist class. Fares were divided into four categories: deluxe, increased comfort, tourist and youth special. The lowest rate for the 1968 season was $84 in youth special quarters.

The *Caribia*'s commercial career ended on 24 September 1972 when her starboard diesel failed and caused her to strike some submerged rocks at Cannes. Her 880 passengers were taken ashore in her lifeboats as the engine room began to flood. She was towed into nearby La Spezia on 29 September and, following a thorough inspection, was estimated, at the age of forty-four, to be uneconomic to repair. Sold to local Italian breakers, she was later resold to Spanish scrappers, who had her towed to Barcelona. In January 1974, she was resold once again, this time to the ever-busy Taiwanese. Although towed out to the Far East, she never felt the breaker's torch – on 20 July, while awaiting a berth at Kaohsiung, a leak developed and she sank in the harbour.

LAURO LINE

ACHILLE LAURO AND ANGELINA LAURO

Two of the most elaborate passenger ship conversions and modernizations of the 1960s involved the former Dutch liners *Willem Ruys* and *Oranje*. Originally built for the colonial trade to Java, the *Willem Ruys* was completed in 1947 by the De Schelde Shipyards at Flushing; the *Oranje* arrived just before the war, in

1939, and came from the Netherlands Shipbuilding Company at Amsterdam. In their final years under the Dutch flag, they plied an unsuccessful around-the-world route. They were sold to Lauro in late summer, 1964.

The *Willem Ruys* became the *Achille Lauro* and *Oranje* the *Angelina Lauro*, and together they were sent to separate Italian shipyards for a thorough rebuilding. Ironically, the *Angelina Lauro* was badly damaged by a shipyard fire at Genoa on 24 August 1965; five days later, at Palermo, the *Achille Lauro* was also seriously damaged while at her shipyard berth. Later repaired and then completed, they entered Lauro service from Europe to Australia via the Suez in March and April 1966 respectively.

In 1973, by which time much of their original tourist and migrant passenger trade had been lost to the airlines, both ships were assigned to full-time cruise operations and given all-one class accommodation. They sailed in the Mediterranean as well as northern European waters. In 1977, the *Angelina Lauro* began a three-year charter to the Costa Line and, in addition, to Mediterranean cruising from Genoa, she spent her winters in the Caribbean, on seven-day cruises from San Juan, Puerto Rico. She was advertised in the US simply as the *Angelina*, although she was never officially renamed. It was during one of these Caribbean voyages that the forty-year-old vessel met her end. While berthed at St Thomas, on 31 March 1979, she was gutted by fire and became a total loss. Salvaged in the following summer, she was put under tow for delivery to the scrappers on Taiwan. Unfortunately, on 24 September, she developed a list while still in the Pacific and then sank.

In January 1982, the Lauro Line unexpectedly declared themselves bankrupt. The *Achille Lauro*, about to set off on a long cruise to Africa, was seized and laid-up at Tenerife and later moved to Genoa. In 1985, as part of a Lauro reorganization, with a secure charter in hand to Chandris Cruises for Mediterranean cruises from Genoa, the liner was brought back into service. Several months later, on 7 October, she made headline news around the world. She was seized by terrorists off Port Said and held for two days. One passenger, an American, was killed in the incident. Rumours were that the ship would be renamed and possibly even retired in order to overcome the sinister tarnish of this event. Instead, however, she resumed Mediterranean cruising for Chandris in the following spring. Her still modern silhouette is deceptive of her forty years of service.

Antonio Scrimali

Formerly the Dutch liner *Oranje* of 1939, the *Angelina Lauro* is shown at anchor off Capri during a week's cruise from Genoa.

Antonio Scrimali

When she was hijacked by the Palestine Liberation Organization, in October 1985, the *Achille Lauro* made headline news around the world.

COSTA LINE

FRANCA C.

The Costa Line ran its first passenger sailing on the migrant run to Latin America in 1948 and by the early 1980s had become the largest cruise operator in the Western world. In all, they and their agents were selling cruises on no less than ten liners. Their first pure cruise ship joined the schedules in 1959. She was the little *Franca C.*, a 6500-tonner.

In 1914, the Newport News Shipbuilding & Drydock Company in Virginia completed what appeared to be quite an ordinary freighter, the *Medina* – they could not have realized that she would continue sailing past her seventieth year. Now in her fourth career, she sails as the *Doulos*.

Although there is very little that obviously hints of her true age, the *Doulos* is, at the time of writing the oldest remaining passenger-carrying ship (or former commercial passenger ship) and is still going strong. She was completed as the freighter *Medina* for the American-flag Mallory Lines, survived both World Wars and did considerable peace-time service before being put up for sale in 1948. Bought by a Panamanian firm, Compania Naviera San Miguel, she was rebuilt as the immigrant ship *Roma*. She sailed mostly between the Mediterranean and Latin America and had a stint on the North Atlantic to New York in 1950 for Holy Year traffic. She was fitted with accommodation for 850, in something similar to steerage class. In 1952, she hoisted the Italian flag for the then expanding Costa Line. Her new name was *Franca C.* and she continued mostly on immigrant sailing to Rio de Janeiro, Santos, Montevideo and Buenos Aires. Then, in 1959, despite being forty-five years old, she was thoroughly converted to a high standard cruise ship and even given new Fiat diesel engines. Her capacity was listed as 354, all first class. Evidently, there was still more life (and profit) ahead. Costa sent her on cruises in the Mediterranean, and she was among the very earliest ships to sail from Port Everglades to the Caribbean. Years later, in 1968, while sailing out of San Juan, she inaugurated the first American air-sea combination sailings. Near the end of her career with Costa, in the mid-seventies, she was kept closer to home, in Adriatic and Aegean waters. Almost deservedly, in winter 1977 she was laid-up, apparently out of service forever.

However, a year later, in 1978, the *Franca C.*, aged sixty-four, found yet a new career, as a floating missionary book and evangelical centre. I visited her at Tenerife in the summer of 1983 in her role as the Maltese-registered, West German-owned *Doulos*. My host was Tom Dyer, the young second officer, who like the 300 others onboard, from the captain to the last assistant baker and greaser, worked as a volunteer.

Tom, a native of California and a graduate of the US Merchant Marine Academy at Kings Point, New York, was a most enlightening host.

Operation Mobilization actually began to think of acquiring a ship for worldwide work in the mid-sixties. The organization itself had been created to promote Christian brotherhood and distribute literature. It took much

Nearing her seventieth year, the floating 'book-fair' *Doulos* sails outbound past London's Tilbury Landing Stage.

patience until the proper and appropriately priced vessel came along. She was the *Umanak*, a 2500-ton passenger-cargo ship that had worked the Danish supply run to Greenland. She was renamed *Logos* (Greek for living word) and put under the Singapore flag. Refitted for her missionary work, she first set sail in February 1971, bound for Africa and then Asia. The results were beyond our wildest expectations. In the following June, at Madras, for example, she had 15,000 visitors in a single day. In the summer of 1972, she moved to Southeast Asia. Two years later, she heroically sailed into Saigon, just as the Vietnam War was grinding to a close.

Tom continued his chronological narration of this novel operation.

The *Logos* was so very successful that, in 1978, we bought the cruise ship *Franca C.* from the Costa Line and had her refitted as well – first at Genoa and then at Bremen – for long-range missionary work. Renamed *Doulos* (Greek for bonded servant) and refitted with permanent exhibit space for 4000 books (replacing the original Italian outdoor pool and lido), she set sail on a four-year trip around South America. We have just completed [July 1983] that very successful voyage, crossing from Vittoria in Brazil to Tenerife in two weeks at a leisurely 11 knots.

The *Doulos* is manned by a company of 300 volunteers, including several families of four or more. Some thirty-three nations are currently represented. We each receive $15 personal money per month. The operation itself is financed through a combination of book sales and contributions – approximately 25 per cent from the former and 75 per cent the latter. We also receive 'in kind' contributions such as

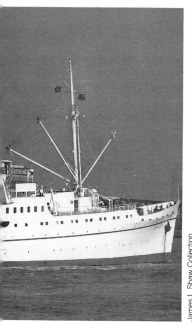

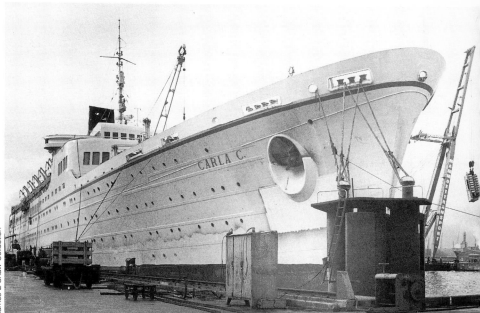

James L Shaw Collection

clothing and food. [In Tenerife, we lunched on some of the ton of fresh fish given by a local donor.]

Our Captain Isaacson and his wife live most of the year onboard. Both are retired; he after over fifty years in the American Merchant Marine, spent mostly with the American President Lines. The other officers include a South African first mate, a chief engineer from Singapore, his assistant from England and two doctors from West Germany and Spain. We are a happy group, learning to live together. We are a mini United Nations that is indeed united!

Now well into her seventies, the *Franca C.*, which continues to sail on her missionary duties, has proved to be the most long-lived contemporary cruise ship.

ANNA C. AND ANDREA C.

Two other early Costa liners were the 12,030-ton *Anna C.* and the 8604-ton *Andrea C..* Though initially used only in the Latin American trades, they were later used quite extensively for cruising. In the 1960s, the *Anna C.* was sent to Port Everglades, Florida for three- and four-day cruises to Nassau and Freeport. Minimum fares began at $59. In later years, she was kept in the Mediterranean, sailing mostly on weekly runs out of Genoa to Cannes, Barcelona, Palma de Majorca, Tripoli, Naples and Capri. She was built by Lithgows of Glasgow in 1929, for the Furness Prince Line as the *Southern Prince*. In 1947, after war-time trooping, she was bought by Costa and rebuilt for Italian-flag passenger service. She was scrapped at La Spezia in 1972.

The *Andrea C.* was completed in 1942 as the war-time freighter *Ocean Virtue* at Richmond, California, for a British Government account and was acquired by Costa in 1947 for cargo service. However, due to the pressing demand for passenger space, especially by westbound migrants to South America, she was rebuilt for passenger operations. Periodically improved and modernized, she underwent a very thorough refit, was given a new engine in 1959 (her original steam turbines were replaced with a new Fiat diesel) and thereafter was occasionally used for cruising. The *Andrea C.* sailed not only from Italian ports to the Mediterranean and Atlantic Isles, but from Rio de Janeiro to ports along the South American east coast and from Cartagena in Colombia to the Caribbean islands. In her final years, in the late seventies, she cruised mostly from Venice to the Dalmatian coast and the Greek isles. Kept in reserve in her last years, she was finally broken-up at La Spezia in 1982.

FEDERICO C.

Apparently content with refitted, second-hand tonnage during their first decade of passenger sailings, by 1958 Costa's great initial success had led to the creation of their first brand-new liner. This extremely beautiful 20,400-tonner was built at the Ansaldo yards at Genoa, the creators of several of the big Italian Line transatlantic liners including the ill-fated

The Costa flagship *Eugenio C.* arrives in New York for the first time, in August 1977, during a special four-week cruise across the North Atlantic from Genoa.

Andrea Doria. The new Costa flagship was named *Federico C.* and was almost immediately acclaimed the finest liner on the South American trade to Rio de Janeiro, Santos, Montevideo and Buenos Aires. Eight years later, in 1966, this distinction passed to another new Costa liner, the 30,500-ton *Eugenio C.* which was, in fact, the last passenger ship to be built for line voyages across the South Atlantic to Brazil, Uruguay and Argentina.

In 1966 the *Federico C.*, which had three-class accommodation for 1279 passengers, was reassigned to a more mid-Atlantic service, sailing to the Caribbean and Florida, and then, four years later, given over completely to one-class cruising with approximately 800 berths. Like all of the Costa cruise ships, she was frequently re-routed, sailing, for instance, from Genoa to the Mediterranean and Atlantic Isles, from Port Everglades or Miami to the Caribbean, on other West Indies trips from either San Juan or La Guaira and South American coastal cruises from Rio and Buenos Aires.

In late 1983, at the age of twenty-five, the *Federico C.* was sold to the Greyhound Bus Company, an American interest, for their newly created Panamanian-flag cruise subsidiary, Premier Cruise Lines. Refitted, upgraded and painted with a distinctive orange-red hull, she was renamed *Royale* and placed on three- and four-day Bahamas cruises out of Port Canaveral, Florida. In spring 1986 she was joined by another Italian-built flagship, Home Lines' *Oceanic.* For advertising purposes, the two ships are now referred to as the *Starship Royale* and *Starship Oceanic.*

BIANCA C., ENRICO C. AND CARLA C.

In the decade between 1958 and 1968, the Costa Line acquired three French liners, all of which were used for cruising. In October 1958, they bought the Panamanian-flag, Swiss-owned *Arosa Sky*, which had been used briefly on the North Atlantic trade. Previously she had worked as the Messageries Maritimes *La Marseillaise.* She had been the last large flagship on the colonial run out to Indochina. Lavishly rebuilt and redecorated by her new Italian owners and renamed *Bianca C.*, she was used in regular passenger service between Italy and West Indies, but also cruised from New York and later Port Everglades to Caribbean ports. Unfortunately, her Costa career was shortlived. On 22 October 1961, while at Grenada in the British West Indies, she was swept by fire. Two days later, in an attempt to beach the scorched hull, she sprang a leak and sank.

The *Enrico C.* joined Costa in 1965. She had worked as the *Provence* for another French shipping firm, Transports Maritimes, and worked the same South American run as Costa. In 1962, she was placed under joint management with Costa and three years later was bought outright. She remains in Italian service at the time of writing, as a full-time cruise ship, sailing mostly on seven-day voyages from Genoa to Barcelona, Palma de Majorca, Tunis, Palermo and Naples. It is rumoured, however, that she is soon to be replaced and retired.

The third of the French purchases was the former *Flandre*, built in 1952 for the French Line's transatlantic service between Le Havre and New York and a winter service to the Caribbean. She joined Costa in early 1968. She was also rebuilt, and almost immediately chartered out to Princess Cruises of Los Angeles for Mexican, Caribbean and later, Alaskan cruises. Although she was renamed the *Carla C.*, she was advertised as the *Princess Carla*. It was on board her that author Jeraldine Saunders later penned the first chapters of the 'Love Boat', which led to the popular television series. The *Carla C.* rejoined the Costa schedules in 1970 and, ever since, has sailed in weekly service from San Juan to Curacao, La Guaira, Grenada, Martinique and St Thomas.

EUGENIO C.

One of the finest looking, most attractively decorated liners of the 1960s was Costa's new flagship and largest liner, the *Eugenio C.*, built by Cantieri Riuniti dell'Adriatico at Monfalcone and delivered in August 1966. She had twin uptakes placed aft similar to Holland's *Rotterdam* and Britain's *Canberra*, and a hull and deck design closely fashioned after the innovative *Oceanic*. Designed primarily as a three-class ship (with 1636 berths) for the traditional liner run to South America, this exceptional ship was also used for periodic long, luxurious cruises around South America, to North America (including visits to Miami, New York, Montreal and San Francisco), around Africa and around the world (a service begun in 1977). In the early 1980s, as line voyages to South America began to wane, the *Eugenio C.* was used almost full-time as a cruise ship, particularly between May and October, sailing from Genoa to Alexandria, Port Said, Ashdod, Cyprus and Rhodes. The minimum fare for one of these ten-day voyages was listed as $1075 in 1986.

FLAVIA AND ITALIA

To strengthen their ever-expanding cruise operations, Costa acquired two Italian-flag cruise ships, the 15,464-ton *Flavia* in 1968, and some years later the 12,219-ton *Italia*. The *Flavia* was built at John Brown's on the Clyde in 1947 and she sailed as Cunard's *Media*, a 250-passenger combination ship on the Liverpool–New York route. Since 1962 she had been used on the Australian run for the Cogedar Line,

A night-time view of the *Eugenio C.* during a cruise visit to New York in August 1985.

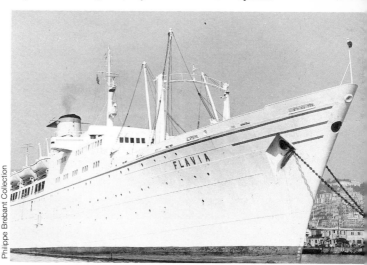

Converted from the Cunarder *Media*, the Italian *Flavia* sailed first for the Cogedar Line and then for the Costa Line. She has spent the years since 1982 at Far Eastern anchorages as the *Flavian*.

another Italian passenger company, later absorbed by Costa. Under Costa she retained her Cogedar-selected name and was assigned to the very lucrative, continuously expanding, overnight Bahamas trade, on three- and four-day cruises out of Miami. She remained in Costa service until early 1982, when she was sold to Hong Kong buyers listed as the Flavian Shipping Company. Renamed *Flavian*, she sailed out

Antonio Scrimali

The Costa cruise ship *Costa Riviera* preparing to sail on her maiden voyage from Genoa to Port Everglades, Florida in November 1985. She was radically rebuilt from the former Lloyd Triestino liner *Guglielmo Marconi*.

Michael Cassar

The *Italia* was built in the mid-1960s, with accommodation for one jumbo jet-load of passengers, so was ideally suited for fly and sail cruises. She is shown arriving at Valletta on Malta.

to Hong Kong, but has done little apart from changing her moorings. Reports were that her original turbines, now nearing forty years of age, were faulty. (Another former transatlantic liner, Norwegian America's *Oslofjord* of 1949, was time-chartered to Costa for two years between 1968–70, as the *Fulvia*. Another victim of fire, she was abandoned and later sunk off Tenerife in July 1970.)

The *Italia*, built in 1967 at the C N Felszegi yards at Trigoso, joined the Costa cruise schedules in 1974. A sleek-looking, engines-aft vessel, specially created for about one jumbo jet-load of air-sea passengers, she has been built under special account and primarily for charter work. She was owned by several Italian banks, who joined together to form Crociere D'Oltramare, which was registered at Cagliari. One of her first assignments was to sail for the Los Angeles-based Princess Cruises, by then part of the P&O

Group, for Mexican, trans-Panama Canal and Alaskan cruises. She was dubbed *Princess Italia*, but never officially renamed.

For Costa, the *Italia* sailed on a variety of cruise runs – on the Greek islands trade out of Venice, sailings from San Juan within the Caribbean and even on some more exotic trips such as along the Amazon from Rio and to the Straits of Magellan from Buenos Aires. In a reorganization of their cruise fleet made at the end of 1983, the *Italia* was sold to Greek buyers, the newly formed Ocean Cruise Lines, for whom she presently sails as the *Ocean Princess*.

DAPHNE AND DANAE

Rebuilt from Port Line freighters, which had been used on the British-flag 'meat runs' from Australia and New Zealand, the former *Port Sydney* and *Port Melbourne* became the Greek *Daphne* and *Danae*. They were highly luxurious and had been very extensively converted and rebuilt with just over 400 berths each. They sailed for a new venture in ocean travel, Carras Cruises, a specially created subsidiary of the Carras Group, which had sizeable holdings in freight and tanker shipping as well as sea-side resorts. They were placed on a worldwide schedule of rather expensively priced voyages in 1975–76 and proved less than the expected success. In 1979 they were leased to Costa who bought them outright five years later. At present they sail on Costa cruises, to the Caribbean, Alaska and in the Mediterranean. They have retained their Greek names and non-Italian registry.

seven

THE
GOLDEN
GREEKS

GREEK LINE

OLYMPIA

When completed in October 1953, the 22,979-ton *Olympia*, owned by the Greek Line, a member of the giant Goulandris Group, was the first brand-new liner to be built for Greek owners and the largest yet to be owned in that country. Unfortunately she was not able to fly the Greek colours (until 1968) because of a dispute about regulations. Instead, she was placed under the Liberian flag and Monrovia was her home port. Used on the Atlantic run to New York, she first sailed out of Northern Europe (until 1955) and later from the Mediterranean. Her accommodation was divided between 138 in first class and 1169 in tourist.

By the late sixties she was used increasingly for cruise sailings, so in 1970 she was converted to a full-time cruise ship and relisted as having an all one-class capacity for 1037 passengers. Her voyages, mostly out of New York, included a considerable number of seven-day trips to Bermuda and/or Nassau as well as three-day weekend jaunts 'to nowhere',

popular trips priced from $75, which left New York on Friday evenings and returned early on Monday morning. Often, during these latter sailings, the *Olympia* cruised at a casual 6–8 knots off the New Jersey coast.

The Greek Line decided to open an Aegean cruise service from Piraeus in spring 1974 and use the *Olympia* in what was thought would be a very profitable, and expanding trade. Unfortunately, the schedule never began and the *Olympia* was sent instead to temporary lay-up at nearby Perama. The dramatic increase in fuel oil costs and the rise in transatlantic airline fares cut sharply into her projected American tourist market and contributed strongly to her withdrawal.

The *Olympia* remained at Perama for eight years – rusting, neglected and beset by rumours she was destined for scrapping. The Lauro Line, Carnival Cruise Lines and others had a look over her. It was rumoured the Sheraton Hotel Corporation wanted her to sail on weekly Caribbean cruises as the *Sheraton Caribbean* but the chances of selling her remained remote. However, in 1982, she was bought by the Sally Line of Finland. Captain Rolf Bassenberg was among those who took delivery of the twenty-nine-year-old ship.

She was of very solid construction, mostly because her hull had originally been intended to be a Royal Navy aircraft carrier that was to be completed in 1945. With the war over, the completed hull section was shunted aside until 1951, when it was used by the Fairfield shipyards at Glasgow to build the new *Olympia*.

The Sally Company bought her primarily as a hotel ship that would remain stationary for most of the year. She would make only two or three voyages for positioning, say from Europe to the Caribbean. The Company had also bought the *Navarino* [17,392 gross tons, the former Swedish American *Gripsholm* of 1957 then owned by Karageorgis Cruises] for Miami–Caribbean cruising. Most unfortunately, just one hour before the final deal was consummated, the *Navarino* capsized in a floating drydock. There seemed to be little hope for a useful salvage. Consequently, we had to revise our plans and rebuild the long idle *Olympia* for active weekly service.

Captain Bassenberg remained with the ship for eleven months, until her entry into service. He has been her master ever since.

When we first reached Perama, the outside of the ship was shocking, with at least a foot of growth along her sides. Internally, she was in poor condition, the plumbing was very old and all while forty-five Greeks had been her caretakers. In fact, just three days before we took

Although it was rumoured she would be scrapped, the Greek *Olympia* found new life, after eight years at her Perama moorings. as the *Caribe I* with Miami's Commodore Cruises.

Following the collapse of the Greek Line the *Queen Anna Maria* was laid-up at Perama (as shown) but unlike her fleetmate *Olympia*, for only ten months. She was quickly sold, in late 1975, sailing thereafter as the *Carnivale* for Miami's Carnival Cruise Lines.

ownership, all of the original Greek Line china was removed and taken away in launches.

We remained at Perama for five months for initial repairs and then set off for Hamburg for the major refitting. We were towed to Germany by the tug *Wotan* for seventeen days, averaging about 8 knots and with a crew of thirty-one including myself. Afterward, we were at a Hamburg shipyard for four months. Among other changes, we had to reduce the ship's draught from 28 to 25 foot. The original 20-ton mast was removed and replaced by a new one-ton stump mast. The original funnel, which had actually begun to crumble, was removed as well and a new stack

arrangement placed farther aft to give the ship a more modern look. Stabilizers and two bow thrusters were added and the engine room was extensively modernized. The original steam turbines were removed and replaced by brand new Deutz diesels. Previously, she used 200 tons of fuel each day; it was now reduced to 45 tons. We were quite impressed that she managed 21 knots during her trials in that first summer of 1983.

The *Olympia* resumed sailing in August 1983, as the *Caribe I*, flying the Panamanian flag for Commodore Cruises of Miami, working on the seven-day shuttle to Cap Haitien, St Thomas, San Juan and Puerto Plata.

QUEEN ANNA MARIA

To supplement their transatlantic services and cruise schedules, the Greek Line bought Canadian Pacific's *Empress of Britain* in 1964 for $9 million. Extensively modernized and given increased accommodation (from 1046 to 1254 berths), she was rechristened the *Queen Anna Maria* by Her Majesty Queen Anne of Greece in a ceremony held at Piraeus on 15 March 1965.

The *Queen Anna Maria* remained in Greek Line service for a full decade, until early 1975, by which time the Company had fallen on hard financial times. Although she was on average 80 per cent full on her New York cruises, this was not enough to offset her mounting costs, particularly the cost of fuel oil which had rocketed from $35 a ton in 1972 to $120 by late 1973. In pursuit by various creditors, the *Queen Anna Maria* 'fled' from New York, in January 1975, without passengers, for the supposed safety of home waters. Once at Piraeus, she was laid-up in Perama Bay, not far from the *Olympia*, and the Greek Line passenger division closed its doors.

Unlike the *Olympia*, the slightly newer *Queen Anna Maria* quickly found a new career (in November 1975) when she was sold to the Carnival Cruise Lines and was renamed *Carnivale* for Caribbean cruising out of Miami. She too now flies the Panamanian flag. In December 1983, while sailing aboard the *Caribe I*, the former *Olympia*, we were berthed at a San Juan pier across from the *Carnivale*. Both former Greek Line ships had had new lives.

ARKADIA AND LAKONIA

During their early years in passenger shipping Greek Lines owned mostly old, second-hand, and often, rebuilt passenger ships. Some were nearing their prime, others were old and creaking. Two of the latter type were the 20,259-ton *Arkadia* and the 20,314-ton *Lakonia*. The *Arkadia*, built in 1931 at Vickers-Armstrongs of Newcastle, had been the *Monarch of Bermuda*, owned by the Furness Bermuda Line. During her postwar refit, after having served as a trooper, she caught fire and was sold off, only to be bought by the British Government and rebuilt as the migrant carrier *New Australia*. The Greek Line bought her in 1958. The *Lakonia*, completed in 1930 at Amsterdam, had been the *Johan van Oldenbarnevelt* for the Netherland Royal Mail Line's colonial run out to Java. She was later used for migrant and low-fare tourist services, and first hoisted the Greek Line banner in 1963.

As cruise ships, both the *Arkadia* (in the off-season winters only) and the *Lakonia* were employed out of Southampton on 'sunshine sailings' to Lisbon, Gibraltar, Casablanca, Las Palmas, Tenerife and Madeira. The *Arkadia* sailed for some six seasons in this trade, until sold for scrapping in Spain in late 1966; the *Lakonia* survived for only a few months. In December 1963, while on her first Greek Line Christmas cruise, she was destroyed by fire while at sea, with 128 fatalities. Days later, while empty and under tow, she capsized and sank. (The Greek Line resumed its Southampton cruise service until 1968, using the chartered Norwegian America liner *Oslofjord* of 1949. Thereafter, they concentrated on their Mediterranean and Caribbean services only.)

TYPALDOS LINES

ACROPOLIS, ATHINAI AND ATLANTICA

By the mid-sixties, the Typaldos Brothers of Greece (as they were often called) had the biggest and busiest passenger fleet in the eastern Mediterranean. They began in passenger shipping in the late forties and quickly assembled an extensive fleet, mostly of older, second-hand tonnage. The largest units were the 9200-ton sisters *Acropolis* and *Athinai*, and a further running-mate, the 13,800-ton *Atlantica*. The first pair were formerly named the *Santa Paula* and *Santa Rosa* respectively and had been built in 1932 for the Grace Line's New York–Caribbean–South America services. Laid-up after being retired in the summer of 1958, the pair was bought by Typaldos in 1961 and then towed across the mid-Atlantic to Piraeus for refitting. The *Atlantica*, acquired in 1964, was the former *Colombie*, built in 1931 for the French Line's West Indies trade.

The *Acropolis* was fitted with 450 one-class berths and used for more diverse cruising, from Piraeus, Genoa and Venice in the Mediterranean, and to Scandinavia and the Atlantic Isles from Zeebrugge. The *Athinai* was made into a three-class ship, with quarters for 240 in first class, 180 in cabin class and 200 in tourist class, and used mostly on the two-week 'express service' from Venice to Split, Piraeus, Limassol, Haifa, Larnaca, Rhodes, Piraeus and then return to Venice. Peter Hagmann, recently cruise director aboard Cunard-Norwegian America's *Vistafjord*, served aboard these ships as a member of the

The former Dutch liner *Johan van Oldenbarnevelt* being converted at Genoa, in 1963, to the Greek Line's *Lakonia*.

Giorgio Ghiglione

The *Athinai* was used as a prop in the film *Raise the Titanic*. She is shown here at Eleusis in June 1984, the name *Titanic* still painted across her bows.

In the 1970s, rusted and neglected at their Perama moorings, the *City of Mykonos*, the former *San Marco* of the Adriatica Line, and the *Athinai*, the former *Santa Rosa* of the Grace Line.

cruise staff. 'I remember them as especially charming old ships and particularly recall the balcony for an orchestra in the main restaurant.'

The Typaldos passenger-cruise fleet also consisted of the 11,300-ton converted ferries *Hania* and *Iraklion* which were the former Bibby combination liners *Warwickshire* and *Leicestershire*; the 10,100-ton sisters *Mount Olympos* and *Poseidon*, which were the former *Ville d'Oran* and *Ville d'Alger* of the French Line; the 5100-ton *Hellas*, once the one-time Australian passenger ship *Taroona*; the 4200-ton *Electra*, once the French *Sidi Okba*; and the 3000-ton sisters *Mykonos* and *Rodos*, both converted war-time seaplane tenders. Peter Hagmann sailed aboard many of these ships and recalled,

They were quite popular for some time with the increasing tourist bonanza in the eastern Mediterranean and also with cruise passengers. I especially recall sailing in the little *Hellas*, which was always full to the very last upper berth. She sailed from Venice outwards to Piraeus and then Rhodes, but always bypassed her scheduled call at Brindisi simply because she was so overcrowded.

By 1965, however, the Typaldos image was becoming tarnished. There were frequent reports of cancelled or delayed sailings, ill-kept ships and poor sanitary conditions. A year later, the Company was ruined completely and closed down. On 8 December 1966, the *Iraklion* sank in an Aegean storm with 241 casualties. In the inquest that followed, the ship was found to be unsafely loaded and therefore not in compliance with Greek maritime law. The Typaldos Brothers, in a test case, were sent to jail and their ships seized, mostly by the National Bank of Greece which was the mortgage holder.

Like most others in the fleet, the three largest units went to Perama Bay and sat at anchorage, rusting and forlorn. The *Acropolis* is reported to have been broken-up in 1972 (actual documentation is most difficult to obtain), and the *Atlantica* broken-up two years later. For some reason, the *Athinai*, the former *Santa Paula*, was not scrapped. In 1978–79, she had a spark of renewed life; she was leased to a film company, who wanted an elderly floating prop to serve as the salvaged *Titanic* in a fictional tale entitled *Raise the Titanic*. The long-neglected, rust-streaked *Athinai* was ideal. She was taken out to the Aegean for some filming sequences and later moored alongside the Piraeus Ocean Terminal for others. Afterwards, she was returned to her Perama Bay moorings, one of the last reminders of the once large Typaldos fleet.

CHANDRIS LINES

The Chandris Group of companies has come to control one of the largest passenger fleets of all time. Their ships have always been second-hand, and some quite elderly, but the tonnage range has been extreme,

△ Antonio Scrimali

▽ Alex Duncan

The *Atlantica*, the former French liner *Colombie* of 1931 joined the sister ships *Acropolis* and *Athinai*, as the most important passenger ships in the Greek Typaldos Lines' fleet. She was broken-up in 1974 after some years in lay-up.

varying from the 3600-ton *Fiesta*, which sailed locally in the Aegean, to the 34,449-ton *Australis*, the Company's flagship which plied an around-the-world service. Because of the limitations of space, I will concentrate mostly on the larger ships, mentioning the smaller cruise ships in far less detail.

QUEEN FREDERICA

It is appropriate that this section on Chandris should begin with the 16,435-ton *Queen Frederica*, a highly successful and profitable ship that survived for just over fifty years. Built in 1927, at Philadelphia as the *Malolo* for the Matson Lines, she was the first major liner for the Hawaiian tourist trade. She was renamed *Matsonia* in 1937. In 1948 she was sold to the Home Lines and sailed as the *Atlantic* on the transatlantic run to both New York and the St Lawrence. She was transferred to the Greek flag in 1954, and to a Home Lines' subsidiary, the National Hellenic American Line. Renamed *Queen Frederica*, she was, for a time, the largest Greek liner of all.

A decade later, in late 1965, she was bought by Chandris, and used not only for Atlantic crossings to New York, but on cruises and migrant and tourist voyages out to Australia and New Zealand from Southampton. Vincent Messina sailed aboard the *Queen Frederica* in 1967, and was later employed by Chandris, serving in the cruise staff of another ex-Matson liner, the *Britanis*.

The *Queen Frederica* was the favourite ship of Mr

Antony Chandris, one of the two brothers that controlled the Chandris passenger fleet. The old *Queen*, however, represented tattered glory by the late 1960s. She was venerable, but hardly venerated. I especially remember the forward lounge, which was pure American Greek Revival, dating from the mid-twenties. Everything else had either been redone or removed. She was, of course, a fire trap with leaking steampipes and badly weathered decks. She was not sparkling clean and even had a hint of seediness about her. She was old and indeed past her best. Everyone – Matson, the Home Lines and now Chandris – made money on her.

On her Australian migrant voyages, she was constantly overbooked, which was true of all Chandris liners on the 'Aussie run'. The *Queen Frederica* had one major disadvantage: she could not carry enough water. For example, on the long run from Durban to Fremantle, she would arrive practically empty of water.

All the profits of these busy liners went into first class hotels, in Greece mostly, which were also a part of the Chandris empire. The Chandris Brothers actually viewed long-distance sea travel as having a limited future and the ships were literally 'run into the ground' and given minimal repairs. Antony Chandris thought American-built liners were the best built and with the greatest potential, and, in particular, he preferred the Matson liners. More specifically, he bought the aged *Queen Frederica* especially to enter the American market out of New York and use the well known National Hellenic American Line name.

In her final years, in the early seventies, the *Queen Frederica* sailed as a Mediterranean cruise ship.

The veteran *Queen Frederica* in the mid 1970s, nearing the end of her days at Perama, an area near Piraeus that is noted for its large collection of out-of-work and elderly vessels. Her funnels are painted with the logos of Sovereign Cruises, her final charter for Mediterranean cruising.

Built in 1931 as the Matson liner *Monterey*, the Chandris *Britanis* reached her fifty-fifth year in 1986 while still in service as an American-based cruise ship.

Brenton Jenkins, now with the Royal Caribbean Cruise Lines in Miami, was a member of her staff.

At the time, I was employed by Captain 'Ted' Langton, a multi-millionaire entrepreneur of the British travel industry. He began 'Blue Cars', a continental coach system in prewar days. Later, he owned the largest hotel on Palma de Majorca and was one of the genius minds behind Skytours. In the late sixties, he developed a high density, low-cost cruising concept – £39 for eleven days from Gatwick Airport, London to the Mediterranean and return. We chartered the *Queen Frederica*, a wonderful old tub that seemed to just sit in the water. I was hired by Captain Langton to be ths cruise director, actually something of a

jack-of-all-trades. I helped to create the entire Sovereign Cruises' concept and even designed the logos that went on the *Queen Frederica*'s stacks. We lasted until 1973, when the fuel crisis made low-cost cruise operations just about impossible.

The *Queen Frederica* was sent to that Greek limbo, the anchorages in Perama Bay and placed between other aged and out-of-work liners, ferries, freighters and tankers. She would never sail again. Sold to local scrappers in May 1977, she was gutted further by a fire at the breakers' yard at Eleusis, on 1 February 1978. Her twisted remains were then promptly cut-up.

ELLINIS AND BRITANIS

The Chandris Company's interest in American-built liners extended to two of the *Queen Frederica*'s fleet mates, the *Lurline* and her twin sister, the *Monterey*, both built by the Bethlehem Steel Co at Quincy, Massachusetts, in 1932. They were long-time favourites on the Matson Line services to Hawaii and the South Pacific. The *Lurline* was sold to Chandris in 1963 and refitted as the *Ellinis* for the Australian migrant run. In the process, her passenger capacity was more than doubled, from 761 first class berths to 1642 berths, all in tourist class. The *Monterey* did war-time service as a trooper and was not back in service until 1957, as the improved *Matsonia*. In 1963, when the original *Lurline* was sold to Chandris the *Matsonia* adopted her very popular name. The *Lurline* (ex-*Matsonia*, ex-*Monterey*) was sold to Chandris in 1970, and, like the original *Lurline*, was refitted primarily for the Australian trade and her capacity was greatly increased from 761 to 1632 berths.

In the mid-seventies, as the Australian trade began to wane and when the British Government's lucrative migrant contract was finally given over to the airlines, both the *Ellinis* and *Britanis* were used increasingly for cruise service. They sailed not only in European waters, but from South Africa and Australia as well. Virtually exhausted, the *Ellinis* was laid-up in Perama Bay, in October 1980, never to sail again. By 1981, the *Britanis* had been moved to the American East Coast to run charter sailings for a New York-based firm known as Fantasy Cruises. Vincent Messina served in her cruise department.

The Chandris-Fantasy cruise concept was 'down market', not fancy but fun. It was, of course, exciting to work on such an old vessel [then just over fifty years old]. In September 1983, she served as a review ship for the

Antonio Scrimali

Luis Miguel Correia

Antonio Scrimali

A fascinating photograph taken in the summer of 1984 of four Chandris liners, all laid-up, with little hope of further service. The *Ellinis* (ex-*Lurline*) is on the left with the *Ariane* (ex-*Ariadne*) and *Regina Prima* (ex-*Panama*) in the centre. The larger former *Australis* (ex-*America*) is on the right.

America's Cup Races at Newport, Rhode Island. During the first races, she was moored so close to the finish line that she was actually blocking the wind. It was, quite understandably, very difficult to manoeuvre a 638-foot long ship amongst several thousand yachts, sailboats and pleasure craft. From those races, as I recall, we 'dead-headed' to New York, where we embarked 1600 passengers – 200 were 'walk-ons' without cabins – for an overnight cruise to nowhere. On the following day, we had 1100 passengers for a two-day cruise. There were times when there wasn't even a full count of passengers. Some of the two-day cruises were actually one-day cruises. We would return to New York for an hour, offload 400–500 passengers and then take 400–500 others. We even had passengers who would buy their tickets as the ship was already outbound, in the middle of the Hudson River.

The Captain and some of his officers had enormous pride in the ship. On one of the Bermuda trips, she raced at 22.14 knots, which was just slightly lower than her paces on her trial runs made fifty years earlier. Her career had been most diverse, sailing on almost every major route in the world and once even serving as the Saudi Arabian royal yacht. She was used especially for the rededication of the Grand Mosque at Mecca and the King used, quite appropriately, the King Kamehaha Suite for the occasion.

Gambling was the whole ship on these short, inexpensive American cruises. It was the real profit. The whole concept was different from most cruises. It was all fun, party and casualness. The disco, for example, opened from 8.30pm until 6am. Many passengers never, ever slept. An overnight cruise might cost as little as $39.95 [in 1983], although without a cabin, but which included dinner, a midnight buffet, casino, cabaret, gambling and breakfast. These overnight cruises would remain off the New Jersey coast, about 70–100 miles east of Atlantic City, and very casually sail at a scant 3 knots.

The ship is, of course, a great testament to American shipbuilding and design. Some of the American installations are still in excellent condition, such as the flooring and the air conditioning system. Spare parts have, of course, been shipped over from the laid-up *Ellinis*. Even the Xs on the twin funnels are original. They are cut-up pieces from the M's from the Matson days!

THE VICTORIA

In 1975, wishing to strengthen its European and later Caribbean cruise services, Chandris saw great potential in the highly reputed *Victoria*. Her owners, the Incres Line, had just gone bankrupt and the opportunity to acquire her seemed ideal. Originally built in 1936, by Harland & Wolff at Belfast, she had sailed as the *Dunnottar Castle* on Union-Castle's Round Africa service out of London. In 1958–59 Incres radically rebuilt her as a cruise ship. In 1986, having reached her fiftieth year, she still sails for Chandris, as *The Victoria*, in their service from San Juan to the Caribbean.

A group of Chandris Cruises' passenger ships in lay-up at Perama. The *Radiosa*, a little Aegean 'feeder' ship, is moored on the left alongside the *Bon Vivant*, next to which lies the *Fiorita*, *Romanza* and *Fiesta*.

CARINA, FANTASIA, ROMANTICA, FIESTA, FIORITA AND ARIANE

Chandris Cruises employed a large fleet of smaller cruise ships, particularly in eastern Mediterranean waters, for one- and two-week cruises. The 4000-ton *Carina* had formerly been the *Princess Helene*, built in 1930 for Canadian Pacific; the 4500-ton *Fantasia*, dating from 1935, had been the British Railways ferry *Duke of York*; the 3700-ton *Romantica* was the former *Fort Townshend*, built in 1936 for Furness Withy; the 3600-ton *Fiesta* was a postwar vessel, completed in 1946 as the Isle of Man Steam Packet Company's *Mona's Queen*; the 5100-ton *Fiorita* was the former *Amsterdam* of 1950 for British Railways; and the 6600-ton *Ariane* of 1951 had been Swedish Lloyd's *Patricia* and later the Caribbean cruise ship *Ariadne*.

Vincent Messina travelled in one of these converted cruise ships, the *Fiorita*.

In those days, in 1970, Chandris offered almost unbelievable bargains for Mediterranean cruising, especially for young students travelling in Europe. The fare was $125 for 11 days, from Venice to Corfu, Itéa, Piraeus, Istanbul, Kusadasi, Rhodes, Piraeus and return to Venice.

The ship was a shocker, however. She actually looked like a floating bath-tub. There was no open deck space at all, except on the Boat Deck. The three upper decks had been modernized in cheap, flashy 'flower power' themes. She was, after all, the 'little flower' – the *Fiorita*.

I was shocked to be taken down to my cabin. I thought it was the crew quarters, along a metal stairwell with a bare lightbulb, to a two-berth inside cabin without private facilities. The room had been painted over in off-white, had no closets but instead four hooks on the wall and a sink with a mirror and another bare bulb. There were two bunks. It was British Rail overnight décor – no frills, just a place to sleep. The shower was on our deck, but the toilets were one

deck up. She rode terribly and bounced endlessly, but I would not have traded that trip for anything.

Peter Hagmann served in another member of this Chandris armada, the *Carina*.

She never managed to keep her schedule. She was an aged old tub that just could not keep speed. I recall that they were still painting the cabins on her maiden cruise [in 1965] and, quite sadly, the work crews actually painted over one passenger's suitcases and shoes!

By the mid-seventies, most of these ships had been retired from active cruising. Some went, quite appropriately, to the breakers, others to lay-up at Perama and the rest to non-sailing roles as hotel and accommodation ships.

REGINA PRIMA AND ROMANZA

Both built in 1939, the *Regina* (later refitted as the *Regina Prima*) had been the *Panama* sailing on the Panama Line's New York–Canal Zone service, and the *Romanza* had been the *Huascaran* for Hamburg American, the *Beaverbrae* for Canadian Pacific and latterly the *Aurelia* for Italy's Cogedar Line. The *Regina* joined Chandris in 1965, the *Romanza* five years later. Both have been used in Mediterranean and Caribbean cruising. The *Regina Prima*, after some years in lay-up, was broken-up in 1985; the *Romanza* still sails, on seven-day cruises from Venice.

REGINA MAGNA

The French *Pasteur* was also built in 1939. She was designed to be one of the largest and most luxurious liners on the South American run, but never entered commercial service. Instead she spent all of her days under the tricolor as a troop ship, sailing mostly out to colonial Indochina. She was sold to North German Lloyd in 1957, and came back into service two years later as their transatlantic *Bremen*. She joined Chandris in late 1971, and began cruising to Scandinavia, the Mediterranean and later the Caribbean as the *Regina Magna*. Her time in Greek service was rather short-lived – she was laid-up in 1974, a victim primarily of increased fuel oil costs. In 1977 she was sold to the Philippine Singapore Ports Corporation for use as a workers' accommodation ship at Jeddah in Saudi Arabia, and renamed *Saudi Phil I* and later *Filipinas Saudi I*. By the spring of 1980 her task had been completed and she was sold to Taiwanese breakers. However, she never reached her Eastern destination. On 9 June, while under tow, the empty former liner heeled over and sank.

AUSTRALIS

The largest of all Chandris liners, the 34,449-ton *Australis* was acquired in 1964, especially for the Australian migrant and around-the-world tourist trades. She was built at the Newport News Shipyards in Virginia in 1940 and previously called the *America*, a famous transatlantic liner for the United States Lines. Once in Greek hands, she too was altered and her capacity increased from 1046 to 2258 berths.

She was used for periodic cruising until she ended the Chandris Australian service in November 1977. Then, in the following spring, renamed *America*, she was brought to New York in a highly unsuccessful attempt to run a series of inexpensive cruises 'to nowhere'. A year later, she briefly resumed service, but within the Mediterranean only, as the *Italis*. She has been laid-up at Perama since late 1979, and, amidst various reports that she would be sold or sail again, has been renamed *Noga* and more recently *Alferdoss*. However, at the time of writing, she has not left her Perama Bay moorings.

AMERIKANIS

'A fantastic conversion, by far the finest yet for a Chandris liner', according to Vincent Messina, describing the 19,377-ton *Amerikanis*, built in 1952 as the Union-Castle liner *Kenya Castle* and then rebuilt in 1967–68.

Chandris wanted a better, more competitive image in

Michael Cassar

Chandris Cruises' *Romanza* has had four careers sailing as the Hamburg American Line combination ship *Huascaran*, the Canadian Pacific migrant ship *Beaverbrae*, Cogedar Line's *Aurelia* and then as a Greek cruise ship.

Antonio Scrimali

The ageing, fuel-hungry *Regina Magna* was a victim of the sudden fuel oil price increases of 1973–74. She spent several years in lay-up at Perama, quite near another out-of-work Chandris passenger ship, the *Queen Frederica* (on the right).

Luis Miguel Correia

The *Australis* arriving at Lisbon, on her final Australian voyage, in November 1977. She had twin funnels – the forward one was a dummy.

Antonio Scrimali

The Chandris *Amerikanis* is shown arriving at Genoa during a series of weekly cruises around the western Mediterranean. She bears little resemblance to her earlier years as the Union-Castle liner *Kenya Castle.*

the US, especially after the aged *Queen Frederica*, and so produced this liner. The superb décor, in a rebuilt series of fine public rooms, was most impressive. All of the cabins had been rebuilt and included not only private bathrooms, but televisions as well. She was a radical change from all previous Chandris liners. There was hardly a trace of her past except, of course, behind-the-scenes, which was still pure Union-Castle: wooden bunks for the crew, heavily cluttered and very cramped.

The *Amerikanis* was leased to the Costa Line for a time but has now resumed Chandris service and divides most of her cruise schedules between New York and Miami.

ATLANTIS

In 1970, as a follow-up to the lavish *Amerikanis*, Chandris bought a vessel with the same high standard of décor and onboard facilities, American President Lines' *President Roosevelt*. She was an 18,920-ton ship and had previously sailed as the *General W P Richardson* for the US Navy, the *Laguardia* for American Export Lines and the *Leilani* for Hawaiian-Textron Lines. In June 1971, having been thoroughly rebuilt and modernized, she entered service as the *Atlantis*. Unfortunately, she was unsuccessful and was the first ship in the Chandris fleet to slip deeply into the red. Among other factors, her fuel-hungry turbines were far too expensive. She was sold, in little over a year, to the Eastern Steamship Lines of Miami and was renamed the *Emerald Seas*.

GALILEO

The great success of the veteran *Britanis* in short, inexpensively-priced cruises out of American East Coast ports led to the addition, in 1983, of the 27,900-ton *Galileo*. Formerly the *Galileo Galilei* of Italy's Lloyd Triestino, she sailed on the Australian run until its decline in the mid-seventies. She and her sister, the *Guglielmo Marconi*, were then assigned to cruise services, but later withdrawn and then offered for sale. The *Marconi* joined the Costa Line and, radically refitted, sails as the *Costa Riviera*. With her original name shortened, the *Galileo* presently cruises, on one- to seven-day voyages from American East Coast ports.

The 1963-built *Galileo* is now the newest member of the remaining Chandris fleet, which includes the *Britanis* (1932), the *Victoria* (1936), *Romanza* (1939) and the *Amerikanis* (1952).

EPIROTIKI LINES

ATLAS, PEGASUS, WORLD RENAISSANCE, OCEANOS, JUPITER, ORPHEUS, JASON, ARGONAUT AND NEPTUNE

Another Greek giant in Mediterranean cruising is the Epirotiki Lines, owned by the Potamianos family. Reputed to have offered the first Greek islands cruise from Piraeus, in 1955, using the 1900-ton *Semiramis*, the Company has long since expanded to other cruise areas as well: the western Mediterranean, West Africa, Scandinavia, the Caribbean and South America, South Africa and, more recently, to more adventurous areas such as the Amazon and the Galapagos. They have also begun summer-time cruising in Alaskan waters. The fleet is composed of second-hand passenger ships, most of which have undergone high standard conversions for all-first class service. The 15,000-ton flagship *Atlas* is the former transatlantic liner *Ryndam*, built in 1951 for the Holland-America Line; the 12,500-ton *Pegasus* was built in 1975 as the Baltic ferry *Svea Corona* and later used as the Alaska cruise ship-ferry *Sundancer*; the 11,700-ton *World Renaissance* was built in 1966 as the *Renaissance* for France's Paquet Lines; the 10,900-ton *Oceanos*, completed in 1952, was the former *Jean Laborde* of Messageries Maritimes and then had a string of names under Greek owners, including *Mykonos*, *Ancona* and *Eastern Princess*; the 6300-ton *Jupiter* was completed in 1961 as the Zim liner *Moledet*; the 5000-ton *Orpheus* was the *Munster*, completed in 1948 for the British & Irish Steam Packet Company; the 3700-ton *Jason* of 1967 had been built as the ferry *Eros* for the Greek Government; the 3000-ton *Argonaut* was the luxury yacht *Vixen*, built in 1929, and the 2800-ton *Neptune* of 1954, the former *Meteor* of the Bergen Line. Both the *Pegasus* and *Neptune* were bought damaged and rebuilt for further service and, coincidentally, both ships were delivered at Vancouver, although in 1970 and 1984 respectively.

Author's collection

The Epirotiki Lines' *Jason* was rebuilt as a cruise ship from the ferry *Eros*, which had been built by the Italians in 1967 for the Greek Government.

ROYAL CRUISE LINES

GOLDEN ODYSSEY AND ROYAL ODYSSEY

The Royal Cruise Lines, formed in the early seventies for the growing air-sea tour market, ordered Greece's first brand-new cruise ship, the 6757-ton *Golden Odyssey*. Built at the Helsingors Shipyard in Denmark, the ship was designed for a maximum of 509 passengers, just over the capacity of a jumbo jet. Initially she was used alternately on the Greek islands trade and out of the American West Coast. Since, the Company's

Designed especially for 'fly'n sail' cruising, the yacht-like *Golden Odyssey* was the first passenger ship in the Royal Cruise Lines' fleet.

George Devol

Undergoing a major refit and modernization at a Greek shipyard in 1982, the former *Doric* of the Home Lines becomes the *Royal Odyssey* for the Royal Cruise Lines.

Antonio Scrimali

schedule has expanded to include sailings to Scandinavia, Alaska, Eastern Canada, the Far East and the South Pacific. The 25,300-ton *Royal Odyssey* was added in 1982, having been refitted to accommodate 817 passengers. She had been bought from the Home Lines, for whom she had sailed as the *Doric* (since 1973), and earlier still as the *Hanseatic* (1967–73) of the German Atlantic Line and the *Shalom* (1964–67) of the Zim Lines.

In the summer of 1985, Royal Cruise announced the building of not one but two 40,000-tonners from the Meyer-Werft shipyards at Papenburg, West Germany. They are to be delivered during 1988, and the first is to be named *Crown Odyssey*.

SUN LINE

STELLA SOLARIS, STELLA OCEANIS AND STELLA MARIS II

Another Greek firm which has developed a strong reputation in Mediterranean cruising is the Sun Line, which began cruise service in 1958. Their first ship was the 1924-ton *Stella Maris*, a converted Canadian corvette. Subsequent expansion included the addition of the 10,500-ton *Stella Solaris*, formerly the *Cambodge* of 1952 of Messageries Maritimes and rebuilt in 1973; the 3900-ton *Stella Oceanis* of 1966, the former ferry *Aphrodite* for the Greek Government; and the 2600-ton

Stella Maris II, built in 1961 as the German coastal passenger ship *Bremerhaven*. Grace Line's *Santa Paula* of 1958 was purchased in 1972 for conversion as their fourth cruise ship, the *Stella Polaris*. However, this project never materialized and this ship has since been used as a floating hotel in Kuwait.

The Sun Line runs cruises not only in the Mediterranean, but to the Caribbean and South America.

EFTHYMIADIS LINES

PATRAS, MELINA AND DELOS

The story of the Efthymiadis Lines has a similar pattern to that of the aforementioned Typaldos Lines. The Company rose quickly to a prominent position in the eastern Mediterranean trade, and was particularly notable for a series of unique tanker-to-ferry conversions. The firm also dabbled in regular passenger shipping as well as cruising. Their three primary cruise vessels were the 11,000-ton *Patras*, formerly the Messageries Martimes combination liner *Pierre Loti* of 1952, and then two other former Frenchmen, the 4500-ton sisters *Melina* and *Delos*, which had been built in 1949 for the Paquet Lines as the *Azrou* and *Azzemour* respectively. Efthymiadis cruises were run mostly out of Piraeus. It was, however, the tragic loss

The half-dismantled Efthymiadis Lines' *Melina* is shown at the end of her days at Perama in Greece. She was the former French *Azrou*.

Antonio Scrimali

The Sun Line rebuilt the former German coastal passenger ship *Bremerhaven* as the cruising yacht *Stella Maris II*.

of one of their converted ferries that finished-off the Company and its ships. In 1977, the *Heleanna* sank in the Adriatic and was found, in the inquest that followed, to have been unsafely loaded. Similar to the Typaldos fleet, all of the Efthymiadis ships were seized for negligence and the owners sent to prison. The *Patras* was auctioned-off to other Greek owners and became the *Chrysovalandou II* and later the *Eros*, before being scrapped in 1986. The *Melina* and *Delos* were laid-up in Perama Bay; the former having been scrapped in 1980 and the latter still afloat at the time of writing. Antonio Scrimali added to the history of the *Delos*.

In 1980, she was sold to the Acquaviva Shipping Co and renamed *Bella Maria*, for cruises in the Adriatic. After her second sailing, she developed engine troubles at Patras

and was later towed to Piraeus and laid-up there. In September 1983, she was reportedly sold to the Arab Emirates and renamed *Khalid I*, but in very poor, neglected condition. Earlier, in July 1980 and just before she was scrapped, part of the *Melina*'s engines were removed and placed in the *Delos*.

MED SUN LINES

ATALANTE

Operating cruises within the Mediterranean, quite often sailing from Venice, is the 12,614-ton *Atalante*, owned by the Med Sun Lines (the abbreviated name of Mediterranean Sun Lines Ferry Ltd). The ship has been used in ferry services as well, across the Adriatic between Italy and Greece, and to the Aegean islands.

The *Atalante* (shown here) once sailed on the long-distance passenger run between France, the South Pacific and Australia as the *Tahitien*. She was rebuilt for Mediterranean cruising under the Greek flag.

Michael Cassar

For some years, the 6000-ton *Orion* was the flagship of the K Lines' Aegean cruise fleet.

She is the former *Tahitien* built in 1953 at Brest, and was once used on the long-haul passenger and cargo run for Messageries Maritimes from Marseilles out to the South Pacific via the Caribbean and Panama. She was bought by the Greeks in 1972, refitted for her present service and was first listed under the ownership of Aphrodite Cruises.

HELLENIC MEDITERRANEAN LINES

AQUARIUS

The Hellenic Mediterranean Lines had long been involved in local Mediterranean passenger and ferry services (Marseilles to the Eastern Mediterranean, across the Adriatic etc) before they built their first cruise ship in 1972. She was the first brand-new liner to be designed specifically for the local Aegean trade. Constructed at the United Shipyards at Perama, the 4800-ton *Aquarius*, commissioned in June 1972, has accommodation for 280 passengers. She was used mostly on weekly runs that included calls as far as Istanbul and sometimes on winter services to the Caribbean. By 1987, however, Hellenic Mediterranean declared bankruptcy and the *Aquarius* was laid-up.

K LINES

CONSTELLATION, ORION, ATLANTIS, GALAXY AND KENTAVROS

Yet another important Aegean-eastern Mediterranean cruise firm is the K Lines, named after its parent company, the Kavounides Shipping Company. Similar to most of their Greek flag competitors, they too maintain a fleet of second-hand but radically converted and improved passenger ships. The 12,400-ton *Constellation* is the flagship and was added in 1978. She

was the *Anna Nery*, built in 1962, and registered at Rio de Janeiro for the South American coastal services of Lloyd Brasileiro. Renamed *Danaos* for a brief time, she was later recommissioned under her present name, mostly for twice weekly three- and four-day cruises out of Piraeus. The 6000-ton *Orion* is a much older ship, built in Italy in 1953. She was originally named *Achilleus*, and she and her twin sister, the *Agamemnon* (which capsized at her Piraeus berth in 1968 and then was later salvaged and scrapped) were built as part of an Italian war-time reparations account for the Greeks. They sailed first for the Nomikos Lines, then Olympic Cruises (an Onassis affiliate) and finally Dorian Cruises. Laid-up for a time, the *Achilleus* was bought by the K Lines in 1968, and refitted as the *Orion*. Cruise director Peter Hagmann served in the ship in her earlier days as the *Achilleus*.

She had been chartered quite frequently by Her Majesty Queen Frederika of Greece for 'matchmaking cruises'. The Queen, with three eligible children of her own [her son is presently the exiled King Constantine of Greece, her eldest daughter is now Queen Sofia of Spain and the youngest is Princess Irene of Greece, also living in exile], invited endless members of the European royal houses, but particularly the unmarried members. They'd sail off on extravagant, almost idyllic cruises through the Aegean isles.

Other ships in the K Lines' cruise fleet included the 4300-ton *Atlantis*, the former Greek ferry *Adonis* of 1965, which was burnt out at Perama in March 1983 and was later scrapped; the 5500-ton *Galaxy*, originally built in 1957 as the Irish Sea passenger ship *Scottish Coast*, then rebuilt in 1969 and presently laid-up; and the 2800-ton *Kentavros*, a converted former seaplane tender, built in 1941 and rebuilt in 1964–65, but scrapped in 1986.

The K Lines have other, mostly smaller passenger ships and ferries. Their cruise services have included periodic voyages in the Caribbean and from South Africa. One, experimental service, offered the first cruises to China, using the 9600-ton *Aquamarine*. She was the former Brazilian liner *Princesa Isabel* of 1962 and later the Dominion Far East Line's *Marco Polo*, a well known Australian-based cruise ship. Financially unsuccessful, she too has been laid-up, since 1981, in the anchorages of Perama Bay.

Few nations can lay claim to as many converted cruise ships, with as many former name and ownership changes, as the Greeks.

eight

THE

SOVIETS

fueled by cheap domestic oil and manned by sailors who work for one-fourth the $1110-a month wages of a US merchant seaman. Even when the ships operate at a loss, they provide the Kremlin with much needed foreign currency (more than $2 billion in 1984). Their military usefulness is indisputable as well. Several Soviet liners are equipped with side ports for vehicles, which are of little use on a cruise but of great value for troop carriers. Sailing from such ports as Genoa, Tilbury [London] and Rotterdam, these liners offer rates 15 per cent to 20 per cent below those of most Western ships. Travellers give the Soviet cruises high marks, however. A group from Lisieux, France, who sailed the Norwegian fjords on the *Leonid Brezhnev* in May, was enchanted by everything from crew members who danced 'Russian', to inexpensive vodka and frog's legs for dinner.

The first deep-sea Soviet liners to be used periodically for cruising consisted of no less than nineteen sister ships and near-sisters. Built in a six-year period beginning in 1958, at the Mathias-Thesen Werft shipyard at Wismar in East Germany, these 5000-tonners, with capacities for as many as 333 passengers each, include the *Mikhail Kalinin* (1958), *Felix Dzerjinsky* (1958), *Grigori Ordjonikidze* (1959), *M. Uritzkij* (1959), *Vazlav Vorovsky* (1959), *Vladivostock* (1959), *Maria Ulyanova* (1960), *Estonia* (1960), *Latvia* (1960), *Litva* (1960), *Turkmenia* (1961), *Petropavlovsk* (1961), *Khabarovsk* (1962), *Nikolaevsk* (1962), *Baikal* (1962), *Armenia* (1963), *Nadeshda Krupskaja* (1963), *Bashkiria* (1964) and the *Adsharia* (1964). All these vessels are frequently used by the government for internal, military, scientific, and supply services, but only the *Nadeshda*

MIKHAIL KALININ CLASS

The Soviet passenger fleet is now the largest in the world, with no less than three dozen deep-sea passenger ships. It began primarily with some ex-German liners, acquired after the Second World War, and grew when the country began to build their own passenger ships in the late fifties. Not all of their ships can be covered within the scope of this book. Those discussed are those that have sailed under tourist charters or to the rather well-known Soviet affiliate, the CTC Lines of London.

Cruise ships wearing the hammer and sickle are common sights throughout the world – from Southampton to Sydney and from North Africa to the North Cape. According to *Time* magazine, in an article published on 23 September 1985,

When Britain took the *Queen Elizabeth 2* out of commercial service to send troops to the Falkland Islands in 1982, the Soviets moved in and within two years upped their share of the British cruise market from 10 per cent to 42 per cent. Soviet ships can afford to underbid other fleets [particularly in cruising] because they are state insured,

One of nineteen sister ships and near-sister ships, the *Adsharia*, completed in 1964, was the last of this series of Soviet passenger ships, most of which have been used for some cruise sailings.

Alex Duncan

Port of Le Havre Authority

During a cruise, the *Taras Schevchenko* calls at Le Havre, France.

Krupskaja has been officially transferred to the Soviet Navy (in 1976) and renamed *Kuban*.

IVAN FRANKO, ALEXANDR PUSHKIN, TARAS SCHEVCHENKO, SHOTA RUSTAVELLI AND MIKHAIL LERMONTOV

The *Mikhail Kalinin* class was followed by another group, of larger liners, each some 20,000 tons. They were also built at Wismar in East Germany. The first was the *Ivan Franko* (1964) followed by the *Alexandr Pushkin* (1965), the *Taras Schevchenko* (1967), the *Shota Rustavelli* (1968) and finally, the *Mikhail Lermontov* (1972). They are large ships, with even greater adaptability for cruising than the *Mikhail Kalinin* class and each can accommodate approximately 700 passengers. They have sailed on a variety of services including cruises in the Mediterranean and Black Seas, to South America and the Caribbean, to Scandinavian and Baltic waters, on CTC Lines' service out to Australia and around the world, and, until 1981, the *Mikhail Lermontov* and *Alexandr Pushkin* have sailed on transatlantic voyages to New York and Montreal, respectively.

Vincent Messina, who has sailed on over three dozen liners and also been employed aboard some of them, has made several quite different voyages with the Soviets.

The *Mikhail Lermontov*, while a modern looking ship, used a design that was quite dated for the early 1970s. For example, the promenade decks were covered and there were old fashioned wooden benches on deck. Her cabins, all of which were outside but most of which were without private facilities, were among her nicest features, although they always reminded me of railway compartments. I recall that she rolled madly during an 8-day cruise to Bermuda from New York, a voyage which [in 1975] cost only $275. The food was plain and sometimes awful, and the crew on this Leningrad-based ship were more dour than the warm-hearted Ukranians on the Odessa-based *Maxim Gorky* and *Odessa*.

Frank Braynard was quite delighted with the same ship during a transatlantic round voyage in 1980.

Hapag-Lloyd Shipyards

The enclosed swimming pool aboard the refitted *Mikhail Lermontov*.

So few ships seem like real ships anymore and so it was a joy to be aboard one that is truly a ship, bow to stern, and makes no pretense at being a Las Vegas nightclub or a Broadway show. To start with, the *Lermontov* and her four sisters have more sheer than most modern ships; you have to struggle uphill at either the bow or stern, whatever deck you are on. And then the wonderful smokestack – what a beauty it is, what a symbol of power and thrust. I loved the glass-enclosed promenade decks. You can walk completely around it and many do. When we sailed on this 20,000-ton liner, we were surprised to spot a very large Russian lady on the Promenade Deck one day and wearing a very large 'I Love Sea Cliff' button. Coming from Sea Cliff [on Long Island, New York], I endeavoured to talk with her, but the language barrier was too much. She had obviously been visiting my hometown, proud of its 200 White Russian families. We travelled roundtrip to London on the *Lermontov* and had hoped to make another voyage on her one day.

Unfortunately, during a cruise out of Sydney, on 16 February 1986, she sank off Cape Jackson, at the northern end of New Zealand's South Island. She had struck the local rocks, was holed and then flooded.

Hapag-Lloyd Shipyards

The modernized verandah area aboard the *Mikhail Lermontov*.

LEONID SOBINOV, FEODOR SHALYAPIN, MAXIM GORKY AND ODESSA

In the early 1970s, to supplement their fast-growing cruise services, the Soviets acquired four foreign-flag liners: the 22,600-ton sisters *Carmania* and *Franconia*

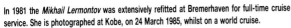

In 1981 the *Mikhail Lermontov* was extensively refitted at Bremerhaven for full-time cruise service. She is photographed at Kobe, on 24 March 1985, whilst on a world cruise.

Y Fukawa

from Cunard which, in 1973, became the *Leonid Sobi-nov* and *Feodor Shalyapin* respectively; then, later the same year, the luxurious 24,900-ton *Hamburg* (which, in her final months with the Germans had been renamed *Hanseatic*) of the German Atlantic Line, which the Soviets renamed the *Maxim Gorky*; and finally, during 1975, the 13,700-ton *Copenhagen*, a brand new cruise ship which was sold whilst still under construction for her financially-troubled Danish owners and renamed the *Odessa*.

Vincent Messina travelled in the *Maxim Gorky* and later served as a member of the limited American cruise staff aboard the *Odessa*.

I sailed in the *Maxim Gorky* in 1974, when she was cruising out of New York to Bermuda and the Caribbean for the Soviets' North American agents, March Shipping Company. The Soviet ships were always good bargains, always undercutting everyone else. It wasn't especially elaborate, however, just good 'Intourist service'. It seemed that the Russians were somehow out of their league with the very fancy former *Hamburg*. She seemed too luxurious. In many ways, she was still a German ship. All of the glassware, for example, was from the German Atlantic Line and the china was Rosenthal. The ship wasn't very clean, however, and there were lots of problems with the staff. Many of the bartenders, for example, did not know how to mix cocktails and I recall a few passengers stepping behind the bars to help. The service was also in contrast to the luxurious surroundings. Most of the crew were from the

Ukraine and had never left the Black Sea area. There was, however, a stark change in crew between my two voyages [in May and November 1974]. Earlier, the staff was very Soviet with ill-fitting, oversized clothes whereas later the men wore jeans and the women used much more make-up. The ship had become, in fact, much more Westernized. After being damaged in a bombing incident [at San Juan, in November 1975] the ship secured a long-term charter for European cruising to the giant Neckermann Co of Frankfurt. At New York, she was eventually replaced by the *Odessa* and the *Mikhail Lermontov*. One other memory of the *Maxim Gorky* is seeing her rendezvous at Martinique, for crew changes, with the prewar Soviet liner *Rossia* [the former Hamburg American *Rossia* of 1939], which had arrived from Odessa.

Vincent Messina was employed aboard the smaller *Odessa* in 1976–77.

There were 170 women and 100 men in the crew aboard the *Odessa*. It was quite interesting for an American working on a Soviet liner. The Soviets could discuss and debate the American system, but were not allowed to discuss the Soviet system. Any form of friendliness with the crew was actually frowned upon. Fully a third of the crew 'watched' one another and, as I recall, the staff captain was the advisor to the captain on political matters.

The Soviets were still quite inexperienced when operating the little *Odessa*. Food preparation and presentation, for example, was quite poor. For dinner, there might be boiled fish, boiled potatoes and white asparagus on a white plate – no colour whatsoever! Every Wednesday night, duck was offered, but which we began to call 'Rubber Duck Night'. During the Christmas cruise in December

Preparing for her first outward voyage to Australia via the Suez, the Feodor Shalyapin, *the former Cunarder* Franconia *of 1955, at Southampton's Ocean Terminal on 19 November 1973.*

Touropa

The *Belorussiya* during a call at Funchal, Madeira. She is one of the five Soviet sister ships that have been used extensively for cruising.

1976 [from New Orleans to Mexico and Central America], the ship was short of both food and water.

The Soviets did, however, become increasingly experimental in fine tuning their cruise ships. However, they suffered also from other infirmities. During the height of the bitter Afghanistan invasion, for example, the *Odessa* sometimes sailed with as few as forty passengers.

Frank Braynard also made a voyage in the *Odessa*, a cruise in the Mediterranean in 1985.

I visited the home offices of the huge Black Sea Shipping Co [the owners of the *Odessa*] at Odessa and relished the air of pride in their work that the building somehow evoked. Ship pictures on the wall, nautical symbols on the doors and floors, a smart feeling of ship-shapeness everywhere. The same is true of shipboard activity. Whether varnishing the scuppers or painting a thick blue line at about deck level on each promenade, the cleanly-uniformed seamen seemed to be enjoying their work. There seemed to be no feeling of 'overtime for the sake of overtime' here, little evidence of 'feather bedding' or living only by the union rules. We were given hand-typed menus because most of the passengers were German and therefore the regular menus were printed in that language. We loved the 'Russian Night' singers, the dancers and their exotic costumes, and the marvellous master of ceremonies, who began each performance with a blunt 'I tell joke!'

BELORUSSIYA, GRUZIYA, AZERBAYDZHAN, KAZAKHSTAN AND KARELIYA

According to Vincent Messina

The *Belorussiya* and her four sisters are actually ferries that are used for cruising. Many of their cabins, for example, have shared bathroom facilities, which is quite common for ferries. They are not really suited for two-week passages, but instead much shorter trips.

All these 16,600-ton ships were built by Finland's Wartsila Shipyards at their Turku plant. The *Belorussiya* was commissioned first, in January 1975, the *Gruzia* in the following June, the *Azerbaydzhan* by December, the *Kazakhstan* in June 1976 and the *Kareliya* in December. Each ship had a capacity for about 500 passengers in cabins as well as 114 additional passengers in aircraft-type reclining seats and 391 on deck. As cruise ships, their capacities were limited to about 350 cabin passengers. Their leisure sailings have taken them not only throughout European waters, but to the Caribbean, around South America and even on cruises around the world. Most of them have since been modernized and refitted for increased cruise service and in 1982 the *Kareliya* was renamed the *Leonid Brezhnev*.

Vincent Messina was aboard the *Kazakhstan* in the early summer of 1979, for a transatlantic 'positioning cruise' from New York to the Mediterranean.

We sailed on Saturday, June 30th, the day of the Harbor Festival procession of liners which included the *Oceanic*, *Doric*, *Statendam*, *Rotterdam*, *Canberra* and the little coastal cruise ship *America*. Ours was primarily a diplomatic crossing, carrying the Soviet delegation to the United Nations. The itinerary was from New York to Odessa via Ponta Delgada, Cadiz, Naples and Piraeus. Ambassador Dobrynin joined us at Cadiz. Otherwise, there were only 40 regular passengers onboard. It was rather surprising to note that the most popular pastime during the crossing was the board game Monopoly. It has, of course, very capitalistic themes.

Several years later, in the summer of 1981, Vincent Messina travelled in one of the *Kazakhstan*'s sister ships, the *Gruzia*, which was being used on the Black Sea express route.

We sailed from Odessa on a seven-day round voyage to Novorossisk, Sukhumi, Batumi, Sukhumi again, Sochi, Yalta and then a return to Odessa. I was the only Western passenger onboard – the others were Soviets, Czechs and East Germans. I felt quite isolated. Originally, I was to have sailed on the veteran *Admiral Nakhimov* [the prewar German liner *Berlin* of 1925], but this was denied because she had no English-speaking staff members and because it was preferred that I sail on a more modern ship. On the *Gruzia*, the food was awful and portioned out in very exact amounts. The passengers varied from overnight to full seven-day round trippers. Some actually lived in aircraft reclining seats on the lower decks for the full seven days!

AIVAZOVSKY

Another acquisition to strengthen the Soviet cruise fleet was the 7100-ton *Aivazovsky*, built at Nantes in France in 1976. With a capacity for 328 passengers, she is unlike the other deep-sea liners in being registered to the Soviet Danube Steamship Co (the rest are registered to one of three firms, the Baltic State Steamship Co of Leningrad, the Black Sea State Steamship Co of Odessa or the Far East State Steamship Co of Vladivostock). The *Aivazovsky* cruises primarily in the Black Sea.

DIMITRI SHOSTAKOVICH, GEORG OTS, MIKHAIL SUSLOV, LEV TOLSTOY AND KONSTANTIN SIMONOV

This series of five 9800-ton sister ships, like the earlier *Belorussiya* class, are dual-purpose and can be used for ferry services and one-class cruising. They were built at the Stocznia Szczecinska shipyards in Poland and were completed in 1980–81. They have cabin accommodation for 212 passengers, but additional certificates for as many as 989 deck passengers. These vessels have been chartered to Western tourist firms and voyaged in Scandinavia, the Baltic, the Mediterranean and the Black Sea.

The Soviets are bound to add new passenger ships, including some that will be used for highly lucrative Western cruises. At the time of writing, several 10,000-tonners are believed to have been ordered and it is rumoured that even larger passenger ships are also on the drawing boards.

nine
UNDER
FLAGS OF
CONVENIENCE

CARNIVAL CRUISE LINES

MARDI GRAS, CARNIVALE AND FESTIVALE

When the Norwegians were investing heavily in Caribbean cruising from Florida in the early seventies, they used only brand-new, specifically designed passenger ships, such as the innovative *Song of Norway* trio and the four 'white ships' of Norwegian Caribbean Lines. Other companies, like the Carnival Cruise Lines, felt that this ever increasing market could also sustain refitted, second-hand ships – thus began what would, within fifteen years, become 'the busiest cruise line in the world'. For some years, all Carnival Cruise Lines' voyages were on average at least ninety-five per cent full.

The Company was formed by the Arison Shipping Company, which had been the agents for the Norwegian Caribbean Lines. Their first acquisition was the 27,200-ton *Empress of Canada*, built in 1961 for Canadian Pacific's transatlantic service between Liverpool and the St Lawrence, and winter cruising from New York. However, she had become uneconomic and was decommissioned by the end of 1971. In the following February she was acquired as the first Carnival Cruise liner and was promptly renamed *Mardi Gras*. She was placed immediately on seven-day cruises out of Miami and her initial refit and modernization was carried out as the ship sailed with commercial passengers. Sections of the vessel were sealed off as work and repair crews made the necessary alterations. The *Mardi Gras* was soon averaging as much as 100 per cent occupancy.

In little more than three years, the Company acquired a second liner, the 21,700-ton *Queen Anna Maria*, which had just been laid-up (in early 1975) following the collapse of her owners, the Greek Line. She too had previously been a Canadian Pacific liner, the *Empress of Britain*, built at Glasgow in 1956. After dry-docking and repairs at Newport News, Virginia, the ship was renamed *Carnivale* and entered Caribbean service in February 1976.

As the Carnival success story continued, a third, even larger liner was acquired, the 32,600-ton *S A Vaal* of South Africa's Safmarine Lines, formerly Union-Castle's *Transvaal Castle* of 1961. She was in need of a very thorough transformation and expansion, so, in a most unusual step, was sent out to Kobe, Japan, rather than a closer European yard, for conversion. She was rebuilt, renamed the *Festivale* and recommissioned in the autumn of 1978. Her capacity had been increased from 728 to 1432 passengers. Rumours were that Carnival would next attempt to purchase another former Union-Castle liner, the 36,200-ton *Windsor Castle* of 1960, which had just been

sold to the Greeks and was to be used as an accommodation ship in Saudi Arabia. Another rumour was that Carnival would build their first brand-new cruise liner in Japan, a nation largely inexperienced in creating large cruise ships.

Even with three large cruise ships in service, the Carnival operation continued to expand. Their formula has been explained by George Devol, the president of the World Ocean & Cruise Liner Society.

Basically, Carnival found a very successful way to attract first time passengers and to give them an activity-filled week of fun. On board their ships, the emphasis is always on fun and on informality. They also offered excellent value for money. They were especially strong in attracting younger passengers as well. Carnival is very competitively priced, but always good value. They remain [in 1986] in the very, very popular air-sea Caribbean and Mexican markets and they recruit their passengers from all parts of North America rather than just concentrating on one geographic area.

TROPICALE

Delivered in January 1981, the 30,000-ton *Tropicale* was Carnival's first brand-new cruise ship. She was built at the Aalborg Vaerft shipyards in Denmark and has a maximum capacity of 1422 passengers. She was first used in the Caribbean, then on the summer-time Alaska trade and is presently employed year-round out of Los Angeles on weekly cruises to the

Carnival Cruise Lines' *Festivale* **was recommissioned in autumn 1978, following an extensive refit at Kobe, Japan during which her capacity was doubled for the Caribbean cruise trades.**

Alex Duncan

In July 1985, Carnival Cruise Lines' 46,052-ton *Holiday*, then the largest liner yet built for cruising, arrives in Miami for the first time.

At Sweden's Kockums shipyard, the bow section is being fitted to the 48,000-ton *Jubilee* in the spring of 1986. Using a revolutionary construction technique, the ship was built in twenty-two different sections, which were later moved to a dock for final assembly.

Mexican Riviera. Her owners are a special holding company, AVL Maritime of Monrovia (the earlier Carnival ships are under the Panamanian flag).

HOLIDAY, JUBILEE AND CELEBRATION

These vessels are known as part of the contemporary cruising fleet of 'mega-cruise ships'. Each member of this Carnival trio is larger than celebrated liners of the past such as the *Ile de France*, the *Caronia* and even the famous *Titanic*. The 46,052-ton *Holiday*, commissioned in July 1985, was, like the *Tropicale*, built by the Danes, at the Aalborg Vaerft yards. A vessel with an enormously high-standing superstructure and a winged funnel (also similar to the earlier *Tropicale*), she has space for as many as 1800 passengers and carries a staff of 620.

Her near-sisters, the slightly larger *Jubliee* completed in 1986 and the *Celebration* of the spring of 1987, are placed at over 48,000 tons. They were constructed by the Swedes, at the Kockums shipyards at Malmo. All three of these 'super cruisers', are used in the Caribbean. The *Holiday* flies the Panamanian flag whereas the other pair have been placed under the Bahamian flag. They are noted for their exceptionally contemporary and 'high tech' design and décor. George Devol noted,

The design of these newer ships is even closer to a shoreside resort. The atmosphere often resembles that of a big tropical hotel. There are large showrooms, for example, and the emphasis is on lots of entertainment. The Carnival philosophy seems to be to keep its passengers busy and to always have something happening. There is no stuffiness about the Carnival ships. It's all fun-in-the-sun. The service and other standards are relatively good as well.

The newer ships also have the added advantage of larger staterooms, with as much as 180 square feet whereas most other cruise ships have a maximum of 140–150 square feet. At the same time, these cabins are handsomely decorated and well fitted-out.

Carnival's success is unparalleled within the contemporary cruise industry, with three new super cruise ships built within three years and all for a fifteen-year-old firm. Extraordinarily, Carnival now has seven liners and over 8,000 weekly berths to sell.

EASTERN STEAMSHIP LINES

EVANGELINE AND YARMOUTH

The pioneer of Caribbean cruising out of Miami, which is presently (in 1986) the busiest cruise port in the world, was the Eastern Steamship Lines, a firm that was American-owned but used foreign registry for its ships. They began leisure sailings to the tropics in the mid-fifties. Operations started with two out-of-work American coastal liners, the 5000-ton sisters *Evangeline* and *Yarmouth*. The latter was renamed *Yarmouth Castle* in 1954, then *Queen of Nassau*, until 1957, then *Yarmouth Castle* for a short time before reverting to *Yarmouth*. Both were built at Philadelphia in 1927 and each had accommodation for approximately 365 first class passengers. They were used on a variety of eastern services: three- and four-day cruises to the Bahamas as well as weekly runs to Puerto Rico and the Virgin Islands, Cuba, the Dominican Republic, Haiti and very often to Jamaica. Having been very successful and earned great profits, they were sold, in 1964 and 1962 respectively, to the specially created Yarmouth Cruise Lines, again with Panamanian registry. The *Evangeline* was renamed *Yarmouth Castle*, a ship that would later join the annals of passenger ship disasters. Both continued in Miami service as well as on charter operations, and in 1964 the *Yarmouth Castle* made summer cruises from New York.

On 12 November 1965, whilst on an overnight cruise from Miami to Nassau, the thirty-eight-year-old *Yarmouth Castle* caught fire in a blaze that broke out in a passenger cabin. The old ship became an inferno, burning from end to end and sank in the early daylight of the following day. Eighty-nine people

Antonio Scrimali

The badly rusted, Cypriot-registered *Elisabeth A* (the former *Yarmouth* of 1927) spent her final years in lay-up at Perama, Greece.

were lost and the rest were rescued by the nearby cruise ship *Bahama Star* and the freighter *Finnpulp*. The poor press resulting from this tragedy soon greatly affected bookings for the *Yarmouth*. Her passenger lists dropped by over 50 per cent. Quite soon, she was retired and then offered for sale. Later she was sold to Colombian interests and renamed *San Andres*, then resold to Greeks, the Hellenic International Lines, and renamed *Elisabeth A*. Beginning in the spring of 1968, she ran two-week cruises from Venice, but there are few records of these. Instead, she was soon sent to lay-up in Perama Bay and remained there, neglected and deteriorating, until scrapped locally in Lavrion, in July 1979.

BAHAMA STAR

For the Eastern Steamship Lines, the success of the earlier *Evangeline* and *Yarmouth* led to the acquisition, in 1959, of the transatlantic liner *Arosa Star*, which had been put up for auction following the bankruptcy of her Swiss owners, the Arosa Line. Originally built in 1931, by the Bethlehem Steel Company at Quincy, Massachusetts, she had sailed as the American cruise ship *Borinquen* until 1949 and then for other American owners until 1954 as the *Puerto Rico*.

She was refitted with a capacity for 735 passengers, modernized with complete air-conditioning, and renamed *Bahama Star*. She began to sail on three-and four-day cruises to Nassau from Miami. Despite her age and lack of such facilities as an open-air pool and vast lido decks, she was a great success. Her three-day cruises cost from $59, the four-day runs from $69.

She was finally forced out of service, in 1968, by newly enforced, very strict US Coast Guard regulations aimed particularly at aged passenger ships. Without a very extensive, very costly refit, the thirty-seven-year-old *Bahama Star* could not reach the required standards. She was laid up for a time and later sold to a previously unknown Panamanian-flag concern known as the Western Steamship Co who sent her out to the American West Coast for use as a floating hotel. Unfortunately, she never opened for business. On 13 April 1970, while at Oxnard, California, she was lashed by a ferocious hurricane, capsized and then was wrecked. She was a complete loss and had to be scrapped on the spot.

ARIADNE

In order to replace the veteran sisters *Evangeline* and *Yarmouth*, the Eastern Steamship Lines bought the 6600-ton *Ariadne*, in May 1961. At the time, with rather personal accommodation for only 239 passengers, she was Eastern's most luxurious ship and certainly one more akin to a private yacht. She had been built in 1951 by Swan, Hunter & Wigham Richardson of Newcastle, as the *Patricia* for Swedish Lloyd. She ran a seasonal service across the North Sea, between Tilbury and Gothenburg, and then spent the winters cruising. In 1957 Swedish Lloyd sold her to the Hamburg American Line. She sailed as their only postwar passenger liner, but retained her original name for full-time cruising in Scandinavia, the Mediterranean and to the Caribbean and South America. She joined the Eastern fleet, with Liberian registry, four years later.

The *Ariadne* sailed mostly out of Miami or Port Everglades to the Caribbean. She was periodically refitted and improved, and later given a domed funnel. She also did some charter work, sailing from New York and other American East Coast ports. However, by the early 1970s, she had been outstripped in the Florida cruise trades. When Eastern bought the Chandris *Atlantis* in 1972, she was included in the transaction. Hoisting the Greek colours, she became the *Freeport II*, later the *Bon Vivant* and still later the *Ariane*. After further cruise service in the Mediterranean as well as use in Arabia as an accommodation ship, she has been laid-up more recently in Perama Bay.

NEW BAHAMA STAR

Because the original, highly popular *Bahama Star* of 1931 was being withdrawn in late 1968 (primarily because of strict, new safety codes for American-based cruise ships), Eastern sought an almost immediate replacement for the very profitable overnight trade to the Bahamas. An offer was made for the 9900-ton Israeli liner *Jerusalem*, built at Hamburg in 1957 for the Zim Lines, and which was under charter to another Miami cruise firm, the P&O Steamship Co, as the *Miami*. The offer was accepted, the charter abruptly cancelled and the ship sold and placed under the Liberian flat for Eastern. She began service in March 1969, as the *New Bahama Star*, sailing on the same pattern of three- and four-day cruises, with twice weekly departures from Miami, on Mondays and Fridays. In a nostalgic act, the steam whistle

In 1975 the Eastern Steamship Lines sold the former *Bahama Star* of 1957. She was renamed *Bonaire Star* and it was planned she would sail as a Venezuelan-based cruise ship, but was, in fact, sent to lay-up. She sank in the Pacific, in October 1979, while empty and under tow, bound for scrappers on Taiwan.

Alex Duncan

from the earlier *Bahama Star* was fitted to the funnel of this newer, replacement vessel. In 1972, her name was shortened to *Bahama Star*.

By 1974 she had become plagued by boiler problems so she was sold a year later, to a newly created firm, Venzolana de Cruceros del Caribe, for service under the Venezuelan flag as the *Bonaire Star*. It was planned she would run Caribbean cruises out of La Guaira in company with the former *Santa Rosa* of the Grace Line, which had just been bought by a related company and renamed *Samos Sky*. Neither ship ever entered this service. The *Bonaire Star* was sent to Mobile, Alabama and soon laid-up. Four years later, she was sold to nearby New Orleans scrappers for $322,000. Soon afterwards, she was resold to the Taiwanese for delivery to the breakers at Kaohsiung. Sadly, on 3 October 1979, while empty and under tow in the Pacific, she developed leaks and sank.

The *Emerald Seas* was built in 1944. Here, in her sixth career, sailing for Eastern Steamship Lines she departs from Miami on a four-day cruise to the Bahamas. Frequently modernized and refitted, she bears little trace of her long career and true age.

EMERALD SEAS

When added to the Eastern fleet in 1972, the 24,458-ton *Emerald Seas* had already had five previous careers working as the American troop ship *General W P Richardson*, American Export Lines' *Laguardia*, Hawaiian-Textron Lines' *Leilani*, American President Lines' *President Roosevelt* and as the Chandris *Atlantis*. She was built originally in 1944. She had been altered and refitted on so many occasions that over $100 million has been spent on her. She had undergone more refits than any other cruise ship of comparable size. However, she consumed much fuel and was rarely profitable in any of her earlier careers. At present she sails in Eastern's overnight cruise trade to the Bahamas at a leisurely 14–15 knots. This, her sixth career, is certainly her most financially successful.

BAHAMA CRUISE LINES

VERA CRUZ

The Bahama Cruise Lines, owned by Britain's Common Brothers, was formed in the late sixties for the short-sea Miami–Nassau–Freeport run. Their first ship was the 10,400-ton ferry-cruise ship *Freeport*, which later became Commodore Cruise Lines' *Caribe* and presently sails as the *Scandinavian Sun* for Scandinavian World Cruises. The Company's second ship, acquired in 1974, was the 10,500-ton former Zim liner *Theodor Herzl*. Built at Hamburg in 1957, she was laid-up in 1970. It was rumoured that she

would be rebuilt as the *Carnivale* for Miami cruise interests but this project never materialised. Instead she was recommissioned in 1975 for Bahama Cruise as the *Freeport*, on the Miami–Bahamas trade. A year later, she was renamed *Vera Cruz I*, later changed to *Vera Cruz Primero* and still later shortened to *Vera Cruz*. She was used for both Caribbean cruises from Montego Bay and Alaskan cruises from Vancouver. She has since been reassigned, spending about eight months of the year sailing from Tampa to the western Caribbean and the remainder travelling from New York to the St Lawrence region.

BERMUDA STAR

The 23,800-ton *Bermuda Star* added to Bahama Cruise services in 1984, is leased from the C Y Tung Group and flies the Panamanian flag. She, like the *Vera Cruz*, sails in summer from New York, on weekly seven-day cruises to Bermuda; for the rest of the year, she sails from New Orleans to the western Caribbean. She was built in 1958, for the Moore McCormack Lines as the *Argentina*. In 1969 she was laid-up until 1972 when she was sold to the Holland-America Line and renamed *Veendam*. In 1975, she was briefly chartered to a Brazilian travel firm sailing as the *Brasil*, and then to the Monarch Cruise Lines, based at Miami, who sailed her as the *Monarch Star*. She was returned to the Holland-America cruise fleet in 1978 and withdrawn in 1983. When she was sold to the Tung Group, it was rumoured that she might be used in Hawaiian cruise service for Tung's passenger

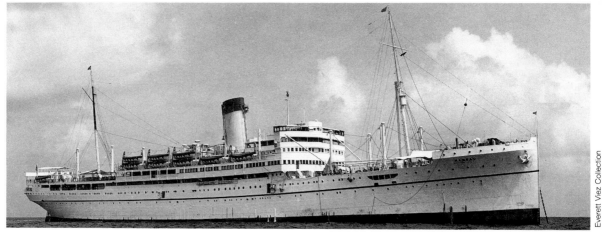

Everett Viez Collection

subsidiary, American Hawaii Cruises. The charter to Bahama Cruise was arranged instead and runs for six years, to the end of 1989.

INCRES LINE

NASSAU

During the week before Christmas 1961, there was to be a new addition to the customary flotilla of Caribbean-bound liners sailing from New York. Sporting a modernized look, unfamiliar funnel colours and flying the distinctive Mexican flag (the first time a cruise ship had ever done so), this new addition was the *Acapulco*. Her owners, the state-formed Natumex Line (Naviera Turistica Mexicana), had planned a gala send-off for the ship which would make one of the earliest trans-Panama Canal voyages, heading for Acapulco, her new home port. It was felt by the Mexicans that sufficient publicity and attention would be generated by a maiden sailing from Manhattan, then still flourishing as the ocean liner capital of the world. Instead, the entire event failed amidst deep embarrassment.

The *Acapulco* was, in 1961, in the last phase of a long, varied career. She had been, in fact, quite familiar to New Yorkers as the *Nassau*, one of the first cruise ships to offer weekly sailings throughout the year. At the time, during the fifties, most liner operations to Europe were still thriving and cruising was considered more of a secondary or alternative trade. The ship had been built originally for P&O Lines as the *Mongolia*, for their London to Sydney via Suez run. She was of sturdy and sensible construction, created by some of the master shipbuilders of the day, the Scots. The Fairfield yards of Glasgow handed her over to P&O in the spring of 1924.

The *Mongolia* was a practical combination of a large cargo capacity (five holds in all) and 410 passenger berths (divided between first and second class). She seems not to have attracted much attention, except in being P&O's first passenger ship to be driven by steam turbines, for bringing home an exceptionally large gold shipment from Bombay on one sailing in the late twenties and, at another time, for colliding with a tanker near Copenhagen during a summer-time Baltic cruise.

When P&O added the first of their innovative and luxurious 'Strath' liners (the *Strathaird* and *Strathnaver*) in 1931, the *Mongolia* was relegated to a less luxurious role: the Australian migrant trade. Her accommodation was reorganized to take 800 all-third class passengers. Then, in 1938, she was again transferred, this time to a P&O subsidiary, the New Zealand Shipping Company. Renamed *Rimutaka*, she was assigned to the long-haul run between London and Wellington via Curacao, the Panama Canal and Tahiti. Even through most of the war, she continued to sail on this route, often returning to Britain with precious meat in her freezer compartments. Then, in 1950, as new tonnage was added to the New Zealand service, the *Rimutaka* was withdrawn and offered for sale.

Her new owners were then an unknown firm, Compania de Navigacion Incres (which was later reformed as the Incres Line), who used Panamanian registry. She was refitted once again and renamed *Europa*. Her owners hoped to profit from the booming business then on the North Atlantic and placed her (for two consecutive seasons) in service between New York, Plymouth and Antwerp. Then, in autumn 1951, Incres decided to enter the cruise business. Yet another refit followed, this time adding two outdoor pools, a large lido deck and making general improvements to the accommodation. She was rechristened the *Nassau*, and worked a seven-day pattern, sailing mostly on Friday nights, between New York and Nassau, occasionally extending her voyages to include either Havana or Port-au-Prince. Minimum fares for the week-long cruises started at $160. The *Nassau* developed a good reputation and strong following, particularly from the 'just married' honeymoon set. By 1960 the Company had added an even more luxurious ship for longer Caribbean cruises, the *Victoria*.

The *Nassau* was retired from New York service in 1961 – a victim of old age, economic constraints and fresh competition from Home Lines' *Italia*, which had just begun seven-day cruises. However, to the Mexicans, she was ideal to begin their new West Coast operations between Los Angeles and the Mexican Riviera. She went back to the Fairfield yards at Glasgow, where she had been built nearly forty years previously and had yet another major refit. The Mexicans glowed with confidence as the *Nassau* became the *Acapulco*.

Unfortunately, the ship's last career was marred by problems. The New York maiden sailing was cancelled almost at the very last moment because the Coast Guard did not certify the vessel. Among other faults, she was said to be quite unsafe and therefore was not allowed to carry passengers from an American port. Her woes continued even in Mexico, as she failed to attract sufficient passengers. Instead, she passed her first summer under the Mexican flag on charter along the Seattle waterfront. She was used as a hotel ship for World's Fair tourists and was moored

just across from another floating hotel, the former *Dominion Monarch* of the Shaw Savill Line. But, when the Fair ended, so did the charter. The *Acapulco* went back to the Mexican run, but with little further success. Her owners even offered dock-side 'businessmen's luncheons' at Los Angeles between voyages – but to no avail. Much of her final year was spent riding at anchor at Manzanillo. In October 1964, in her fortieth year, she was towed to Osaka, Japan and scrapped.

VICTORIA

Wanting to expand into longer, more expensive Caribbean cruising, Incres purchased, in 1958, the 15,000-ton *Dunnottar Castle*, built in 1936 for Union-Castle's Round Africa service. She was extensively rebuilt and modernized at Schiedam in Holland and was recommissioned, in January 1960, as the very fine *Victoria*. With 600 all-first class berths, praise and great popularity soon came her way.

In 1964, Incres was bought by the Swedish-flag Clipper Line, owners of the cruising yacht *Stella Polaris*, but were changed very little by their acquisition. However, the *Victoria* did begin to divide her cruise services, between the Caribbean run out of New York, and European services, mostly to Scandinavia from Copenhagen.

Hard-hit by the enormous oil price increases of 1973–74, the single-ship Incres operation began to fall on hard times. They were forced to increase their fares and as a result even some of their loyalist following diminished. In the summer of 1975, the

Christmas cruise departures from New York on a snowy afternoon in December 1968. From left to right: the *Oceanic* (foredeck only), *Victoria*, *United States* (just sailing), *France*, *Leonardo di Vinci* (mostly obscured) and (in the distance) the *Empress of Canada*.

Sitmar Cruises

In May 1977, in preparation for a special three-week cruise to the Caribbean, Panama Canal and Peru, Sitmar's *Fairwind* made a special maiden visit to New York.

Company closed and the *Victoria* was laid-up at New York, amidst rumours that she would be auctioned-off to buyers who wanted to use her as a floating hotel along the Amazon. Instead, in that November, she was bought by the Chandris Group, placed under the Greek flag (later changed to Panamanian) and began cruising in the Mediterranean. She is presently employed in year-round Caribbean cruising, sailing out of San Juan under the name *The Victoria*.

SITMAR CRUISES

FAIRSTAR

Sitmar Cruises (an abbreviation of Societa Italiana Trasporti Marittimi) had a Russian-born owner with a base at Monte Carlo. The Company was previously known as the Sitmar Line. For many years they had been involved in the Australian migrant and around-the-world low fare tourist trades. In 1973 they began full-time cruising out of Sydney, just as their passenger services were beginning to suffer from airline competition. Though most of their previous all-tourist class liners had been retired, the 23,700-ton *Fairstar*, formerly the British troop ship *Oxfordshire* of the Bibby Line (which had been rebuilt for commercial service in 1963–64) was refitted as a year-round cruise ship. Her original capacity of 1910 berths was

reduced to take approximately 1400 cruise passengers. She has been cruising from Sydney ever since, mostly on two-week voyages to the South Pacific islands.

FAIRSEA AND FAIRWIND

Just as Sitmar was retiring most of its older, converted passenger ships from the Australian migrant trade, they purchased two out-of-work Cunarders, the 22,900-ton sister ships *Carinthia* and *Sylvania*, which had been built in 1956 and 1957 respectively by the John Brown Shipyard on the Clyde. They had been used on the North Atlantic, sailing to the St Lawrence out of Liverpool. Sitmar planned to extensively rebuild both liners for year-round cruising, one ship out of Sydney and the other, in a new, quite experimental venture for the company, in American service from San Francisco and Los Angeles. However, there were some initial delays. Although repainted with Sitmar funnel colours and renamed the *Fairland* (then *Fairsea*) and *Fairwind* respectively, they sat for nearly two years along the Southampton Docks. They were not moved to Trieste for rebuilding until early 1970. They reappeared commercially in December 1971 and July 1972 as greatly altered, highly improved ships. They had new upper decks and funnels, lido areas with three outdoor pools, closed circuit television, a gymnasium and sauna, and modern cabin accommodation for 910 cruise passengers. The plan to sail the *Fairwind* out of Australia never materialized and instead she too went into American cruising, first from California like the *Fairsea*, but later from a permanent base at Port Everglades, Florida.

FAIRSKY

Sitmar's experimental years, in the early seventies in North American cruising, proved to be highly successful. George Devol said,

> Sitmar's greatest success in US cruising has been their stress on the family aspect of sea travel. They offer a strong and very serious welcome to children. They have one of the very best programmes not only for younger children, but for teenagers as well. The Italian flavour aboard their ships has also been very important.

The success of the two converted former Cunarders led, by the late seventies, to serious thoughts of acquiring a third additional liner. In 1980, Sitmar bought, through a subsidiary, the Fairline Shipping Co of Panama, the 19,300-ton former *Principe Perfeito* of 1961. Until 1976 she was used in the African colonial trades. More recently she had been used, by other Panama-flag owners, as the Middle Eastern accommodation ship *Al Hasa*. Sitmar's plan was to lavishly rebuild her as the *Fairsky*. However, the plans were abandoned and the vessel was laid-up under the temporary name *Vera*. Instead, a brand-new *Fairsky* was ordered from the French, at a cost in excess of

$150 million. The *Vera* was sold off within a year, in 1982, to the Greek Latsis Group and returned to the Middle East as the hotel ship *Marianna IX*.

The new *Fairsky*, at 38,786 gross tons and with a capacity for 1212 cruise passengers, was delivered by the CNIM shipyards at La Seyne, in the spring of 1984. In the summer she cruises from San Francisco to Alaska and British Columbia, and during other months on trips to the Mexican Riviera, trans-Panama Canal or on an extensive schedule of weekly Caribbean trips out of Port Everglades, Florida. Impressed and encouraged by the success of their very first brand-new cruise ship, Sitmar announced, in April 1986, plans to build as many as three 62,000 tonners with capacities for 1600 passengers each. To be delivered in 1988–89, they will replace the earlier *Fairsea* and *Fairwind* in American services. At least one of these older ships will then be moved to Australia, to replace the *Fairstar*, which will have passed her thirtieth year. The three new Sitmar 'mega-cruise ships' will be built by the French as well, at Chantiers de L'Atlantique at St Nazaire. They are to be constructed alongside an even larger cruise ship that is also destined for North American waters, the 74,000-ton *Sovereign of the Seas* for the Royal Caribbean Cruise Lines.

Arriving at the Port of Los Angeles for the first time in May 1984, Sitmar's first brand-new passenger liner, the 38,700-ton *Fairsky*, which divides her cruise sailings between Alaska, Mexico and the Caribbean.

CRUISE
SHIP
MISCELLANY

TRANSPORTS MARITIMES

BRETAGNE AND PROVENCE

In the early 1960s, the French sister ships *Bretagne* and *Provence*, built for the Latin American run, from Marseilles and Genoa to Rio de Janeiro, Santos, Montevideo and Buenos Aires, were chartered to the American-based Caribbean Cruise Lines and used mostly on summer-time weekly trips between New York, Nassau and Bermuda. At 16,000 tons each, they had been the largest postwar French liners trading to South America and their accommodation had been divided into three classes: first, tourist and third. The *Bretagne* had been built by Chantiers et Ateliers de St Nazaire and commissioned in 1952; the *Provence* came from Swan, Hunter & Wigham Richardson of Newcastle and was delivered two years earlier.

Their service on American cruise sailings was brief. The *Bretagne* ran cruises in 1960 and 1961. The following summer she was sold to the Chandris Group and sailed under her new name *Brittany* on their Australian migrant trade. However, this career was short-lived – she caught fire and capsized on 8 April 1963, while undergoing repairs at a Greek shipyard at Skaramanga. The wreck was later salvaged, and delivered to Italian breakers at La Spezia in March 1964. The *Provence* cruised from New York during the summer of 1963, and then returned to the South American trade under joint Transports Maritimes-Costa Line management. She was bought outright by the latter company in 1965, raised the Italian flag and became the *Enrico C.*, as which she still sails.

VIKING CRUISE LINES

VIKING PRINCESS

Completed in 1950, by Ateliers et Chantiers de la Loire of St Nazaire, the 11,900-ton motor liner *Lavoisier* was, like the *Bretagne* and *Provence*, built for the Latin American route (although sailing from Le Havre) and for French owners, Chargeurs Réunis. She was a combination passenger-cargo liner and carried 324 passengers in two classes, first and tourist.

A decade or so later, in August 1961, she was sold to unknown Italian buyers, Commerciale Marittime Petroli SpA of Palermo, and extensively rebuilt as the 600-passenger cruise ship *Riviera Prima*. She resumed service, in November 1962, sailing periodically under the so-called banner of Riviera Cruises, or under extensive charter to the Caribbean Cruise Lines for two- to fourteen-day cruises out of American East Coast ports, including New York and Miami. When, in the summer of 1964, Caribbean Cruise Lines suddenly collapsed, the ship was seized for debt and later auctioned-off. That October, she joined the Norwegian fleet, with a new firm called Viking Cruise Lines, a special subsidiary created by Norwegian shipper A/S Sigline Berge Sigval Bergesen of Oslo. At 12,800 tons, she then ranked as the third largest liner under the Norwegian flag. She was modernized and improved, and renamed *Viking Princess*.

Once again she was used mostly for Bermuda, Nassau and Caribbean cruising out of American East Coast ports. It was during one of these voyages, on 8 April 1966, that she was swept by fire while off the Cuban coast. Two passengers perished in the disaster. The blistered, blackened wreck was towed into Port Royal on Jamaica, declared a total loss and gently towed across the mid-Atlantic to ship-breakers at Bilbao, Spain. The Viking Cruise Lines ceased trading thereafter.

Jeff Blinn, Moran Towing & Transportation Co

EMPRESA INSULANA

FUNCHAL

Delivered in October 1961, by Denmark's Helsingor Shipyards, the 9800-ton *Funchal* became the flagship of Portugal's Empresa Insulana fleet. Carrying three classes of passengers, she was assigned to the short-sea service between Lisbon, Madeira, the Azores and the Canary Islands. Later, however, she spent increasing time in cruise service, sailing often in summer in Scandinavian waters under a Swedish charter and in winter to South America.

Marine photographer Luis Miguel Correia is the best authority on Portuguese shipping. He recalled the history of the 400-passenger *Funchal*.

She was specially chartered by the President of Portugal in the mid 1960s and used by Admiral Thomaz as his yacht on his state visit to Madeira, the Azores, the Cape Verde Islands and Guinea. She was used once again, in 1972, for the state visit to Brazil. Withdrawn from three-class liner service in July 1972 and then refitted (her original turbines were replaced by diesels), the *Funchal* began cruising extensively in Europe and South America by 1973. Owned by Compania Transportes Maritimos since 1974, she changed from Portuguese to Panamanian registry in 1985, following her sale to 'European interests'. Still based at Lisbon, but with a Portuguese crew and with Swedish, Greek and Portuguese management, the *Funchal* presently cruises to Scandinavia, in the Mediterranean and to the Caribbean. Extensively refitted once again, in 1986, this handsome vessel is now one of the last classic luxury liners in cruise service.

Photographed on 4 July 1963, the French liner *Provence* arrives at New York during a series of charter cruises to Bermuda and Nassau.

PAQUET CRUISES

RENAISSANCE, MERMOZ AND RHAPSODY

France's Paquet Cruises began cruising in 1966, with the delivery of their 11,700-ton *Renaissance*. Built at Chantiers de L'Atlantique of St Nazaire, this new vessel, with accommodation for 416 passengers, was designed for Mediterranean cruising out of Marseilles and was later used in the Caribbean, Scandinavia and in Alaskan waters. She also ran an annual cruise around continental South America from Port Everglades, Florida. Her original owners were listed as Compagnie Francaise de Navigation and were

Portugal's only cruise ship, the *Funchal*, spends summers on charter cruises in Scandinavian waters and winters in South America.

Luis Miguel Correia

The first cruise ship in the Paquet fleet, the *Renaissance* of 1966, was first employed mostly in the Mediterranean, but later extended her sailings to Scandinavia, the Caribbean, South America and Alaska. She is shown during her maiden visit to Le Havre.

reorganized, in 1970, as Nouvelle Compagnie de Paquebots, although the marketing and sales arm in North America was always listed as Paquet Cruises.

The success of this ship led to the conversion of the 12,400-ton motor liner *Jean Mermoz*, at Genoa in 1970. She had previously been a four-class passenger vessel, built in 1957 at St Nazaire and trading on the colonial West African routes from Marseilles. Refitted for approximately 500 cruise passengers (with a maximum of 757 berths), her tonnage was relisted as 13,800 and her name shortened to *Mermoz*. She too divided her time, spending approximately eight months in European waters and the rest of the year in the Caribbean, first out of Port Everglades and later from San Juan.

The *Renaissance* was unexpectedly sold out of the Paquet fleet in 1977, and became the Greek-flag *Homeric Renaissance* for the Epirotiki Lines. A year or so later, her name was modified to *World Renaissance* and she began to do a considerable amount of charter cruising for Italy's Costa Line. She has since rejoined the Epirotiki fleet and presently sails mostly in North and South American waters.

The Paquet Company added, in 1982, the 24,200-ton Holland-America liner *Statendam* of 1957 which was renamed *Rhapsody* and placed under the Bahamian flag. She was acquired primarily to strengthen Paquet's North American operations: sailing in summers to Alaska from Vancouver and the remaining time to the Caribbean from Florida. She was also used for Mexican Riviera cruises from Los Angeles. However, bookings were not particularly encouraging and the vessel

was sold, in March 1986, to Regency Cruises, a Greek-owned firm. She was refitted extensively, and joined the *Regent Sea*, the former *Gripsholm*, also dating from 1957, in North American services.

At the time of writing (spring 1986), it is rumoured that the *Mermoz*, which has also been transferred to the Bahamian flag and is the sole remaining Paquet cruise ship, is to be sold off as well.

JUGOLINIJA

DALMATIA AND ISTRA

Though there have been several smaller cruise ships under the Yugoslavian flag, the primary and best known units were the 5600-ton sisters *Dalmatia* and *Istra*, which were built in home waters, at the Brodogadiliste Uljanik shipyards at Pula, and delivered in 1965. Yacht-like vessels, their maximum capacity is for 315 passengers and they are staffed by 175.

Built for the boom in Mediterranean cruising in the 1960s, they have also sailed in Northern waters, in the Caribbean, and to South America. Peter Hagmann served aboard both ships and recalled some of their cruise sailings.

They were nice ships then still quite new [in 1968–69] and had maximum capacities for only 180 passengers. They were like private yachts, but later altered to carry as many as 316 travellers. We had diverse itineraries, often according to special charters, and I recall visiting such ports of call as Spitzbergen and Rio, Leningrad and Dakar. I especially remember a charter nudist cruise aboard the *Istra* that sailed to Rio de Janeiro out of San Juan. Each ship had a top-deck pool, on which twin cranes could lift a double cover over it for cold weather cruising. Both the *Dalmatia* and *Istra* were very popular ships, especially liked by Germans on air-sea tours in the Mediterranean. They offered good service and a fine staff, and were certainly superior to most Greek cruise ships of that time.

RUMANIAN GOVERNMENT

TRANSILVANIA

The 6600-ton *Transilvania*, certainly Rumania's best known cruise ship, was built by the Burmeister & Wain shipyards at Copenhagen, in 1938. She had been created especially for the express passenger run between Constantza and Alexandria. Even after the war her passenger accommodation remained divided into four classes with 20 deluxe, 60 first class, 100 second class and 216 tourist class berths. Her twin sister, the *Basarabia*, was sold to the Soviets in 1948, and became their *Ukraina*.

Rumania's popular cruise ship, the *Transilvania* of 1938 berthed at Istanbul.

Completed in 1965, *Dalmatia* (shown here) and her twin sister ship *Istra* are certainly the best known cruise ships under the Yugoslavian flag.

Peter Hagmann served in the *Transilvania* during the mid-sixties.

She was then used in the summers between Constantza and Istanbul on overnight trips, and also to Mamaia, the first of the big Rumanian seaside resorts. In the spring and fall, we ran the so-called 'dream cruises', the first inexpensive sea tours to be marketed in Germany since 1939. It quickly became a very popular market and was one

The American Export liner *Exochorda* of 1931 was transferred to Turkey after the Second World War and became the national flagship *Tarsus* (shown here). She survived until 1960.

of the earliest offerings by the huge Neckermann Co of Frankfurt. We ran three-week cruises from Constantza to Yalta, Istanbul, Piraeus, Rhodes, Alexandria, Crete, Malta, Naples and Genoa or to Venice, and then we would exchange passengers. At the end of each voyage, the ship was thoroughly searched at Constantza.

I especially recall that the ship had been designed originally to also serve as a royal yacht, with specially fitted suites for King Carol and his mistress Madame Lupescu. The best suites onboard were on the top deck aft. I remember all sorts of entrances, offices, dining rooms and interconnecting bedrooms. The staff, usually tightly 'squeezed' on board, were sometimes assigned to one of the royal bedrooms.

As a courier-guide onboard these *Transilvania* cruises, I had to perform many extra duties such as entertain the passengers, dance with the ladies, organize quizzes and arrange a costume ball.

During my visit to Budapest in the summer of 1985, aboard the *Danube Princess*, we were moored alongside a Rumanian river boat. One of the bartenders on board told me that the *Transilvania*, by then well past forty, had capsized at Constantza.

TURKISH MARITIME LINES

TARSUS AND ANKARA

These two well-known prewar American passenger ships did considerable cruising after being turned over to Turkey in the late 1940s. The 9400-ton *Tarsus*,

the flagship of the Turkish Maritime Lines, had been American Export's *Exochorda* of 1931, one of the original 'Four Aces', and served during the Second World War as the troop transport USS *Harry Lee*. Under Turkish colours, her accommodation was enlarged from the original 125 first class berths to 189 in first class, 66 in second class and 210 in third class, all of which could be combined into one class for cruising. The 6100-ton *Ankara* dated from 1927 and had sailed as Clyde Mallory Lines' *Iroquois* and later the war-time hospital ship *Solace*. Her passenger configuration was listed as 170 in first class, 148 in second class and 88 in third class.

Both ships cruised periodically in both the Mediterranean and Black Seas. The *Tarsus* revisited New York in the summer of 1960, for a series of weekly seven-day cruises to Bermuda for the short-lived Fiesta Cruise Lines. The *Ankara* was perhaps best known for her charter to Swan's Hellenic Cruises, for which she became a popular passenger ship to many British tourists.

The *Tarsus* was lost in December 1960, after being rammed by a blazing tanker in the Bosphorous and catching fire herself. The *Ankara* had a far longer career, sailing in the early 1970s until being scrapped in 1977.

REGENCY CRUISES

REGENT SEA

In 1975 the Greek-flag Karageorgis Lines purchased Swedish American Line's highly reputed 23,200-ton *Gripsholm* of 1957. It was their first attempt at Mediterranean cruising. Refitted as the *Navarino*, she cruised largely on two-week itineraries, mostly from Venice and Piraeus, but also did some winter sailings from South Africa and South America. Once again, she developed a high reputation. She was, however, sold quite unexpectedly in the autumn of 1981, to Finland's Sally Line, who planned to use her on seven-day Caribbean cruises out of Miami for their North American subsidiary, Commodore Cruises. Unfortunately, on 26 November, just before the sale arrangements were completed, she capsized whilst in a floating dry-dock at Skaramanga. At first, it was reported that she was a complete loss and would go to the scrappers. However, by the following March, she had been refloated and was renamed *Samantha*. Her future was thereafter clouded in rumours. She was, in fact, refitted at La Spezia and then at Piraeus and returned to cruise service, in November 1985, for Regency Cruises. She was their first ship and was renamed *Regent Sea*. Within little more than a year she was joined by a second liner, Paquet's former *Rhapsody*, which had previously been Holland-America's *Statendam* of 1957. She has been renamed *Regent Star* and placed in Caribbean cruise service, but as a converted diesel-driven liner. Further, the Company purchased two Swedish-flag Johnson Line freighters and plans to rebuild them as the cruise ships *Regent Sun* and *Regent Sky*.

SUNDANCE CRUISES

SUNDANCER AND STARDANCER

Prompted by the continuing boom in summer-time Alaskan cruising, Seattle-based businessman Stanley McDonald (who had created Princess Cruises in the mid-sixties and later sold it to the P&O Group), formed Sundance Cruises in 1983. There were several other partners in this venture, including Finland's Effoa Steamship Co and Sweden's Johnson Line. The Company's first ship was, in fact, a Johnson-owned vessel, the 12,500-ton *Svea Corona*, a 799-passenger ferry that had been completed at Nantes in 1975 for Baltic service between Stockholm and Helsinki. She was refitted for cruising, although still had space for 150 cars, for passengers who wanted, in a rather novel approach for Alaska cruising, to 'cruise and drive'. However, on 29 June 1984, soon after entering service

The *Regent Sea* being refitted at a Greek shipyard in preparation for her North American cruise sailings, which began in November 1985.

the *Sundancer* (as she had been renamed) struck the rocks off Maud Island at the entrance to Seymour Straits while northbound from Vancouver to Alaska. Badly damaged, she went to a wharf at nearby Duncan Bay, but sank stern first.

In August, the badly damaged vessel was raised and was later towed to Vancouver and placed on auction as a constructive total loss. Though it was assumed that she would go for scrap, she was in fact towed that December to Greece via the Panama Canal and the Caribbean for her new owners, the Epirotiki Lines. She has since been thoroughly restored as the *Pegasus*. In December 1985, she began charter cruising out of Rio de Janeiro and, in the following summer, returned to the Alaskan trade. Ironically, she has become a competitor to Sundance Cruises' replacement ship, the 26,700-ton *Stardancer*.

Once the largest ferry afloat, the *Stardancer* had also been built at Nantes, in 1981. She was commissioned for a new subsidiary of Denmark's DFDS known as Scandinavian World Cruises. Renamed *Scandinavia*, she was to run New York's first deep-sea ferry-cruise service, sailing every five days to Freeport in the Bahamas. Though her sailings were linked to other ships sailing out of Miami and Port Canaveral, the anticipated success of the Bahamian-registered ship did not materialize. Her first sailing had been in October 1982 and her last sailing departed little more than a year later. Recalled by DFDS, she was assigned to the local overnight trade between Copenhagen and Oslo for a short time. She was sold to Sundance in late 1984 and then refitted for North American service, sailing to Alaska in the summer and the Mexican Riviera for the rest of the year.

Antonio Scrimali

eleven

IN PACIFIC
WATERS

She is a marvellous little ship that is well fed, well served and very comfortable. She is like an intimate floating club [in much of the marketing she is advertised as 'Club Pearl'] gone to sea in a remote part of the world. She also represents a very fine conversion [from ferry to cruise ship], where the former car decks have been thoughtfully transformed into cabins, the laundry, crew quarters and storage. Her crew is divided between Danish in the deck and engine departments, Italian and Swiss in hotel administration and Filipinos in the hotel department. Her itineraries are superbly planned, with an emphasis on 'sea time' for enrichment and relaxation.

CHINA NAVIGATION COMPANY

CORAL PRINCESS

Built in Spain 1962, as the Brazilian coastal liner *Princesa Leopoldina*, this 9600-ton vessel has been owned by the Hong Kong-based China Navigation Company since 1970. She has been sailing ever since as their *Coral Princess*. With space for 480 passengers, she sails mostly in Australian and Far Eastern waters.

ORIENT OVERSEAS LINES

ORIENTAL JADE AND ORIENTAL PEARL

In the mid-sixties, Hong Kong-based shipping tycoon C Y Tung began to create one of the largest contemporary Pacific Ocean passenger fleets. His earlier ships were, however, mostly of the combination passenger-cargo type and, while they offered one-way passages, their sailings were also sold as round-trip cruises. All of the Tung passenger ships were second-hand.

The first of these passenger-carrying vessels joined Tung's ever growing Orient Overseas Lines subsidiary in 1964. They were the 9600-ton former *Excalibur* and *Exeter*, the last of American Export Lines' postwar 'Four Aces' to sail to the Mediterranean. They had first class quarters only, for 124 passengers, were renamed *Oriental Jade* and *Oriental Pearl* respectively, placed under Liberian colours and began to offer monthly sailings from San Francisco to Yokohama, Kobe, Pusan or Yosu (in South Korea), Inchon, Keelung, Kaohsiung and Hong Kong, and then return via Kobe, Nagoya and Yokohama to San Diego and then to San Francisco. The round voyage took approximately fifty-six days.

However, within a decade they became among the first casualties of Tung's early passenger fleet. In

PEARL CRUISES

PEARL OF SCANDINAVIA

By the early 1980s, the Pacific was being called 'the untapped cruise market of the world'. There was a special fascination with cruising in Far Eastern and Southeast Asian waters, and among those who took almost immediate interest were two well-known shippers, Denmark's DFDS and Norway's Skaugen Company. Together they formed Pearl Cruises and created a Bahamian-flag subsidiary for their first cruise ship, the 12,500-ton *Pearl of Scandinavia*. She was built in 1967 for Finnlines' Baltic service and named *Finnlandia*. In 1978 she was converted, with 576 one-class berths, to the cruise ship *Finnstar*. She joined her present owners in 1981, and until recommissioned a year later, she bore the name *Innstar*.

The *Pearl of Scandinavia*, sailing mostly on two-week cruises out of Kobe, Hong Kong or Singapore, has developed a high reputation. Vincent Messina has been a passenger aboard her on two occasions.

1974 with their important revenues from cargo greatly reduced by the transition to containerized shipping and with the sudden increase in fuel oil costs, they were sent to the breakers at Kaohsiung, Taiwan.

ORIENTAL CARNAVAL AND ORIENTAL ESMERALDA

In 1968–69, wanting to expand to an around-the-world passenger service, the Tung Group bought the 21,800-ton sister ships *Rangitoto* and *Rangitane* from Britain's New Zealand Shipping Company. They were refitted to carry 300 first class passengers (decreased from the 436 tourist class passengers previously carried), renamed *Oriental Carnaval* and *Oriental Esmeralda*, placed under the Liberian flag and employed on four-month long circumnavigations. Their itinerary, though often changed to suit cargo requirements, read: Los Angeles to Acapulco, the Panama Canal, Port Everglades, Rio de Janeiro, Santos, Buenos Aires, Capetown, Durban, Lourenco Marques, Singapore, Hong Kong, Kaohsiung, Keelung, Kobe, Yokohama, Vancouver and return to San Francisco.

In the early 1970s this pair were briefly used in both a short-lived Central American as well as trans-pacific service, but were hard-hit by 1973–74, when the price of oil increased. Both were broken-up in 1976 on Taiwan.

ORIENTAL RIO

Another out-of-work New Zealand Shipping Company vessel, the *Ruahine*, built on the Clyde in 1951, joined the Tung fleet in 1968. She was refitted with 267 berths, all in first class, renamed *Oriental Rio* and joined the Orient Overseas Lines' around-the-world service and her two earlier fleet-mates. She survived for about four years and then was broken-up in early 1974 at Kaohsiung.

ORIENTAL AMIGA AND ORIENTAL FANTASIA

The last combination ships to be built for the Holland-America Line's service between Northern Europe, the Caribbean and Panama and to the North American West Coast were the *Diemerdyk* of 1950 and her near-sister, the *Dinteldyk* of 1957. Both were just over 11,000 tons and each had comfortable accommodation for about sixty passengers. The *Diemerdyk* was sold to the Tung Group in 1968, renamed *Oriental Amiga* and placed on the around-the-world run. Two

A converted Baltic car ferry, the cruise ship *Pearl of Scandinavia* has established a very favourable reputation for Far Eastern cruising. She is seen arriving at Hong Kong.

World Ocean & Cruise Society Collection

years later, the *Dinteldyk* was acquired as well and became the *Oriental Fantasia*. The two ships were then assigned to extensive 120-day itineraries out of New York, Baltimore, Charleston, New Orleans, Houston, Galveston and then Los Angeles to Yokohama, Nagoya, Kobe, Pusan, Yosu or Inchon, Keelung, Kaohsiung and Hong Kong; they returned more directly from Kaohsiung and Keelung to Los Angeles and then via the Panama Canal to New York.

Alex Duncan

The *Oriental Jade*, the former American Export liner *Excalibur*, is docked at San Francisco, soon to take on cargo and passengers for a round voyage to the Far East. She and her sister ship, the *Oriental Pearl*, were the first passenger ships in the C Y Tung fleet.

In the mid-seventies, as the passenger runs declined, both ships were downgraded to all-freight sailings and altered slightly to handle small numbers of containers. They survived until 1979, when they too went to the Taiwanese scrappers.

ORIENTAL HERO, ORIENTAL INVENTOR, ORIENTAL LADY, ORIENTAL MUSICIAN, ORIENTAL RULER AND ORIENTAL WARRIOR

In the early 1950s, as Allied shipbuilding restrictions were eased, the first brand-new passenger ships were built for the West Germans. They were a series of six eighty-six-passenger combination ships. Three were assigned to the well-known North German Lloyd and

three to their long-time rival, the Hamburg American Line. Together with a series of twelve-passenger freighters, these ships were used on a weekly service from Northern Europe to the Far East via the Mediterranean, Suez and Southeast Asia. They were sold to the Tung Group in 1966, just before they were replaced by larger, faster and more advanced German freighters. The *Frankfurt*, *Hannover* and *Hamburg* of the Hamburg American Line became the *Oriental Hero*, *Oriental Inventor* and *Oriental Warrior* respectively; the *Bayernstein*, *Hessenstein* and *Schwabenstein*, having sailed for the North German Lloyd, became the *Oriental Lady*, *Oriental Musician* and *Oriental Ruler*. They were assigned to the four-month Far Eastern run, sailing from New York and other American ports, and were later joined by the aforementioned *Oriental Amiga* and *Oriental Fantasia*.

For a while they were rather popular ships, especially with passengers who preferred the casual, informal atmosphere of freighters. By the mid-seventies these ships had been downgraded to pure cargo vessels and used in worldwide tramp trades. The *Oriental Warrior* was destroyed by fire off Florida in 1972 and the other five were broken-up in the Far East in 1978–79.

UNIVERSE

In the summer of 1970, the Tung Group made a rather extraordinary leap in passenger shipping by acquiring the world's largest liner, Cunard's 82,900-

The combination liner *Oriental Esmeralda*, formerly New Zealand Shipping Company's *Rangitane*, departs from Vancouver for a four-month cruise around the world.

Michael D J Lennon

Alex Duncan

The vessel built for Holland-America Line's North American West Coast service as the *Dinteldyk* was used in passenger-cargo service for the Orient Overseas Line as the *Oriental Fantasia* (shown here). She later became a victim of increased containerized shipping and was scrapped finally in 1979.

ton *Queen Elizabeth*, which had been laid-up since being withdrawn from transatlantic service in the autumn of 1968. The Tung Group's plan was to reactivate the legendary giant as a combination cruise ship-floating university while heavily advertising her glorious past. Renamed *Seawise University* and placed under the Bahamian flag, she was brought out to Hong Kong to undergo an extensive refit and overhaul. Unfortunately, on the eve of her first sailing

(to a Japanese dry-dock), on 8–9 January 1972, she was swept by as many as five fires while at anchor. She was badly burned and so overloaded with water used for firefighting that she later capsized. She had to be scrapped where she laid.

The *Universe Campus* (renamed *Universe* in 1976), purchased in 1971 from the American Export Lines for whom she had sailed as the *Atlantic* on the New York–Mediterranean trade became, to some extent, a replacement for the fire-gutted former *Queen Elizabeth*.

The handsome combination passenger-cargo ship, the *Oriental Ruler*, the former *Schwabenstein* of the North German Lloyd, worked Orient Overseas Lines' Far East run from North America. She and her sisters had fine accommodation for eighty-six first-class passengers.

Alex Duncan

She was only 14,000 tons and had been built in 1953 as the freighter *Badger Mariner* and rebuilt in 1957–58 for passenger service for the short-lived American Banner Lines. She joined American Export in 1960 and retained the name *Atlantic*. She was laid-up in 1967, first at New York and then at Baltimore, and then refitted for 'floating university' cruises. Her first such sailing was in September 1971. Presently, she divides her schedule between these educational voyages and summer-time cruises to Alaska from Vancouver.

ORIENTAL PRESIDENT AND ORIENTAL EMPRESS

As more and more American passenger ships were retired, C Y Tung seemed to become further enthused and willing to expand his passenger operations. The sister ships *President Cleveland* and *President Wilson* had been built at Alameda, California in 1947–48, and thereafter became well known for their transpacific sailings for the American President Lines. To the Tung managers, they seemed ideal for further use on the transpacific run, cruising, or for around-the-world sailings. In fact, they rarely had any further commercial use. Purchased in early 1973 and assigned to a Panamanian subsidiary, the ships, renamed the *Oriental President* and *Oriental Empress* respectively, were almost immediate victims of the fuel oil crisis. The *Oriental President* went directly to lay-up at Hong Kong and then was sold to Kaohsiung

The *Oriental Empress* (ex-*President Wilson* of 1948) and her sister, the *Oriental President* (ex-*President Cleveland*), were bought by the Tung Group just as the oil price increases began in 1973–74, consequently both ships were poor investments.

scrappers in June 1974. The *Oriental Empress*, after a very few voyages, was laid-up in September 1975 and scrapped a decade later.

INDEPENDENCE AND CONSTITUTION

In spring 1974, the Tung Group expanded even further by adding the 30,300-ton sister ships *Independence* and *Constitution*. These well-known, very popular three-class transatlantic liners, had been built by the Bethlehem Steel Company at their Quincy, Massachusetts yard in 1950–51 and delivered to American Export Lines. They sailed mostly on a three-week express run to the Mediterranean, between New York Algeciras, Cannes, Genoa and Naples. Used in later years for more extended cruising, they were laid-up in 1968–69 as American Export discontinued all of its passenger services. Both ships, while featuring in several rumours, including one that they were to be purchased by the Greek Chandris Group, sat unused until 1974, the *Independence* at Baltimore, the *Constitution* at Jacksonville, Florida.

The exact intended use for these twin sister ships within the Tung fleet remains unclear but they were renamed *Oceanic Independence* and *Oceanic Constitution* and then went directly to lay-up moorings near Hong Kong. They were given Liberian registry for yet another Tung subsidiary, the Atlantic Far East Line. The *Independence* was brought into service briefly in 1975, for some proposed charter cruising from Capetown and Durban, and also made one refugee sailing on lease to the Portuguese Government. She returned to her Hong Kong anchorage in January 1976. A year

Michael D J Lennon

J Fred Rodriguez

American Hawaii Cruises' *Independence* at Honolulu on 3 December 1983.

later, it was rumoured that she would become a Middle Eastern hotel and recreation ship, the *Sea Luck I*. However, this plan never materialized.

In 1979, arrangements were begun to have the ship returned to the American flag for use in a new seven-day cruise service from Honolulu to the Hawaiian islands. Sent to Kobe and then refitted and upgraded to American standards, the *Oceanic Independence* began Hawaiian cruises in June 1980, sailing under the banner of Tung's latest subsidiary, American Hawaii Cruises. The success of this enterprise was encouraging, so the *Oceanic Constitution* was put onto the same service in June 1982. At that time, the names of both ships were abbreviated, as in earlier days, to *Independence* and *Constitution*.

LIBERTE

In 1983, the Tung Group reportedly wanted to expand its Hawaiian cruise operations by, among other plans, offering three- and four-day twice-weekly cruises out of Honolulu and possibly sailings from San Francisco and Los Angeles. The Company had

just purchased the sister ships *Veendam* and *Volendam* from the Holland-America Line, ships that had been built in 1958 as the *Argentina* and *Brasil* for the Moore McCormack Lines. The Tung Company was continuing its fascination with ex-American liners. It was hoped that at least one of these ships would enter Hawaiian service. In fact, soon after the final sales arrangements were completed, both ships went elsewhere: the former *Veendam* went on long-term charter to the Bahama Cruise Lines and became their *Bermuda Star* while the ex-*Volendam* was used briefly as the accommodation ship *Island Sun* before being taken to Sasebo, Japan and then refitted as the *Liberte*. The latter ship resumed sailing in December 1985, on a special weekly Polynesian run from Papeete. This lasted one year. She now sails as the *Canada Star* in North American waters.

CHINESE GOVERNMENT

YAOHUA AND MINGHUA

In the 1960s and 1970s, the government of the People's Republic of China, through a series of holding companies such as the China Ocean Shipping Co of Canton, began to assemble a deep-sea passenger fleet. Some ships were built or acquired especially for the country's extensive coastal network of services, others for duties such as taking engineers, scientists and work crews out to a railway building project in East Africa. In more recent years, in the early 1980s, at least two of these Chinese passenger ships have been used for cruising.

The 10,100-ton *Yaohua* was built at Chantiers de L'Atlantique at St Nazaire in 1967. Initially assigned to the aforementioned East African run, her passenger quarters were divided between 100 in first class, 100 in second class and 118 in third class. Vincent Messina was a passenger during one of her cruises in 1984.

The *Yaohua* was not like a cruise ship in the traditional way, since lectures mostly replaced the standard entertainment forms. She had a very comfortable, almost Old World atmosphere about her, which included dark wood panelling, despite her being built as recently as 1966. She had been especially refitted for cruising [in 1983] and all of the earlier third class dormitory space was closed off. She was restyled for only 180 passengers, all of them in refurbished cabins. The Chinese were so proud of her cleanliness, for example, that her kitchens were open almost constantly for inspection. The bridge was also open very often. I especially recall the excellent Chinese cuisine. We had only fifty-seven passengers on our cruise, from Hong Kong to Xiamen and then to Shanghai. She had been chartered to Salen-Lindblad, but soon after, the Chinese suddenly increased the charter rates and this arrangement was terminated.

Also cruising for the Chinese, under charter, mostly from Australia (for Burns, Philp & Co), was the 14,200-ton *Minghua*. She sailed from Sydney mostly, to the nearby South Pacific islands as well as the Far East and Hawaii. She, also built by Chantiers de L'Atlantique at St Nazaire, joined the Chinese in 1973 and was used initially on the East African run. She had been commissioned in 1962 as the *Ancerville* and sailed for Compagnie de Navigation Paquet, mostly on the Marseilles–West Africa route and also for some cruising. At this time her accommodation was arranged for 171 in first class, 346 in tourist class and 253 in third class. Though she later terminated

A gathering of three Japanese passenger ships at Tokyo on 25 December 1981: the *Shin Sakura Maru* (left), *Sakura* (centre) and *Nippon Maru* (right).

Y Fukawa

her Australian cruise services, it is possible that she and the *Yaohua* will reappear in cruise listings, probably under charter to Western tourist agencies.

MITSUI-OSK LINES

NIPPON MARU AND SHIN SAKURA MARU

Though they have produced an extensive fleet of large ferries and even some smaller 'internal' cruise ships, only two Japanese-flag liners for overseas services are

Rebuilt considerably since her days as a floating industrial trade fair, the *Shin Sakura Maru* was fitted with 550 passenger berths for Pacific cruising.

included here: the 9700-ton *Nippon Maru* and the 16,400-ton *Shin Sakura Maru*. Both sail mostly from Yokohama on government charter cruises to nearby Far Eastern ports, the Pacific islands and on the occasional voyage to Hawaii.

The 532-passenger *Nippon Maru* was built at Split in Yugoslavia, in 1962, for Brazilian owners as the *Rosa da Fonseca*. She was used not only for South American coastal services, but for periodic cruising as well, including a summer-time stint in 1965 for New York–Bermuda cruises. She was later sold in 1975 to Panamanian buyers, the Cosmos Passenger Service, and renamed *Seven Seas* for a four-year charter to the Mitsui-OSK Lines. She was bought outright two years later and placed under the Japanese flag as the *Nippon Maru*.

The *Shin Sakura Maru* was delivered in 1972, by the Mitsubishi Heavy Industries' yard at Kobe. Fitted with ninety-two first class passenger berths for periodic use in commercial service, she was chartered mostly to JIFF, the Japan Industrial Floating Fair, and used in worldwide trade exhibition service. She was rebuilt in 1981, mostly for student cruising, with 550 passenger berths, which replaced many of the original cargo, storage and exhibit areas.

Y Fukawa

Appendix

SPECIFICATIONS
OF CRUISE
SHIPS

Achille Lauro (Lauro Line)
Built by De Schelde Shipyards, Flushing, Netherlands, 1939–47. 23,629 gross tons; 631 feet long; 82 feet wide. Sulzer diesels, twin screw. Service speed 22 knots. Approximately 1652 passengers maximum (reduced to about 900 for cruising).

Acropolis (Typaldos Lines) ex-*Santa Paula*
Built by Newport News Shipbuilding & Drydock Company, Newport News, Virginia, 1932. 9237 gross tons; 508 feet long; 72 feet wide. Steam turbines, twin screw. 450 one-class passengers.

Aivazovsky (Soviet Union)
Built by Ateliers et Chantiers Dubigeon-Normandie, Nantes, France, 1976. 7127 gross tons; 400 feet long; 58 feet wide. Pielstick diesels, twin screw. Service speed 18 knots. 328 passengers.

Alcoa Cavalier (Alcoa Steamship Company)
Built by Oregon Shipbuilding Corporation, Portland, Oregon, 1947. 8481 gross tons; 455 feet long; 62 feet wide. Steam turbines, single screw. Service speed 16½ knots. 95 first class passengers.

Alcoa Clipper (Alcoa Steamship Company) – see *Alcoa Cavalier*

Alexandr Pushkin (Soviet Union)
Built by Mathias-Thesen Werft Shipyard, Wismar, East Germany, 1965. 19,860 gross tons; 577 feet long; 77 feet wide. Sulzer diesels, twin screw. Service speed 20 knots. 666 passengers.

Amerikanis (Chandris Lines) ex-*Kenya Castle*
Built by Harland & Wolff Limited, Belfast, Northern Ireland, 1952. 16,485 gross tons; 576 feet long; 74 feet wide. Steam turbines, twin screw. Service speed 17½ knots. 910 cruise passengers.

Ancon (Panama Line)
Built by Bethlehem Steel Company, Quincy, Massachusetts, 1939. 9978 gross tons; 493 feet long; 64 feet wide. Steam turbines, twin screw. Service speed 17½ knots. 216 one-class passengers.

Andes (Royal Mail Lines)
Built by Harland & Wolff Limited, Belfast, Northern Ireland, 1939. 26,860 gross tons; 669 feet long; 83 feet wide. Steam turbines, twin screw. Service speed 21 knots. 500 first class passengers.

Andrea C. (Costa Line)
Built by Todd-California Shipbuilding Corporation, Richmond, California, 1942. 8604 gross tons; 467 feet long; 57 feet wide. Fiat diesel, single screw. Service speed 16 knots. 482 cruise passengers maximum.

Angelina Lauro (Lauro Line) ex-*Oranje*
Built by Netherlands Shipbuilding Corporation, Amsterdam, Netherlands, 1939. 24,377 gross tons; 672 feet long; 83 feet wide. Sulzer diesels, triple screw. Service speed 21½ knots. 1616 passengers, maximum; approximately 900 one-class cruise passengers.

Ankara (Turkish Maritime Lines)
Built by Newport News Shipbuilding & Drydock Company, Newport News, Virginia, 1927. 6178 gross tons; 409 feet long; 62 feet wide. Steam turbines, twin screw. Service speed 18 knots. 406 passengers, maximum.

Anna C. (Costa Line)
Built by Lithgows Limited, Glasgow, Scotland, 1929. 12,030 gross tons; 524 feet long; 65 feet wide. Fiat diesels, twin screw. Service speed 20 knots. 1066 passengers, maximum.

Aquarius (Hellenic Mediterranean Lines)
Built by United Shipyards, Perama, Greece, 1972. 4800 gross tons; 340 feet long; 45 feet wide. Diesels, twin screw. Service speed 19 knots. 280 first class passengers.

Arcadia (P&O-Orient Lines)
Built by John Brown & Company Limited, Clydebank, Scotland, 1954. 29,734 gross tons; 721 feet long; 91 feet wide. Steam turbines, twin screw. Service speed 22 knots. 1382 passengers (647 first class, 735 tourist class).

Argentina (Moore McCormack Lines)
Built by Ingalls Shipbuilding Corporation, Pascagoula, Mississippi, 1958. 23,500 gross tons; 617 feet long; 86 feet wide. Steam turbines, twin screw. Service speed 23 knots. 553 first class passengers.

Argonaut (Epirotiki Lines)
Built by Krupp Shipyards, Kiel, West Germany, 1929. 4007 gross tons; 306 feet long; 46 feet wide. Krupp diesels, twin screw. Service speed 15 knots. 220 cruise passengers.

Ariadne (Eastern Steamship Lines)
Built by Swan, Hunter & Wigham Richardson Limited, Newcastle, England, 1951. 6644 gross tons; 454 feet long; 58 feet wide. Steam turbines, single screw. Service speed 18 knots. 239 one-class passengers.

Ariane (Chandris Lines) – see *Ariadne*

Arkadia (Greek Line)
Built by Vickers-Armstrongs Shipbuilders Ltd, Newcastle, England, 1931. 20,259 gross tons; 590 feet long; 84 feet wide. Steam turbo-electric, quadruple screw. Service speed 19 knots. 1300 passengers (150 first class, 1150 tourist class).

Ascania (Grimaldi-Siosa Lines)
Built by Ateliers et Chantiers de la Loire, St Nazaire, France, 1926. 9536 gross tons; 490 feet long; 60 feet wide. Steam turbines, twin screw. Service speed 16 knots. 1247 maximum passengers.

Astor (HADAG)
Built by HDW Shipyards, Hamburg, West Germany, 1981. 18,835 gross tons; 535 feet long; 73 feet wide. M.A.N. type diesels, twin screw. Service speed 18 knots. Approximately 500 one-class passengers.

Atalante (Mediterranean Sun Lines) ex-*Tahitien*
Built by the Naval Dockyard, Brest, France, 1953. 12,614 gross tons; 549 feet long; 68 feet wide. Burmeister & Wain diesels, twin screw. Service speed 17 knots. 659 passengers.

Athinai (Typaldos Lines) – see *Acropolis*

Atlantica (Typaldos Lines) ex-*Colombie*
Built by Ateliers et Chantiers de France, Dunkirk, France, 1931. 13,803 gross tons; 508 feet long; 67 feet wide. Steam turbines, twin screw. Service speed 15½ knots. Approximately 900 cruise passengers.

Atlantis (Chandris Lines) ex-*President Roosevelt*
Built by the Federal Shipbuilding & Drydock Company, Kearny, New Jersey, 1944. 24,178 gross tons; 622 feet long; 75 feet wide. Steam turbines, twin screw. Service speed 20 knots. 962 cruise passengers, maximum.

Atlantis (K Lines)
Built by Cantieri Riuniti dell'Adriatico Shipyard, Monfalcone, Italy, 1965. 5000 gross tons; 318 feet long; 52 feet wide. Sulzer diesels, twin screw. Service speed 17 knots. 322 cruise passengers.

Atlas (Epirotiki Lines) ex-*Ryndam*
Built by Wilton-Fijenoord Shipyard, Schiedam, the Netherlands, 1951. 15,051 gross tons; 510 feet long; 69 feet wide. Steam turbines, single screw. Service speed 16 knots. 731 cruise passengers.

Ausonia (Adriatica Line)
Built by Cantieri Riuniti dell'Adriatico Shipyard, Monfalcone, Italy, 1957. 11,879 gross tons; 522 feet long; 70 feet wide. Steam turbines, twin screw. Service speed 20 knots. 690 cruise passengers.

Australis (Chandris Lines) ex-*America*
Built by Newport News Shipbuilding & Drydock Company, Newport News, Virginia, 1940. 34,449 gross tons; 723 feet long; 93 feet wide. Steam turbines, twin screw. Service speed 20 knots. 2258 passengers, maximum.

Azerbaydzhan (Soviet Union)
Built by Wartsila Shipyards, Turku, Finland, 1975–76. 13,200 gross tons; 511 feet long; 65 feet wide. Pielstick diesels, twin screw. Service speed 22 knots. 504 cruise passengers.

Bahama Star (Eastern Steamship Lines)
Built by Bethlehem Steel Corporation, Quincy, Massachusetts, 1931. 7114 gross tons; 466 feet long; 60 feet wide. Steam turbines, single screw. Service speed 15 knots. 735 first class passengers.

Belorussiya (Soviet Union) – see *Azerbaydzhan*

Bergensfjord (Norwegian America Line) later *De Grasse, Rasa Sayang, Golden Moon* and *Rasa Sayang*
Built by Swan, Hunter & Wigham Richardson Limited, Wallsend-on-Tyne, England, 1956. 18,739 gross tons; 578 feet long; 72 feet wide. Stork diesels, twin screw. Service speed 20 knots. 878 passengers, maximum; 420 on cruise voyages.

Berlin (Peter Deilmann Company)
Built by HDW Shipyards, Kiel, West Germany, 1980. 8000 gross tons; 402 feet long; 64 feet wide. Diesels, twin screw. Service speed 18 knots. 275 cruise passengers.

Bermuda Star (Bahama Cruise Lines) – see *Argentina*

Bernina (Adriatica Line)
Built by Ansaldo Shipyards, Leghorn, Italy, 1959. 4400 gross tons; 385 feet long; 54 feet wide. Fiat diesels, twin screw. Service speed 16 knots. 81 first class passengers.

Bianca C. (Costa Line)
Built by Constructions Navales, La Ciotat, France, 1939–49. 18,427 gross tons; 594 feet long; 75 feet wide. Sulzer diesels, triple screw. Service speed 21 knots. 1232 passengers, maximum.

Black Prince (Fred Olsen Line)
Built by Lubecker-Flenderweke Shipyard, Lubeck, West Germany, 1966. 9499 gross tons; 462 feet long; 68 feet wide. Diesel, twin screw. Service speed 22 knots. 591 passengers.

Black Watch (Fred Olsen Line) – see *Black Prince*

Blenheim (Fred Olsen Line)
Built by Upper Clyde Shipbuilders Limited, Clydebank, Scotland, 1970. 10,736 gross tons; 490 feet long; 68 feet wide. Pielstick diesels, twin screw. Service speed 22½ knots. 1107 passengers, maximum.

Brasil (Moore McCormack Lines) – see *Argentina*

Brennero (Adriatica Line) – see *Bernina*

Bretagne (Transports Maritimes)
Built by Chantiers et Ateliers de St Nazaire, France, 1952. 16,355 gross tons; 581 feet long; 73 feet wide. Steam turbines, twin screw. Service speed 19 knots. Approximately 1000 passengers for cruising.

Britanis (Chandris Lines)
Built by Bethlehem Steel Corporation, Quincy, Massachusetts, 1932. 18,254 gross tons; 638 feet long; 79 feet wide. Steam turbines, twin screw. Service speed 20 knots. 1632 one-class passengers.

Canberra (P&O Lines)
Built by Harland & Wolff Limited, Belfast, Northern Ireland, 1961. 45,733 gross tons; 818 feet long; 102 feet wide. Steam turbo-electric, twin screw. Service speed 27½ knots. 2272 passengers (556 or 596 first class, 1616 or 1716 tourist class).

Caribia (Grimaldi-Siosa Lines) ex-*Vulcania*
Built by Cantieri Navale Triestino, Monfalcone, Italy, 1928. 24,496 gross tons; 631 feet long; 80 feet wide. Fiat diesels, twin screw. Service speed 21 knots. 1437 passengers (337 first class, 368 cabin class, 732 tourist class).

Carina (Chandris Cruises)
Built by William Denny & Brothers, Dumbarton, Scotland, 1930. 4055 gross tons; 330 feet long; 51 feet wide. Steam turbines, twin screw. Service speed 19 knots. 200 passengers.

Carla C. (Costa Line)
Built by Ateliers et Chantiers de France, Dunkirk, France, 1952. 19,975 gross tons; 600 feet long; 80 feet wide. Diesels, twin screw. Service speed 21 knots. 754 cruise passengers.

Carmania (Cunard Line) later *Leonid Sobinov*
Built by John Brown & Company Limited, Clydebank, Scotland, 1954. 22,600 gross tons; 608 feet long; 80 feet wide. Steam turbines, twin screw. Service speed 19½ knots. 881 passengers.

Carnivale (Carnival Cruise Lines) ex-*Queen Anna Maria*
Built by Fairfield Shipbuilding & Engineering Company, Glasgow, Scotland, 1956. 21,716 gross tons; 640 feet long; 85 feet wide. Steam turbines, twin screw. Service speed 21 knots. 950 cruise passengers (1350 berths maximum).

Caronia (Cunard Line)
Built by John Brown & Company Limited, Clydebank, Scotland, 1948. 34,172 gross tons; 715 feet long; 91 feet wide. Steam turbines, twin screw. Service speed 22 knots. 932 passengers (581 first class, 351 cabin class).

Celebration (Carnival Cruise Lines)
Built by Kockums Shipyard, Malmo, Sweden, 1987. 48,000 gross tons; 750 feet long; 94 feet wide. Sulzer diesels, twin screw. Service speed 22 knots. 1850 passengers, maximum.

Chusan (P&O Lines)
Built by Vickers-Armstrongs Shipbuilders Limited, Barrow-in-Furness, England, 1950. 24,215 gross tons; 672 feet long; 85 feet wide. Steam turbines, twin screw. Service speed 22 knots. 1026 passengers (475 first class, 551 tourist class).

Columbus C. (Costa Line) ex-*Europa*, ex-*Kungsholm*
Built by De Schelde Shipyards, Flushing, Netherlands, 1953. 21,141 gross tons; 600 feet long; 77 feet wide. Burmeister & Wain type diesels, twin screw. Service speed 19 knots. 802 passengers, maximum.

Constellation (K Lines)
Built by Brodogradiliste Uljanik Shipyard, Pula, Yugoslavia, 1962. 12,433 gross tons; 492 feet long; 66 feet wide. Diesels, twin screw. Service speed 19 knots. 480 passengers.

Constitution (American Hawaii Cruises)
Built by Bethlehem Steel Corporation, Quincy, Massachusetts, 1951. 30,293 gross tons; 683 feet long; 89 feet wide. Steam turbines, twin screw. Service speed 23 knots. 1100 passengers, maximum.

Coral Princess (China Navigation Company)
Built by Compania Euskalduna, Bilbao, Spain, 1962. 9639 gross tons; 478 feet long; 61 feet wide. Burmeister & Wain type diesels, twin screw. Service speed 17 knots. 480 passengers.

Costa Riviera (Costa Line)
Built by Cantieri Riuniti dell'Adriatico, Monfalcone, Italy, 1963. 31,500 gross tons; 702 feet long; 94 feet wide. Steam turbines, twin screw. Service speed 24 knots. 984 cruise passengers.

Cristobal (Panama Line) – see *Ancon*

Cunard Adventurer (Cunard Line)
Built by Rotterdam Drydock Company, Rotterdam, the Netherlands, 1971. 14,155 gross tons; 484 feet long; 71 feet wide. Diesels, twin screw. Service speed 20½ knots. 806 first class passengers.

Cunard Ambassador (Cunard Line) – see *Cunard Adventurer*

Cunard Countess (Cunard Line)
Built by Burmeister & Wain Shipyards, Copenhagen, Denmark and then completed by Industrie Navali Merchaniche Affine Shipyard, La Spezia, Italy, 1976. 17,495 gross tons; 536 feet long; 74 feet wide. B & W diesels, twin screw. Service speed 20½ knots. 750 cruise passengers.

Cunard Princess (Cunard Line) – see *Cunard Countess*

Dalmatia (Jadrolinija)
Built by Brodogadiliste Uljanik Shipyard, Pula, Yugoslavia, 1965. 5651 gross tons; 383 feet long; 50 feet wide. Sulzer diesels, twin screw. Service speed 19 knots. 316 cruise passengers, maximum.

Danae (Carras Cruises/Costa Line)
Built by Harland & Wolff Limited, Belfast, Northern Ireland, 1955 – for specifications see *Daphne*.

Daphne (Carras Cruises/Costa Line)
Built by Swan, Hunter & Wigham Richardson Limited, Newcastle, England, 1955. 16,310 gross tons; 533 feet long; 70 feet wide. Doxford diesels, twin screw. Service speed 17 knots. Approximately 500 cruise passengers.

Del Mar (Delta Line)
Built by Ingalls Shipbuilding Corporation, Pascagoula, Mississippi, 1946–47. 10,073 gross tons; 495 feet long; 70 feet wide. Steam turbines, single screw. Service speed 16½ knots. 119 first class passengers.

Del Norte (Delta Line) – see *Del Mar*

Delos (Efthymiadis Lines)
Built by Ateliers et Chantiers de Bretagne, Nantes, France, 1951. 4500 gross tons; 373 feet long; 49 feet wide. Steam turbines, single screw. Service speed 16 knots. 450 passengers.

Del Sud (Delta Line) – see *Del Mar*

Devonia (British India Line)
Built by Fairfield Shipbuilding & Engineering Company, Glasgow, Scotland, 1939. 12,796 gross tons; 517 feet long; 63 feet wide. Sulzer diesels, twin screw. Service speed 13 knots. 1028 passengers (194 adults, 834 students).

Dimitri Shostakovich (Soviet Union)
Built by Stocznia Szczecinska Shipyard, Poland, 1980. 9878 gross tons; 440 feet long; 70 feet wide. Sulzer diesels, twin screw. Service speed 19 knots. 212 cabin passengers, 989 deck passengers.

Doric (Home Lines) ex-*Hanseatic*, ex-*Shalom*, later *Royal Odyssey*
Built by Chantiers de L'Atlantique Shipyard, St Nazaire, France, 1964. 25,320 gross tons; 629 feet long; 82 feet wide. Steam turbines, twin screw. Service speed 20 knots. 945 cruise passengers, maximum.

Dunera (British India Line)
Built by Barclay Curle & Company, Glasgow, Scotland, 1937. 12,615 gross tons; 517 feet long; 63 feet wide. Doxford diesels, twin screw. Service speed 14 knots. 1022 passengers (188 adults, 834 students).

Ellinis (Chandris Lines)
Built by Bethlehem Steel Corporation, Quincy, Massachusetts, 1932. 24,351 gross tons; 642 feet long; 79 feet wide. Steam turbines, twin screw. Service speed 20 knots. 1642 all tourist class passengers.

Emerald Seas (Eastern Steamship Lines) – see *Atlantis* (Chandris)

Empress of Britain (Canadian Pacific) – see *Carnivale*

Empress of Canada (Canadian Pacific) – see *Mardi Gras*

Empress of England (Canadian Pacific) – see *Ocean Monarch* (Shaw Savill)

Enotria (Adriatica Line)
Built by Ansaldo Shipyards, Leghorn, Italy, 1951. 5173 gross tons; 383 feet long; 54 feet wide. Fiat diesels, twin screw. Service speed 16 knots. 268 passengers (120 first class, 148 tourist class).

Enrico C. (Costa Line) ex-*Provence*
Built by Swan, Hunter & Wigham Richardson Limited, Newcastle, England, 1951. 13,607 gross tons; 580 feet long; 73 feet wide. Steam turbines, twin screw. Service speed 18 knots. 1198 passengers, maximum.

Eugenio C. (Costa Line)
Built by Cantieri Riuniti dell'Adriatico, Monfalcone, Italy, 1966. 30,567 gross tons; 712 feet long; 96 feet wide. Steam turbines, twin screw. Service speed 27 knots. 1636 passengers, maximum.

Europa (1953) (Hapag-Lloyd) – see *Kungsholm* (1953)

Europa (1981) (Hapag-Lloyd)
Built by Bremer-Vulkan Shipyards, Bremen, West Germany, 1981. 33,819 gross tons; 655 feet long; 92 feet wide. M.A.N. type diesels, twin screw. Service speed 21 knots. 758 first class passengers.

Evangeline (Eastern Steamship Lines)
Built by William Cramp & Sons Shipbuilding & Engine Building Company, Philadelphia, Pennsylvania, 1927. 5002 gross tons; 379 feet long; 56 feet wide. Steam turbines, twin screw. Service speed 18 knots. Approximately 350 one-class passengers.

Fairsea (Sitmar Cruises) ex-*Carinthia*
Built by John Brown & Company Limited, Clydebank, Scotland, 1956. 21,916 gross tons; 608 feet long; 80 feet wide. Steam turbines, twin screw. Service speed 19½ knots. 910 cruise passengers.

Fairsky (Sitmar Cruises)
Built by CNIM Shipyards, La Seyne, France, 1984. 46,314 gross tons; 790 feet long; 90 feet wide. Steam turbines, twin screw. Service speed 19 knots. 1212 cruise passengers.

Fairstar (Sitmar Cruises)
Built by Fairfield Shipbuilding & Engineering Company, Glasgow, Scotland, 1957. 21,620 gross tons; 609 feet long; 78 feet wide. Steam turbines, twin screw. Service speed 20 knots. 1400 cruise passengers.

Fairwind (Sitmar Cruises) ex-*Sylvania* – see *Fairsea*

Fantasia (Chandris Cruises)
Built by Harland & Wolff Limited, Belfast, Northern Ireland, 1935. 4595 gross tons; 359 feet long; 52 feet wide. Steam turbines, twin screw. Service speed 20 knots. 426 cruise passengers.

Federico C. (Costa Line)
Built by Ansaldo Shipyards, Genoa, Italy, 1958. 20,416 gross tons; 606 feet long; 79 feet wide. Steam turbines, twin screw. Service speed 21 knots. 1279 passengers.

Festivale (Carnival Cruise Lines)
Built by John Brown & Company Limited, Clydebank, Scotland, 1961. 38,175 gross tons; 760 feet long; 90 feet wide. Steam turbines, twin screw. Service speed 22½ knots. 1432 cruise passengers.

Fiesta (Chandris Cruises)
Built by Cammell Laird & Company Limited, Birkenhead, England, 1946. 3659 gross tons; 345 feet long; 47 feet wide. Steam turbines, twin screw. Service speed 20 knots. 378 cruise passengers.

Fiorita (Chandris Cruises)
Built by John Brown & Company Limited, Clydebank, Scotland, 1950. 5092 gross tons; 380 feet long; 50 feet wide. Steam turbines, twin screw. Service speed 20 knots. 490 cruise passengers.

Feodor Shalyapin (Soviet Union) – see *Franconia*

Flavia (Costa Line)
Built by John Brown & Company Limited, Clydebank, Scotland, 1947. 15,465 gross tons; 556 feet long; 70 feet wide. Steam turbines, twin screw. Service speed 18 knots. 1120 maximum passengers.

Florida (Peninsular & Occidental Steamship Company)
Built by Newport News Shipbuilding & Drydock Company, Newport News, Virginia, 1931. 4956 gross tons; 388 feet long; 56 feet wide. Steam turbines, twin screw. Service speed 19 knots. Approximately 500 one-class passengers.

Franca C. (Costa Line)
Built by Newport News Shipbuilding & Drydock Company, Newport News, Virginia, 1914. 6822 gross tons; 428 feet long; 55 feet wide. Fiat diesel, single screw. Service speed 15 knots. 367 cruise passengers.

Franconia (Cunard Line)
Built by John Brown & Company Limited, Clydebank, Scotland, 1955. 22,637 gross tons; 608 feet long; 80 feet wide. Steam turbines, twin screw. Service speed 19½ knots. 847 passengers, maximum.

Funchal (Compania Transportes Maritimos)
Built by Elsinore Shipbuilding & Engineering Company, Elsinore, Denmark, 1961. 9824 gross tons; 501 feet long; 63 feet wide. Steam turbines, twin screw. Service speed 20 knots. Approximately 500 passengers.

Galaxy (K Lines)
Built by Harland & Wolff Limited, Belfast, Northern Ireland, 1957. 5500 gross tons; 342 feet long; 52 feet wide. Diesels, twin screw. Service speed 18 knots. 349 cruise passengers.

Galileo (Chandris Lines)
Built by Cantieri Riuniti dell'Adriatico, Monfalcone, Italy, 1963. 27,907 gross tons; 702 feet long; 94 feet wide. Steam turbines, twin screw. Service speed 24 knots. Approximately 1100 cruise passengers.

Georg Ots (Soviet Union) – see *Dimitri Shostakovich*

Golden Odyssey (Royal Cruise Lines)
Built by Elsinore Shipbuilding & Engineering Co, Elsinore, Denmark, 1974. 6757 gross tons; 427 feet long; 65 feet wide. Diesels, twin screw. Service speed 22½ knots. 509 cruise passengers, maximum.

Gripsholm (Swedish-American Line)
Built by Ansaldo Shipyard, Genoa, Italy, 1957. 23,191 gross tons; 631 feet long; 82 feet wide. Gotaverken diesels, twin screw. Service speed 19 knots. 842 maximum passengers.

Gruziya (Soviet Union) – see *Azerbaydzhan*

Himalaya (P&O-Orient Lines)
Built by Vickers-Armstrongs Shipbuilding Limited, Barrow-in-Furness, England, 1949. 27,955 gross tons; 709 feet long; 91 feet wide. Steam turbines, twin screw. Service speed 22 knots. 1159 passengers (758 first class, 401 tourist class).

Holiday (Carnival Cruise Lines)
Built by Aalborg Vaerft Shipyards, Aalborg, Denmark, 1985. 46,052 gross tons; 725 feet long; 92 feet wide. Sulzer diesels, twin screw. Service speed 22 knots. 1760 cruise passengers, maximum.

Homeric (1931) (Home Lines)
Built by Bethlehem Steel Company, Quincy, Massachusetts, 1931. 24,907 gross tons; 638 feet long; 79 feet wide. Steam turbines, twin screw. Service speed 20 knots. 1243 passengers, maximum; 730 all-first class for cruises.

Homeric (1986) (Home Lines)
Built by Joseph L Meyer Shipyards, Papenburg, West Germany, 1986. 42,092 gross tons; 668 feet long; 96 feet wide. M.A.N.-Burmeister & Wain diesels, twin screw. Service speed 22 knots. 1085 cruise passengers.

Iberia (P&O Lines)
Built by Harland & Wolff Limited, Belfast, Northern Ireland, 1954. 29,614 gross tons; 719 feet long; 91 feet wide. Steam turbines, twin screw. Service speed 22 knots. 1406 passengers (673 first class, 733 tourist class).

Illiria (Adriatica Line)
Built by Cantieri Navale Pellegrino, Naples, Italy, 1962. 3763 gross tons; 333 feet long; 48 feet wide. Fiat diesels, twin screw. Service speed 17 knots. 180 cruise passengers.

Independence (American Hawaii Cruises) – see *Constitution*

Irpinia (Grimaldi-Siosa Lines)
Built by Swan, Hunter & Wigham Richardson Ltd, Newcastle, England, 1929. 13,204 gross tons; 537 feet long; 67 feet wide. Fiat diesels, twin screw. Service speed 16 knots. 1181 passengers, maximum.

Island Princess (Princess Cruises) ex-*Island Venture*
Built by Nordseewerke Shipyard, Rheinstahl, West Germany, 1972. 19,907 gross tons; 550 feet long; 80 feet wide. Fiat diesels, twin screw. Service speed 20 knots. 646 cruise passengers.

Istra (Jadrolinija) – see *Dalmatia*

Italia (Home Lines)
Built by Blohm & Voss Shipbuilders, Hamburg, West Germany, 1928. 21,532 gross tons; 609 feet long; 78 feet wide. Burmeister & Wain diesels, twin screw. Service speed 17 knots. 680 cruise passengers.

Italia (Costa Line)
Built by Cantieri Navali Feszegi Shipyards, Trieste, Italy, 1967. 12,219 gross tons; 490 feet long; 68 feet wide. Sulzer diesels, twin screw. Service speed 20 knots. 476 cruise passengers.

Ivan Franko (1964) (Soviet Union) – see *Alexandr Pushkin*

Jason (Epirotiki Lines)
Built by Cantieri Riuniti dell'Adriatico, Monfalcone, Italy, 1965. 3719 gross tons; 318 feet long; 53 feet wide. Sulzer diesels, twin screw. Service speed 17 knots. 298 cruise passengers.

Jubilee (1986) (Carnival Cruise Lines) – see *Celebration*

Jupiter (Epirotiki Lines)
Built by Chantiers de L'Atlantique, St Nazaire, France, 1961. 7811 gross tons; 415 feet long; 65 feet wide. S.E.M.T.-Pielstick diesel, single screw. Service speed 16 knots. 473 cruise passengers.

Kareliya (Soviet Union) – see *Azerbaydzhan*

Kazakhstan (Soviet Union) – see *Azerbaydzhan*

Kentavros (K Lines)
Built by Puget Sound Navy Yard, Seattle, Washington, 1941. 2805 gross tons; 311 feet long; 41 feet wide. Diesel, twin screw. Service speed 15½ knots. 220 cruise passengers.

Konstantin Simonov (Soviet Union) – see *Dimitri Shostakovich*

Kungsholm (1953) (Swedish-American Line)
Built by De Schelde Shipyards, Flushing, Netherlands, 1953. 21,141 gross tons; 600 feet long; 77 feet wide. Burmeister & Wain diesels, twin screw. Service speed 19 knots. 802 maximum passengers; 400 cruise passengers.

Kungsholm (1966) (Swedish-American Line)
Built by John Brown & Company Limited, Clydebank, Scotland, 1966. 26,678 gross tons; 660 feet long; 86 feet wide. Gotaverken diesels, twin screw. Service speed 21 knots. 750 passengers; 450 during cruises.

Lakonia (Greek Line)
Built by Netherlands Shipbuilding Company, Amsterdam, Holland, 1930. 20,314 gross tons; 609 feet long; 75 feet wide. Sulzer diesels, twin screw. Service speed 16½ knots. 1210 one-class passengers.

Leonardo da Vinci (Italian Line)
Built by Ansaldo Shipyards, Genoa, Italy. 33,340 gross tons; 761 feet long; 92 feet wide. Steam turbines, twin screw. Service speed 23 knots. 1326 passengers, maximum.

Leonid Sobinov (Soviet Union) – see *Carmania*

Lev Tolstoy (Soviet Union) – see *Dimitri Shostakovich*

Liberte (American Hawaii Cruises) – see *Brasil*

Lurline (Matson Line)
Built by Bethlehem Steel Company, Quincy, Massachusetts, 1932. 18,564 gross tons; 631 feet long; 70 feet wide. Steam turbines, twin screw. Service speed 22 knots. 760 first class passengers.

Lurline (Matson Line) ex-*Monterey*, ex-*Matsonia*
Built by Bethlehem Steel Company, Quincy, Massachusetts, 1932. 18,655 gross tons; 638 feet long; 79 feet wide. Steam turbines, twin screw. Service speed 20 knots. 761 first class passengers.

Mardi Gras (Carnival Cruise Lines)
Built by Vickers-Armstrongs Shipbuilders Limited, Newcastle, England, 1961. 27,250 gross tons; 650 feet long; 87 feet wide. Steam turbines, twin screw. Service speed 21 knots. 1240 maximum cruise passengers.

Mariposa (Matson Line)
Built by Bethlehem Steel Company, Quincy, Massachusetts, 1953. 14,812 gross tons; 563 feet long; 76 feet wide. Steam turbines, single screw. Service speed 20 knots. 365 first class passengers.

Matsonia (Matson Line) – see *Lurline*, ex-*Monterey*

Maxim Gorky (Soviet Union) ex-*Hamburg*
Built by Deutsche Werft, Hamburg, West Germany, 1969. 24,981 gross tons; 642 feet long; 90 feet wide. Steam turbines, twin screw. Service speed 23½ knots. 790 cruise passengers, maximum.

Melina (Efthymiadis Lines) ex-*Azrou*
Built by Ateliers et Chantiers de Bretagne, Nantes, France, 1951. 4500 gross tons; 373 feet long; 49 feet wide. Steam turbines, single screw. Service speed 16 knots. Approximately 500 cruise passengers.

Mermoz (Paquet Lines)
Built by Chantiers de L'Atlantique, St Nazaire, France, 1957. 13,804 gross tons; 530 feet long; 66 feet wide. Burmeister & Wain type diesels, twin screw. Service speed 17 knots. 757 cruise passengers, maximum.

Messapia (Adriatica Line) – see *Enotria*

Meteor (Bergen Line)
Built by Aalborg Vaerft Shipyard, Aalborg, Denmark, 1955. 2856 gross tons; 297 feet long; 45 feet wide. Burmeister & Wain diesels, single screw. Service speed 17 knots. 147 first class passengers.

Michelangelo (Italian Line)
Built by Ansaldo Shipyards, Genoa, Italy, 1965. 45,911 gross tons; 902 feet long; 102 feet wide. Steam turbines, twin screw. Service speed 26½ knots. 1775 passengers (535 first class, 550 cabin class, 690 tourist class).

Mikhail Kalinin (Soviet Union)
Built Mathias-Thesen Werft, Wismar, East Germany, 1958–64 (series of sister ships). 4800 gross tons; 401 feet long; 52 feet wide. M.A.N. diesels, twin screw. Service speed 18 knots. 333 passengers.

Mikhail Lermontov (Soviet Union) 1971 – see *Alexandr Pushkin*

Mikhail Suslov (Soviet Union) 1980 – see *Dimitri Shostakovich*

Minghua (Chinese Government)
Built by Chantiers de L'Atlantique, St Nazaire, France, 1962. 14,225 gross tons; 549 feet long; 71 feet wide. B & W type diesels, twin screw. Service speed 22½ knots. Approximately 750 passengers.

Monterey (Matson Line)
Built by Bethlehem Steel Company, Sparrows Point, Maryland, 1952. 14,799 gross tons; 563 feet long; 76 feet wide. Steam turbines, single screw. Service speed 20 knots. 365 first class passengers.

Nassau (Incres Line)
Built by Sir W G Armstrong-Whitworth & Company Limited, Newcastle, England, 1923. 15,043 gross tons; 573 feet long; 72 feet wide. Steam turbines, twin screw. Service speed 17 knots. 617 first class passengers.

Neptune (Epirotiki Lines) – see *Meteor*

Nevasa (British India Line)
Built by Barclay Curle & Company Limited, Glasgow, Scotland, 1956. 20,746 gross tons; 609 feet long; 78 feet wide. Steam turbines, twin screw. Service speed 17½ knots. 1400 passengers (300 adults, 1100 students).

New Bahama Star (Eastern Steamship Lines)
Built by Deutsche Werft Shipyards, Hamburg, West Germany, 1957. 8312 gross tons; 487 feet long; 65 feet wide. Steam turbines, twin screw. Service speed 18 knots. 755 one-class passengers.

Nieuw Amsterdam (Holland-America Line)
Built by Rotterdam Drydock Company, Rotterdam, Holland, 1938. 36,667 gross tons; 758 feet long; 88 feet wide. Steam turbines, twin screw. Service speed 21 knots. 1187 passengers, maximum.

Nieuw Amsterdam (Holland-America Line)
Built by Chantiers de L'Atlantique, St Nazaire, France, 1983. 33,930 gross tons; 704 feet long; 90 feet wide. Sulzer diesels, twin screw. Service speed 21 knots. 1210 all-first class passengers.

Nippon Maru (Mitsui-OSK Lines)
Built by Split Brodogradiliste Shipyard, Split, Yugoslavia, 1962. 12,433 gross tons; 492 feet long; 62 feet wide. Krupp-Burmeister & Wain type diesels, twin screw. Service speed 19 knots. 532 one-class passengers.

Noordam (Holland-America Line)
1984 – see *Nieuw Amsterdam* (1983)

Nordic Prince (Royal Caribbean Cruise Lines)
Built by Wartsila Shipyards, Helsinki, Finland, 1971. 23,200 gross tons; 644 feet long; 78 feet wide. Sulzer-Wartsila diesels, twin screw. Service speed 21 knots. 1194 cruise passengers.

Northern Star (Shaw Savill Line)
Built by Vickers-Armstrongs Shipbuilders Limited, Newcastle, England, 1962. 24,731 gross tons; 650 feet long; 83 feet wide. Steam turbines, twin screw. Service speed 20 knots. 1437 tourist class passengers.

Norway (Norwegian Caribbean Lines)
Built by Chantiers de L'Atlantique, St Nazaire, France, 1956–61. 70,202 gross tons; 1035 feet long; 110 feet wide. Steam turbines, twin screw. Service speed 16 knots. 2100 cruise passengers.

Oceanic (Home Lines)
Built by Cantieri Riuniti dell'Adriatico, Monfalcone, Italy, 1965. 39,241 gross tons; 774 feet long; 96 feet wide. Steam turbines, twin screw. Service speed 26½ knots. 1600 cruise passengers, maximum.

Ocean Monarch (Furness-Bermuda Line)
Built by Vickers-Armstrongs Shipbuilders Limited, Newcastle, England, 1951. 13,654 gross tons; 516 feet long; 72 feet wide. Steam turbines, twin screw. Service speed 18 knots. 440 first class passengers.

Ocean Monarch (Shaw Savill Line)
ex-*Empress of England*
Built by Vickers-Armstrongs Shipbuilders Limited, Newcastle-upon-Tyne, England; 1957. 25,971 gross tons; 640 feet long; 85 feet wide. Steam turbines, twin screw. Service speed 20 knots. 1372 one-class passengers.

Oceanos (Epirotiki Lines)
Built by Forges et Chantiers de la Gironde, Gironde, France. 10,902 gross tons; 492 feet long; 64 feet wide. Burmeister & Wain diesels, twin screw. Service speed 17 knots. 500 cruise passengers.

Odessa (Soviet Union)
Built by Vickers Shipbuilders, Barrow-in-Furness, England, 1974. 13,758 gross tons; 447 feet long; 71 feet wide. Crossley-Pielstick diesels, twin screw. Service speed 19 knots. 525 cruise passengers.

Olympia (Greek Line)
Built by Alexander Stephen & Sons Limited, Glasgow, Scotland, 1953. 22,979 gross tons; 611 feet long; 79 feet wide. Steam turbines, twin screw. Service speed 22 knots. 1307 passengers maximum.

Orcades (P&O Lines)
Built by Vickers-Armstrongs Shipbuilders Limited, Barrow-in-Furness, England, 1948. 28,396 gross tons; 709 feet long; 90 feet wide. Steam turbines, twin screw. Service speed 22 knots. 1365 passengers (631 first class, 734 tourist class).

Oriana (P&O Lines)
Built by Vickers-Armstrongs Shipbuilders Limited, Barrow-in-Furness, England, 1960. 41,923 gross tons; 804 feet long; 97 feet wide. Steam turbines, twin screw. Servive speed 27½ knots. 2134 passengers (638 first class, 1496 tourist class).

Oriental Amiga (Orient Overseas Lines)
Built by Wilton-Fijenoord Shipyards, Schiedam, Holland, 1950. 11,195 gross tons; 494 feet long; 69 feet wide. Steam turbines, twin screw. Service speed 16½ knots. 61 one-class passengers.

Oriental Carnaval (Orient Overseas Lines)
Built by Vickers-Armstrongs Shipbuilders Limited, Newcastle, England, 1949. 19,567 gross tons; 609 feet long; 78 feet wide. Doxford diesels, twin screw. Service speed 16½ knots. 300 first class passengers.

Oriental Empress (Orient Overseas Lines) – see *President Wilson*

Oriental Esmeralda (Orient Overseas Lines)
Built by John Brown & Company Limited, Clydebank, Scotland, 1949. 19,567 gross tons; 609 feet long; 78 feet wide. Doxford diesels, twin screw. Service speed 16½ knots. 300 first class passengers.

Oriental Fantasia (Orient Overseas Lines)
Built by Wilton-Fijenoord Shipyards, Schiedam, Holland, 1957. 11,366 gross tons; 504 feet long; 69 feet wide. Steam turbines, twin screw. Service speed 16½ knots. 60 one-class passengers.

Oriental Hero (Orient Overseas Lines)
Built by Bremer-Vulkan Shipyards, Bremen, West Germany, 1953–54. 9000 gross tons; 538 feet long; 64 feet wide. M.A.N. diesels, single screw. Service speed 16½ knots. 86 one-class passengers.

Oriental Inventor (Orient Overseas Lines) – see *Oriental Hero*

Oriental Jade (Orient Overseas Lines)
Built by Bethlehem Steel Company, Sparrows Point, Maryland, 1944. 14,983 gross tons; 473 feet long; 66 feet wide. Steam turbines, single screw. Service speed 17 knots. 124 one-class passengers.

Oriental Lady (Orient Overseas Lines) – see *Oriental Hero*

Oriental Musician (Orient Overseas Lines) – see *Oriental Hero*

Oriental Pearl (Orient Overseas Lines) – see *Oriental Jade*

Oriental President (Orient Overseas Lines) – see *President Cleveland*

Oriental Rio (Orient Overseas Lines)
Built by John Brown & Company Limited, Clydebank, Scotland, 1951. 17,730 gross tons; 584 feet long; 75 feet wide. Doxford diesels, twin screw. Service speed 16½ knots. 229 one-class passengers.

Oriental Ruler (Orient Overseas Lines) – see *Oriental Hero*

Oriental Warrior (Orient Overseas Lines) – see *Oriental Hero*

Orion (K Lines)
Built by Ansaldo Shipyards, Leghorn, Italy, 1952. 6200 gross tons; 416 feet long; 55 feet wide. Steam turbines, twin screw. Service speed 17 knots. 335 one-class passengers.

Oronsay (P&O Lines)
Built by Vickers-Armstrongs Shipbuilders Ltd, Barrow-in-Furness, England, 1951. 27,632 gross tons; 709 feet long; 90 feet wide. Steam turbines, twin screw. Service speed 22 knots. 1416 passengers (612 first class, 804 tourist class).

Orpheus (Epirotiki Lines)
Built by Harland & Wolff Limited, Belfast, Northern Ireland, 1948. 5078 gross tons; 365 feet long; 50 feet wide. Diesel, twin screw. Service speed 15 knots. 350 cruise passengers.

Orsova (P&O Lines)
Built by Vickers-Armstrongs Shipbuilders Ltd, Barrow-in-Furness, England, 1954. 28,790 gross tons; 723 feet long; 90 feet wide. Steam turbines, twin screw. Service speed 22 knots. 1503 passengers (694 first class, 809 tourist class).

Oslofjord (Norwegian America Line)
Built by Netherlands Shipbuilding Company, Amsterdam, Holland, 1949. 16,844 gross tons; 577 feet long; 72 feet wide. Stork diesels, twin screw. Service speed 20 knots. 646 passengers, maximum.

Pacific Princess (Princess Cruises)
Built by Nordseewerke Shipyard, Rheinstahl, West Germany, 1971. 19,904 gross tons; 550 feet long; 80 feet wide. Fiat diesels, twin screw. Service speed 20 knots. 750 cruise passengers, maximum.

Panama (Panama Line) – see *Ancon*

Patra (Efthymiadis Lines)
Built by Brest Naval Dockyard, Brest, France, 1952. 10,900 gross tons; 492 feet long; 64 feet wide. Burmeister & Wain diesels, twin screw. Service speed 17 knots. 500 passengers.

Pearl of Scandinavia (Pearl Cruises)
Built by Wartsila Shipyards, Helsinki, Finland, 1967. 12,456 gross tons; 505 feet long; 67 feet wide. Sulzer-Wartsila diesels, twin screw. Service speed 22 knots. 509 cruise passengers.

Pegasus (Epirotiki Lines) – see *Sundancer*

President Cleveland (American President Lines)
Built by Bethlehem Steel Shipyard, Alameda, California, 1947. 18,962 gross tons; 609 feet long; 75 feet wide. Turbo-electric, twin screw. Service speed 20 knots. 511 cruise passengers, maximum.

President Hoover (American President Lines) – ex-*Panama*, see *Ancon*

President Monroe (American President Lines)
Built by Newport News Shipbuilding & Drydock Company, Newport News, Virginia, 1940. 9255 gross tons; 492 feet long; 70 feet wide. Steam turbines, single screw. Service speed 16½ knots. 96 first class passengers.

President Polk (American President Lines) – see *President Monroe*

President Roosevelt (American President Lines)
Built by Federal Shipbuilding & Drydock Company, Kearny, New Jersey, 1944. 18,920 gross tons; 622 feet long; 76 feet wide. Steam turbines, twin screw. Service speed 20 knots. 456 first class passengers.

President Wilson (American President Lines) – see *President Cleveland*

Prinsendam (Holland-America Line)
Built by De Merwede Shipyard, Hardinxveld, Holland, 1973. 8566 gross tons; 427 feet long; 62 feet wide. Werkspor diesel, twin screw. Service speed 21 knots. 374 cruise passengers.

Prinses Margriet (Holland-America Line)
Built by Der Merwede Shipyards, Hardinxveld, Holland, 1961. 9341 gross tons; 456 feet long; 61 feet wide. M.A.N. type diesels, single screw. Service speed 17 knots. 111 one-class passengers.

Provence (Transports Maritimes)
15,719 gross tons – see *Enrico C.*

Queen Anna Maria (Greek Line)
Built by Fairfield Shipbuilding & Engineering Co, Glasgow, Scotland, 1956. 21,716 gross tons; 640 feet long; 85 feet wide. Steam turbines, twin screw. Service speed 21 knots. 1254 passengers, maximum.

Queen Elizabeth 2 (Cunard Line)
Built by Upper Clyde Shipbuilders Limited (formerly John Brown & Company Limited), Clydebank, Scotland, 1969. 65,863 gross tons (later increased to 67,107); 963 feet long; 105 feet wide. Steam turbines, twin screw. Service speed 28½ knots. 1820 passengers, maximum.

Queen Frederica (Chandris Lines)
Built by William Cramp & Sons Ship & Engine Building Co, Philadelphia, Pennsylvania, 1927. 20,553 gross tons; 582 feet long; 83 feet wide. Steam turbines, twin screw. Service speed 21 knots. 1179 passengers, maximum.

Queen of Bermuda (Furness-Bermuda Line)
Built by Vickers-Armstrongs Shipbuilders Limited, Barrow-in-Furness, England, 1933. 22,501 gross tons (later increased to 22,552); 579 feet long (later increased to 590 feet); 77 feet wide. Steam turbo-electric, quadruple screw. 733 first class passengers.

Raffaello (Italian Line)
Built by Cantieri Riuniti dell' Adriatico Shipyard, Trieste, Italy, 1965. 45,933 gross tons; 902 feet long; 102 feet wide. Steam turbines, twin screw. Service speed 26½ knots. 1775 passengers.

Regent Sea (Regency Cruises)
17,391 gross tons – for other specifications see *Gripsholm*

Regina Magna (Chandris Cruises)
Built by Chantiers de L'Atlantique, St Nazaire, France, 1939. 32,336 gross tons; 699 feet long; 88 feet wide. Steam turbines, quadruple screw. Service speed 23 knots. 1122 maximum passengers.

Regina Maris (Peter Dielmann Company)
Built by Lubecker Flenderwerke AG, Lubeck, West Germany, 1966. 5813 gross tons; 390 feet long; 54 feet wide. Diesel, twin screw. Service speed 18 knots. 276 first class passengers.

Regina Prima (Chandris Cruises) ex-*Panama*, ex-*President Hoover*
Built by Bethlehem Steel Company, Quincy, Massachusetts, 1939. 10,603 gross tons; 493 feet long; 64 feet wide. Steam turbines, twin screw. Service speed 17½ knots. 600 cruise passengers.

Reina del Mar (Union-Castle Line)
Built by Harland & Wolff Limited, Belfast, Northern Ireland, 1956. 21,501 gross tons; 601 feet long; 78 feet wide. Steam turbines, twin screw. Service speed 18 knots. 1026 cruise passengers, maximum.

Renaissance (Paquet Lines)
Built by Chantiers de l'Atlantique, St Nazaire, France, 1966. 11,724 gross tons; 492 feet long; 69 feet wide. Burmeister & Wain type diesels, twin screw. Service speed 18½ knots, 375 first class passengers.

Rhapsody (Paquet Lines) – see *Statendam*

Romantica (Chandris Cruises)
Built by Blythswood Shipbuilding Company Limited, Glasgow, Scotland, 1936. 3743 gross tons; 326 feet long; 45 feet wide. Steam triple expansion, single screw. Service speed 13½ knots. 200 first class passengers.

Romanza (Chandris Cruises)
Built by Blohm & Voss Shipbuilders, Hamburg, Germany, 1939. 10,480 gross tons; 487 feet long; 60 feet wide. M.A.N. type diesel, single screw. Service speed 17 knots. 600 cruise passengers.

Rotterdam (Holland-America Line)
Built by Rotterdam Drydock Company, Rotterdam, Holland, 1959. 38,645 gross tons; 748 feet long; 94 feet wide. Steam turbines, twin screw. Service speed 20½ knots. 1356 passengers, maximum.

Royal Odyssey (Royal Cruise Lines)
17,884 gross tons – for other specifications see *Doric*

Royal Princess (Princess Cruises)
Built by Wartsila Shipyards, Helsinki, Finland, 1984. 44,348 gross tons; 761 feet long; 96 feet wide. Wartsila-Pielstick diesels, twin screw. Service speed 22 knots. 1260 cruise passengers.

Royal Viking Sea (Royal Viking Line)
Built by Wartsila Shipyards, Helsinki, Finland, 1973. 21,897 gross tons (later increased to 28,221 gross tons); 581 feet long (later increased to 674 feet); 83 feet wide. Wartsila-Sulzer diesels, twin screw. Service speed 21 knots. 758 passengers, maximum.

Royal Viking Sky (Royal Viking Line)
– see *Royal Viking Sea*

Royal Viking Star (Royal Viking Line)
Built 1972 – for specifications see *Royal Viking Sea*

Sagafjord (Norwegian America Line)
Built by Societe des Forges et Chantiers de la Mediterranee, Toulon, France, 1965. 24,002 gross tons; 615 feet long; 82 feet wide. Sulzer diesels, twin screw. Service speed 20 knots. 789 passengers, maximum.

San Giorgio (Adriatica Line)
Built by Cantieri Riuniti dell'Adriatico, Trieste, Italy, 1956. 4755 gross tons; 367 feet long; 51 feet wide. Fiat diesels, twin screw. Service speed 17 knots. 203 passengers (92 first class, 45 second class, 66 tourist class).

San Marco (Adriatica Line) – see *San Giorgio*

Santa Barbara (Grace Line)
Built by North Carolina Shipbuilding Corporation, Wilmington, North Carolina, 1946. 8357 gross tons; 459 feet long; 63 feet wide. Steam turbines, single screw. Service speed 16 knots. 52 first class passengers.

Santa Cecilia (Grace Line) – see *Santa Barbara*

Santa Clara (Grace Line)
Built by Federal Shipbuilding & Drydock Company, Kearny, New Jersey, 1946. 8710 gross tons; 459 feet long; 63 feet wide. Steam turbines, single screw. Service speed 16 knots. 52 first class passengers.

Santa Isabel (Grace Line) – see *Santa Barbara*

Santa Luisa (Grace Line) – see *Santa Barbara*

Santa Magdalena (Grace Line)
Built by Bethlehem Steel Corporation, Sparrows Point, Maryland, 1963. 14,442 gross tons; 547 feet long; 79 feet wide. Steam turbines, single screw. Service speed 20½ knots. 125 first class passengers, maximum.

Santa Margarita (Grace Line) – see *Santa Barbara*

Santa Maria (Grace Line) 1946 – see *Santa Barbara*

Santa Maria (Grace Line) 1964 – see *Santa Magdalena*

Santa Mariana (Grace Line) 1964 – see *Santa Magdalena*

Santa Mercedes (Grace Line) 1964 – see *Santa Magdalena*

Santa Monica (Grace Line) – see *Santa Clara*

Santa Paula (Grace Line)
Built by Newport News Shipbuilding & Drydock Company, Newport News, Virginia, 1958. 15,371 gross tons; 584 feet long; 84 feet wide. Steam turbines, twin screw. Service speed 20 knots. 300 first class passengers.

Santa Rosa (Grace Line) – see *Santa Paula*

Santa Sofia (Grace Line) – see *Santa Clara*

Sea Goddess I (Sea Goddess Cruises)
Built by Wartsila Shipyards, Helsinki, Finland, 1984. 4200 gross tons; 344 feet long; 58 feet wide. Diesel, twin screw. Service speed 18 knots. 116 first class passengers.

Sea Goddess II (Sea Goddess Cruises)
1985 – see *Sea Goddess I*

Sea Princess (P&O Cruises) – see *Kungsholm* (1966)

Shin Sakura Maru (Mitsui-OSK Lines)
Built by Mitsubishi Heavy Industries, Kobe, Japan, 1972. 13,082 gross tons; 577 feet long; 80 feet wide. Diesel, single screw. Service speed 20½ knots. 550 cruise passengers.

Shota Rustavelli (Soviet Union) 1968 – see *Alexandr Pushkin*

Skyward (Norwegian Caribbean Lines)
Built by A G Weser Shipyards, Bremerhaven, West Germany, 1969. 16,254 gross tons; 525 feet long; 75 feet wide. M.A.N. diesels, twin screw. Service speed 21 knots. 740 cruise passengers.

Song of America (Royal Caribbean Cruise Lines)
Built by Wartsila Shipyards, Helsinki, Finland, 1982. 37,584 gross tons; 703 feet long; 93 feet wide. Wartsila-Sulzer diesels, twin screw. Service speed 21 knots. 1575 cruise passengers.

Song of Norway (Royal Caribbean Cruise Lines) 1971 – see *Nordic Prince*

Southern Cross (Shaw Savill Line)
Built by Harland & Wolff Limited, Belfast, Northern Ireland, 1955. 20,204 gross tons; 604 feet long; 78 feet wide. Steam turbines, twin screw. Service speed 20 knots. 1100 tourist class passengers.

Southward (Norwegian Caribbean Lines)
Built by Cantieri Navali del Tirreno e Riuniti Spa Shipyard, Genoa, Italy, 1971. 16,607 gross tons; 536 feet long; 75 feet wide. Fiat diesels, twin screw. Service speed 21 knots. 918 cruise passengers, maximum.

Sovereign of the Seas (Royal Caribbean Cruise Lines)
Built by Chantiers de L'Atlantique, St Nazaire, France, 1988. 74,000 gross tons; 874 feet long; 103 feet wide. Diesels, twin screw. Service speed 22 knots. 2276 cruise passengers.

Spirit of London (P&O Lines)
Built by Cantieri Navali del Tirreno e Riuniti Spa Shipyard, Genoa, Italy, 1972. 17,370 gross tons; 535 feet long; 75 feet wide. Fiat diesels, twin screw. Service speed 20 knots. 862 cruise passengers, maximum.

Stardancer (Sundance Cruises)
Built by Dubigeon-Normandie SA, Nantes, France, 1981. 26,747 gross tons; 610 feet long; 90 feet wide. Burmeister & Wain diesels, twin screw. Service speed 20 knots. 1606 passengers, maximum.

Starward (Norwegian Caribbean Lines)
Built by A G Weser Shipyards, Bremerhaven, West Germany, 1968. 12,949 gross tons; 525 feet long; 75 feet wide. M.A.N. diesels, twin screw. Service speed 21 knots. 747 cruise passengers.

Statendam (Holland-America Line)
Built by Wilton-Fijenoord Shipyard, Schiedam, Holland, 1957. 24,294 gross tons; 642 feet long; 81 feet wide. Steam turbines, twin screw. Service speed 19 knots. 952 passengers, maximum.

Stella Maris II (Sun Line)
Built by Adler Werft, Bremen, West Germany, 1960. 3432 gross tons; 289 feet long; 46 feet wide. Deutz diesels, twin screw. Service speed 16 knots. 233 one-class passengers.

Stella Oceanis (Sun Line)
Built by Cantieri Riuniti dell'Adriatico, Monfalcone, Italy, 1965. 5051 gross tons; 318 feet long; 52 feet wide. Sulzer diesels, twin screw. Service speed 17 knots. 367 first class passengers.

Stella Polaris (Clipper Line)
Built by Gotaverken Shipyard, Gothenburg, Sweden, 1927. 5209 gross tons; 416 feet long; 51 feet wide. Burmeister & Wain diesels, twin screw. Service speed 15 knots. 165 first class passengers.

Stella Solaris (Sun Line)
Built by Ateliers et Chantiers de France Shipyards, Dunkirk, France, 1953. 10,595 gross tons; 532 feet long; 72 feet wide. Steam turbines, twin screw. Service speed 21 knots. 720 cruise passengers, maximum.

Stelvio (Adriatica Line) – see *Bernina*

Sundancer (Sundance Cruises)
Built by Dubigeon-Normandie SA, Nantes, France, 1975. 12,600 gross tons; 499 feet long; 73 feet wide. Pielstick diesels, twin screw. Service speed 22 knots. 650 passengers.

Sun Princess (Princess Cruises) – see *Spirit of London*

Sun Viking (Royal Caribbean Cruise Lines)
Built by Wartsila Shipyards, Helsinki, Finland, 1972. 18,559 gross tons; 550 feet long; 80 feet wide. Sulzer diesels, twin screw. Service speed 21 knots. 876 cruise passengers, maximum.

Sunward (Norwegian Caribbean Lines)
Built by A S Bergens Shipyard, Bergen, Norway, 1966. 11,000 gross tons; 458 feet lovg; 68 feet wide. Burmeister & Wain diesels, twin screw. Service speed 21 knots. 558 one-class passengers.

Sunward II (Norwegian Caribbean Lines) – see *Cunard Ambassador*

Taras Schevchenko (Soviet Union) 1967 – see *Alexandr Pushkin*

Tarsus (Turkish Maritime Lines)
Built by New York Shipbuilding Company, Camden, New Jersey, 1931. 9451 gross tons; 475 feet long; 62 feet wide. Steam turbines, single screw. Service speed 15 knots. Approximately 500 passengers, maximum.

Transilvania (Rumanian Government)
Built by Burmeister & Wain Shipyard, Copenhagen, Denmark, 1938. 6672 gross tons; 432 feet long; 58 feet wide. B & W diesels, twin screw. Service speed 22½ knots. Approximately 400 passengers.

Tropicale (Carnival Cruise Lines)
Built by Aalborg Vaerft, Aalborg, Denmark, 1981. 36,674 gross tons; 670 feet long; 87 feet wide. Sulzer diesels, twin screw. Service speed 20 knots. 1396 passengers, maximum.

Uganda (British India Line)
Built by Barclay Curle & Company Limited, Glasgow, Scotland, 1952. 16,907 gross tons; 540 feet long; 71 feet wide. Steam turbines, twin screw. Service speed 16 knots. 1226 passengers (306 adults, 920 students).

Universe (Orient Overseas Line)
Built by Sun Shipbuilding & Drydock Company, Chester, Pennsylvania, 1953. 13,950 gross tons; 564 feet long; 76 feet wide. Steam turbines, single screw. Service speed 20 knots. 800 cruise passengers, maximum.

Veendam (Holland-America Line)
Ex-*Argentina*
Built by Ingalls Shipbuilding Corporation, Pascagoula, Mississippi, 1958. 23,395 gross tons; 617 feet long; 88 feet wide. Steam turbines, twin screw. Service speed 21 knots. 671 cruise passengers.

Venus (Bergen Line)
Built by Elsinore Shipbuilding & Engineering Company, Elsinore, Denmark, 1931. 6269 gross tons; 420 feet long; 54 feet wide. Burmeister & Wain diesels, twin screw. Service speed 19 knots. 251 cruise passengers.

Vera Cruz (Bahama Cruise Lines)
Built by Deutsche Werft Shipyard, Hamburg, West Germany, 1957. 10,595 gross tons; 487 feet long; 64 feet wide. Steam turbines, twin screw. Service speed 18 knots. 960 cruise passengers, maximum.

Victoria (Adriatica Line)
Built by Cantieri Riuniti dell'Adriatico, Monfalcone, Italy, 1953. 11,695 gross tons; 522 feet long; 68 feet wide. Fiat diesels, twin screw. Service speed 19½ knots. 431 passengers, maximum.

Victoria (Incres Line)
Built by Harland & Wolff Limited, Belfast, Northern Ireland, 1936. 14,917 gross tons; 573 feet long; 71 feet wide. Fiat diesels, twin screw. Service speed 18 knots. 600 cruise passengers, maximum.

Viking Princess (Viking Cruise Lines)
Built by Ateliers et Chantiers de la Loire, St Nazaire, France, 1950. 12,812 gross tons; 537 feet long; 64 feet wide. Sulzer diesels, twin screw. Service speed 16 knots. 600 cruise passengers.

Vistafjord (Norwegian America Line)
Built by Swan Hunter Shipbuilders Limited, Newcastle-on-Tyne, England, 1973. 24,292 gross tons; 628 feet long; 82 feet wide. Sulzer diesels, twin screw. Service speed 22 knots. 600 cruise passengers, maximum.

Volendam (Holland-America Line) – ex-*Brasil*, see *Veendam*

Volkerfreundschaft (Deutsche Seereederei)
Built by Gotaverken Shipyards, Gothenburg, Sweden, 1948. 12,068 gross tons; 525 feet long; 69 feet wide. Gotaverken diesels, twin screw. Service speed 19 knots. 568 one-class passengers.

World Renaissance (Epirotiki Lines) – see *Renaissance*

Yaohua (Chinese Government)
Built by Chantiers de L'Atlantique, St Nazaire, France, 1967. 10,151 gross tons; 488 feet long; 68 feet wide. Sulzer diesels, twin screw. Service speed 21 knots. 180 cruise passengers.

Yarmouth (Eastern Steamship Lines) – see *Evangeline*

Bibliography

Eisele, Peter (editor). *Steamboat Bill* (1966–86). New York: Steamship Historical Society of America Inc.

Ikeda, Yoshito. *Large Ferries of the World.* Tokyo: 1978.

Kludas, Arnold. *Great Passenger Ships of the World*, Volumes 1–5. Cambridge, England: Patrick Stephens Ltd, 1972–76.

Kludas, Arnold. *Great Passenger Ships & Cruise Liners of the World.* Herford, West Germany. Koehlers Verlagsgesellschaft GmBh, 1983.

Maxtone-Graham, John. *The Only Way To Cross.* New York: Macmillan Co, 1972.

Maxtone-Graham, John. *Liners to the Sun.* New York: Macmillan Co, 1985.

Moody, Bert. *Ocean Ships.* London: Ian Allan Ltd, 1978.

Stindt, Fred A. *Matson's Century of Ships.* Modesto, California: 1982.

Williams, David L & de Kerbrech, Richard P. *Damned by Destiny.* Brighton, Sussex: Teredo Books Ltd, 1982.

Yamada, Michio & Ikeda, Yoshito. *Passenger Ships of the World.* Tokyo: 1981.

Brinnin, John Malcolm. *The Sway of the Grand Saloon.* New York: Delacorte Press, 1971.

Coleman, Terry. *The Liners.* New York: G P Putnam's Sons, 1977.

Crowdy, Michael (editor). *Marine News* (1964–86). Kendal, Cumbria: World Ship Society.

DeLand, Antoinette. *Fielding's Worldwide Cruises.* New York: William Morrow & Co Ltd, 1985.

Devol, George (editor). *Ocean & Cruise News* (1980–86). Stamford, Connecticut: World Ocean & Cruise Society.

Dunn, Laurence. *British Passenger Liners.* Southampton: Adlard Coles Ltd, 1959.

Dunn, Laurence. *Passenger Liners.* Southampton: Adlard Coles Ltd, 1961.

Dunn, Laurence. *Passenger Liners* (revised edition). Southampton: Adlard Coles Ltd, 1965.

Index

Entries in *italics* refer to illustrations